Chasing the Ink

Gregory Magac Sr.

The Odyssey of an Autograph Collector

the Peppertree Press
www.peppertreepublishing.com

ISBN: 978-1-61493-957-3
Library of Congress: 2024911386
Printed: May, 2024

Manufactured in the United State of America

Acknowledgements

◆ ◆

This book goes out with love to all the people who pushed me to write it. First and foremost, to my mother, Marilyn, who was the first one to tell me to write my stories down, and for raising me to be the man I am today. After reading the first draft, my mom wrote me this: "*I am amazed at what you have accomplished in writing this book. Your knowledge of sports and figures you have in your head is astounding. I am so proud of you and what you have accomplished and the wonderful son you are. Love, Mom.*"

To my partner, friend, editor, and love of my life, Robin. To my Dad, and my three children, Daphney, Greg Jr., and Mara—you three were my little autographers!! To my best friends, Cody and Louie—the most awesome Golden Retrievers in the world! To my six grandchildren—I love you more than words can say.

Gregory Magac Sr.

Table of Contents

One, Two, Three ...
The Beginning

In Illinois, my family owned a three-story mansion built in the early 1900s on a wooded hill with twelve acres. My parents had separated and then divorced when I was around ten. In the early seventies, my mom had to contend with harsh winters and after running out of heating oil and having water pipes freeze, she sold the house, loaded up six kids into a VW bus, and drove to the place where it hardly snowed and the sun shined.

Sarasota, Florida

My mother purchased a home in the downtown area of Sarasota, around 4th St. and Orange Avenue. I would be attending the eighth grade at St. Martha's Catholic School, a small school located on Orange Avenue between 8th and 10th streets. Living downtown, there was a lot to explore. It was a great city back then, and Main Street was just four blocks away, running east and west. To the west was a movie theater, Woolworths, Five Points (where three roads intersected to form a five-spoke wagon wheel), and the beautiful bayfront.

To the east was the Maas Brother's department store (comparable to today's Macy's), the courthouse, and the Sheriff's office. The old railway station was at the very east end. It was later demolished for a medical and parking building—a shame. Sarasota city commission loves tearing down the history of its city. Robarts Arena was close to downtown and it hosted music, circus acts, and sporting events.

Behind the police station was Adam's Lane. On this street is where the historic Payne Park used to host spring training for baseball. The stadium was the spring home of the America League Chicago White Sox and Payne Park was one of the original spring training sites for major league baseball.

Twenty-nine acres of land were donated to the City of Sarasota in 1923 to be developed into a ballpark. It was developed with the help of circus owner and real estate developer, John Ringling. He was instrumental in bringing the New York Giants' manager, John McGraw, and the team to Sarasota to be ready for the 1924 spring training opening day.

The Giants were a popular Major League team in the National League, because they had won both the 1921 and 1922 World Series. They would call Sarasota their spring training home until 1927. After the departure of the Giants, the stadium was used by several MLB teams until 1933 when the American League Boston Red Sox came to call Payne Park and Sarasota their spring training home, along with baseball greats, Babe Ruth and Ted Williams.

Ted Williams arrived in Sarasota as a rookie in 1938. He would stay in the Terrace Hotel and it's said he would drive around town in an old jalopy. He loved fishing and would often ignore sports reporters' questions about baseball, but he was always eager to answer questions about fishing. He even once held a fishing seminar in the old Sarasota High School auditorium in 1956.

The Red Sox would leave Sarasota after the 1958 season and move to Scottsdale, Arizona, which was now attracting Major League teams due to the warm weather and dry air. They say the ball travels better there. Myself, I've never been to Arizona, but it's on my bucket list to go and visit a few of the spring training cities.

So, when I moved to Sarasota in 1974, the Chicago White Sox, which had called Sarasota its spring training home since 1960, were still occupying the complex. I decided to start an autograph collection that day, so in my later years of life, I would have some kind of value to cash in on or leave to my children and grandchildren.

I visited Payne Park for a major league game in the fall of 1974. The St. Louis Cardinals were coming to town to play the White Sox for a scheduled night game. I asked my mom if my sister, Maggie, and I could walk to the stadium for the game. She must have said yes because I remember going that night. I was confused about what was going on, as I didn't recognize any of the players that night.

Only weeks later did it register that the big boys were playing up north in the fall, while I went to a minor league game, which were the farm teams of the Grapefruit League. The major league players would come in the spring, after the World Series and a short winter break, reporting to camps in mid-February.

In the meantime, I had been at school in eighth grade. A friend of mine, Mike, asked if I wanted to go see the Harlem Globetrotters with him. They were coming to town and would be playing a night game at Robarts Arena. I went home and asked my mom. She agreed I could go. Before the day of the game, I went down to Woolworth's on Main Street and bought a small notepad. It was my first notion to get an autograph.

I remember being at this grand event. The arena was packed, as everyone knew who the Harlem Globetrotters were—a basketball team made up of some of the best dribblers, passers, and shooters. At the time, it was a team of men who challenged other teams. The Trotters are highly skilled, comical, and are like some kind of magic, beating the opposing teams with their antics and skills.

It was really cool watching Meadowlark Lemon, Curly Neal, Nate Branch, Larry Rivers, Marques Haynes, Geese Augbie, and Dave Lattin. They were the best of the best to hold a basketball.

After a game of skills, tricks, and comedy, the game ended with the Globetrotters winning. We went to the lobby to use the pay phone to call Mike's mom to pick us up. While waiting, we walked around the side of the arena. There the bus was idling with players walking to it. I told Mike I had my notepad and was going walk over to see if I could get some signatures. He said, "Don't be long," and waited for his mom.

I walked up to the bus door. It was open and the inside of the bus was poorly lit. There was a gentleman sitting in the seat by the door. I went up on the first step and asked if I could get an autograph. As he leaned forward into the light, I could see it was Curly Neal. He signed my notepad and then passed it back to other players. I told Mr. Neal it was a fun night and they were great. I remember he thanked me. I then thanked him for passing my notepad around.

When I went back to Mike under the streetlight, he was amazed I'd gotten six or seven autographs. When I returned home, I told my mom, brother, and sisters all about it. It was an exciting night and those were my first autographs.

In the spring of 1975, I returned to Payne Park, still trying to figure out the routine of the stadium and the players. It was a sunny weekend game. The White Sox were playing the Pittsburg Pirates, whose spring training home was in Bradenton, just north of Sarasota, Florida. All I knew about these two teams was that the White Sox was American League and the Pittsburg Pirates was National League.

However, I knew one more thing for sure. Pittsburg had Willie Stargell, as their first baseman. He was a tree trunk of a man, a power hitter who hit tape-measured home runs. Would I see him in person? Playing? That would be awesome! All I had was my notepad. I'd torn out the Globetrotters signatures and left them home in a cigar box.

As I was going down the bleachers to my seat, behind the third base line, some people up the aisles were making a fuss over an older gentleman with white wavy hair, sporting a tan and wearing thick square black glasses. So after a couple of people got his autograph and pictures, I made my way up to him, too. I pulled out my notepad and asked for his signature. He scribbled some phrase on my notebook with a name. When I got to my seat, I sat down to get a better look. It read, "Holy cow, Harry Caray!" Who the heck was this guy?" I wondered.

The Pittsburg Pirates were taking batting practice before game time. A few other players were practicing in the cage surrounding home plate. Up first was Willie Stargell, the one player I knew on the team, because he was one of the most feared power hitters of the 1970s, hitting the most home runs of that era. Some of these were tape measure home runs for the history books, like when Stargell stepped up to the plate inside the cage.

What I mostly remember about that day was how far he hit the ball. In the 50s, 60s, and 70s, a trailer park was behind the stadium, from the left field foul pole to the right side. Residents would put their lawn chairs on the trailers to watch the game. Mr. Stargell was hitting home runs over the wall and three rows of trailer homes back. Amazing power!

During the game, I was lucky enough to retrieve a foul ball. This ball had "Major League American Ball" stamped in ink on it. Wow! Maybe I could get Willie Stargell's autograph on it. After the sixth inning or so, Mr. Stargell was out of the game for the day. I decided to go stand around the back side of home plate by the first base line. This was the gate where the players would leave the field to go to the visiting team's locker room.

In the good ole days, there was no fencing to separate the fans from the players. You could just stand there and get a signature. However, some players would grab their gloves and bats, run past you to the lockers, and then jump on the bus waiting outside the stadium fence.

So here comes Mr. Stargell out the gate next to the first base bleachers. He was not running—just walking by, carrying his bats and glove. Imagine a fourteen-year-old kid standing there. I don't know what I said or what he said. I remember that he stopped, leaned the handles of his bats between his knees, and placed his glove on top. Then he took my ball, smiled, and signed. Finally, he gathered his stuff and stepped into the locker room. Wow! My first baseball superstar autograph! The thing I remember most was the size of his arms and thighs. I could see where all that power was coiled up.

To this day, I don't know why I decided to take that autographed ball outside and play catch with it with a friend. The ball ended up in the bushes or gutters. One of us had missed a throw, so we looked for it for what seemed like hours with no success. To this day, that is my only missing autograph in my collection of early originals. Damn! I should have kept looking.

Willie Stargell was voted by *Sports Illustrated* as Sports Person of the Year in 1979: number 8, 6'2" tall, 187 pounds. He played left field and first base, batted 282 with 475 home runs. He was inducted into the Hall of Fame in 1989 and won the Lou Gehrig Memorial Award. He was born on March 6, 1940 and passed away at the age of 61. He played all of his twenty-one seasons as a Pirate.

As for my autograph on that piece of paper with "Holy cow! Harry Caray," on it, this gentleman was a famous sportscaster from my neck of the woods. He started as a broadcaster with the St. Louis Cardinals in 1954 and remained with them until October 9, 1969. Rumor was that there had been a love affair with the wife of the owner of the Cardinals, A. Bush Sr., of the famous Budweiser Brewing family.

From there, Caray did a stint with the Oakland A's and also the Chicago White Sox, before anchoring down in Wrigley Field, home of the National League Chicago Cubs, across state lines from big-time rival, St. Louis. He would remain with the Cubs from the 1982 season until February 18, 1998, where he would make his famous, "Holy cow! It's a home run! It might be. It could be. It is! A home run!" That was the full statement. *Sporting News* named him Baseball Announcer of the Year seven times. In 1989, he was voted into the American Sportscasters Association Hall of Fame. He was born March 1, 1914 and passed away on February 18, 1998 at the age of 84.

The reason this chapter is called One, Two, Three … The Beginning is that this was what I was able to recall as the beginning of me chasing the ink. As for Payne Park, the final tenants were the Chicago White Sox. The last game was played on March 30, 1988 against the Texas Rangers (score unknown). The stadium was demolished in 1990 (darn!) and replaced with a new one, Ed Smith Stadium. This stadium is currently home to the Baltimore Orioles. Robarts Arena still stands, entertaining crowds with offerings like bands, the County Fair, and car shows. Watch out! Sarasota loves using the wrecking ball.

Robarts Arena today

Meadowlark Lemon Autograph

Payne Park in Sarasota
Before Being Razed

Holy Cow!! Harry Caray Autograph

"Curly" Neal Autograph

Game Program from Robart's Arena East

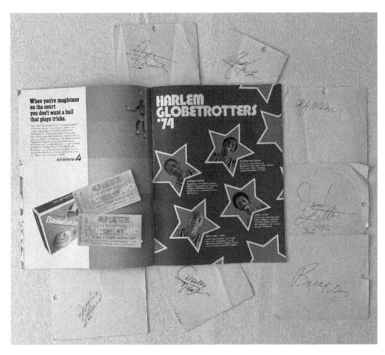

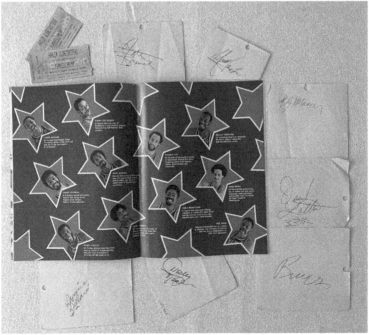

Harm Globetrotters 1974 Line up

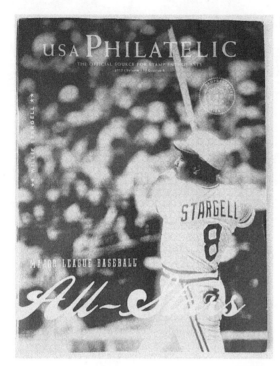

Willie Stargell

*Harlem Globetrotter,
Meadowlark
Lemon's team jersey*

Greg and his five siblings as they picnicked on Lido Beach in 1974, Greg hiding back center of photo and oldest brother Steve buried in the sand.

Baseball Card Autograph Show

A friend of mine in the 80s and 90s, Michael, was a collector of baseball cards. He had cards going as far back as tobacco cards (you would get a baseball card with a pack of cigarettes). When Michael heard that I collected autographs of sports people, he told me about an autograph show that was coming up. These shows would bring in famous figures who would sign autographs to make additional income. This show had advertised that Jose Canseco and Mark McGuire of the Oakland Athletics would be there. I probably said something like, "Darn, yes!"

Both Canseco and McGuire had just won the World Series, so these two were some of the hottest collectable guys of the time. When Saturday morning came around, off we went headed to Tampa from Sarasota. My first baseball card show, so I was really excited! We arrived a little early to buy our tickets and score a good place in line. The show was being held at a mall and into those front doors we went. Lots of 8x8 card tables were set up on both sides of the corridors.

Baseball and football collectable dealers were here selling what was hot and what was rare. Remember, this was before the internet, so if you wanted something for your collection, this was the kind of place to find it. Tickets for the autographs varied—it might cost you ten dollars for a signed 8x10 picture, twenty dollars for a signed ball, or fifty dollars for a signed bat. I bought two balls and two tickets, one for McGuire and one for Conseco.

I was a father of three, so I could only get what my income could afford. Mike and I looked around and purchased some items from the collector's world. The line was forming and getting a little long, so we decided to stand in it … and that's when you stand and stand …. You really don't want to be too far back in the line, because the person signing may become impatient or someone pisses them off, so they leave. Sometimes they even start signing fast and sloppy at the end of the day, too.

We were waiting when the commotion started and realized that McGuire and Conseco had entered the mall. I looked past the people down the corridor, and saw the two making their way to the signing table. I remembered telling Mike as they came through the crowd that they looked like two huge pine trees coming through the forest.

As the line started moving, I was just taking it all in, when I noticed one gentleman, two people ahead of me, who had about a hundred items to autograph—cards, pictures, balls, hats, helmets, cardboard statues, bobble heads—you name it, he had it. I'm like, man, it's gonna be a while.

Luckily, when we got to the front of the line, they decided to take that guy back to the hotel and signed his stuff privately with Conseco later. Once it was my turn, it was over quickly. The balls were signed and I maybe got a hello. I told Conseco, "You're the greatest," and got a handshake. It was a long day when Mike and I headed across the Skyway Bridge back to Sarasota, watching the sun set.

I spent a lot of time and effort autographing these two awesome baseball players. Jerseys, bats, baseballs, cereal boxes—tons of signed items I acquired. But all these treasures were put away, as the black mark of the "steroid period" in baseball killed the collection value. Some of the great ones had amazing records—all tarnished. To do what these players achieved was no easy task, but they got caught doping and paid the price.

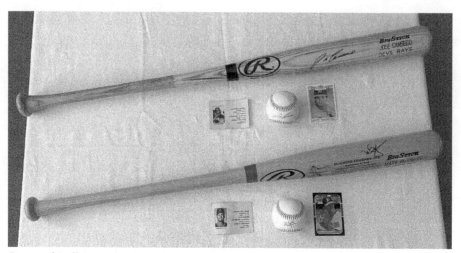

Bats and Ball Signed at the Event

Jose Canseco Collection

Mark McGuire Collection

The Van Wezel and the Pull of a Long Cigar

I'd been chasing autographs on the east side of Sarasota and other locations near and far. However, on the west side of downtown Sarasota sat the Van Wezel (pronounced Van Way-zull). I don't know why I never thought of hanging out there to get autographs. I had this treasure right in my back yard and for years, I didn't take advantage of it.

Many celebrities had performed there: Betty Davis, Ray Charles, Ella Fitzgerald, Jimmy Buffet, and Steve Martin—just to name a few. The Van Wezel is located in a beautiful open-air park on Sarasota Bay. It was constructed in 1968 and was the brainstorm of Lewis Van Wezel and his wife, Eugenia. The building is in the form of a seashell and was designed by William Peters, who worked for Frank Lloyd Wright's firm. It is (as of this writing) still gracing its original color, purple— yes, purple.

Some say the purple was picked to blend with the turquoise waters of Sarasota Bay. Others think that Wright's widow picked the color. Many of the locals just call it, "The Purple Cow." As I write this, Sarasota County is thinking about redeveloping the park, but so far, the Van Wezel has avoided the wrecking ball. Since so many of my stories are tied to the Van Wezel, I thought a short history of it should be included.

The oldest date I can recall autographing there was in 1991. George Burns, the comedian and Oscar-winning actor, was coming to the Van Wezel. I grew up watching Mr. Burns on television in comedy shows. I wanted to autograph him because he was such an icon. I didn't have a ticket to the show, but I had to see this gentleman in real life.

I had a paperback book and a newspaper article about the show to get signed. That afternoon I gathered up my things and headed down to the Van Wezel. I took my son, Greg Jr., with me. I told him that whenever Mr. Burns got out of his limousine, he usually had a long cigar in his mouth and one or two beautiful women with him.

We were waiting for him in the back parking lot near the stage door, when up pulled a black limousine. The driver got out and had everyone stand back. Next, a tall, blonde woman in a *very* red dress got out, followed by George Burns. Sure enough, he was puffing on a long cigar!

We moved along a side path for a chance to get a signature. As Mr. Burns walked by, I asked him to sign his book. He stopped! When he was signing, I also asked him to sign the newspaper Greg Jr. was holding. After he signed that, he walked right into the Van Wezel.

Greg Jr. was only seven years old then and doesn't remember meeting Mr. Burns, who passed away in 1996 at the age of 100. I believe that's what drove me down there that evening to see him. Thank you, Mr. Burns!

George Burns Autograph Collection

Greg Meets George Burns

Greg with youngest daughter Mara and Greg Jr. with his 1957 International Harvester.

Family Day—Spring Break

I was having lunch with my mom at Hooters Restaurant in Sarasota, which is a common event. She was a beautiful woman, who was then 89 years old. We got to talking about my writing and how the book was coming along. I told her that she was in a couple of stories. Then she asked me if I had written about cutting across a field to get Whitey Herzog's autograph. My mom, my little sister, Maggie, and I were together for that one.

Whitey Herzog was hired as manager for the Cardinals in 1980 and he'd taken them to win the 1982 World Series and brought them back in 1985 and 1987. He was named Manager of the Year in 1985.

The St. Louis Cardinals were coming into town from St. Petersburg to play the Chicago White Sox in Sarasota at Payne Park. It was the spring of 1983. The Cardinals had just won the 1982 World Series and I told my mom and Maggie that I wanted to get to the stadium early and both were fine with that. We bought some bleacher seats when we arrived—the cheap seats and, yes, back then the bleachers were made of old wood!

The visiting team dugout was down the third base line, and we could see the Cardinals were warming up on the field. I saw Willie McGee, Ozzie Smith, Keith Hernandez, and other stars from the World Series team that had made the trip. This was great! My sister was ready to get a cold beer and go to our bleacher seats. Me? I wanted to hang out and grab some autographs for a while. My grandmother, Stella, had sent me a Cardinal World Series baseball hat in the mail and I wanted the entire team's autographs on it!

As we stood along the third base line, Maggie and I yelled to players to come sign my hat and the one she was wearing. By the time we went to get a beer, I had gotten signatures from Tommy Herr, Ozzie Smith, Willie McGee, and a couple of others. Even Maggie got Ozzie Smith on her hat!

I don't remember who won that day, but I do remember the end of the game when the place was emptying out. I was looking out onto the field and saw Whitey Herzog talking with the home plate umpire. To reach Mr. Herzog, I needed to get out onto the field. I told my mom and Maggie to follow me to the third base line, where there was a gate that you could walk through to get onto the field.

I opened the gate, and the three of us just walked over to home plate, while Mr. Herzog was talking. He looked at us kind of funny, but continued with his conversation. When he was done talking, I asked him if he would sign my hat and ball.

My mom was so excited! Here was a name she knew from his earlier days as a player. He signed, shook our hands, and headed off the field. The three of us were the last ones on the field, so we started walking toward the first base line and past the White Sox dugout. Wouldn't you know it, but right there on the bench was a baseball bat!

I stepped down to grab it, but my mom asked me if I was going to take it. I told her that I was, as it was a cracked bat and didn't have any player or team name on the barrel. It was a pro-stock model, a Louisville Slugger.

My mom, the bat, and I exited the field and then the stadium. This is the bat that became the first baseball bat of my now-large collection. I would use it later to get a Jack Clark autograph, who played for the Cardinals in the 80s.

Greg with his Mother, Marilyn.

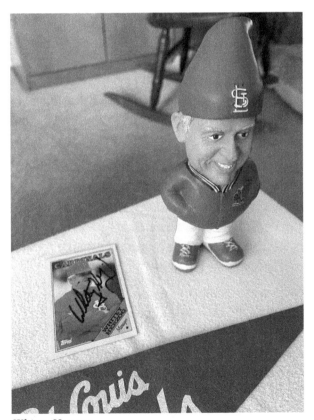

Whitey Herzog

Sleeping in the Spotlight

It was St. Patrick's Day, and Payne Park in Sarasota was still the home of the Chicago White Sox. The Mets were going to be playing in town. I had moved out of my house and was living in my 1979 Grand Prix at the time.

The Cardinals had traded Keith Hernandez to the Mets after defeating the Milwaukee Brewers in the 1982 World Series. I had one thing on my mind: get off work at 3:30, get down to the stadium, find Hernandez, and get a nice autograph in the manager's spot. For collectors, that's the spot on the ball where the stitching runs parallel to each other. Back when I first started chasing players for autographs, this spot was reserved for only the managers of a team. If a manager saw a signature in this spot, the player could be fined or maybe get an ass-chewing.

Nowadays though, jugheads called it the sweet spot and getting one single signature there was worth more than cash. I had a three-mile drive, so after work, I shot down Bahia Vista, hung a right on Highway 301 out to Morrill Street, and parked along Payne Park Way. There the Mets bus should be waiting to load up players for the trip to Vero Beach. So, zoom, zoom and I was off.

When I reached the park, I saw the bus, so I was right on time. I reminded myself that the baseball I brought with me was for the great former first baseman of the St. Louis Cardinals, and the hell with the Met's players. I parked the car and grabbed my shiny new ball. I was heading up to the bus, when I noticed that parked at the side equipment gate was a baby blue '67 or '69 Cadillac. There, at the wheel, sat Keith Hernandez with player, Wally Backman, sitting in the passenger seat.

I walked up to the driver's side door and asked Mr. Hernandez if he would sign my ball. He took the ball and signed a nice autograph. Remember, that was all I wanted—until Daryl Strawberry opened the back door of the Cadillac, threw a case of Budweiser cans on the back seat, and jumped into the car. Damn! It was the first time I had ever seen Mr. Strawberry, so should I ask him to sign the ball or just leave it the way it was?

I couldn't resist. I walked around the side of the car and asked Mr. Strawberry, "Please sign my ball, sir," He took the ball and signed it, too!

Well, damn, I just let a Mets player sign the "Hernandez Only" ball!" I thought, *What the hell—I might as well get Wally Backman, too.* The ball was signed and the beers were popping, when I looked inside the gate. People were autographing for an older gentleman coach. They said it was Johnny Sam of the '69 Miracle Mets, so I asked him sign my ball, also.

Remember it was St. Patrick's Day, and I was living out of my car, so I took a ride out to south Lido Beach where I could shower. What to do next—Bennigan's? Why not? I was all happy that my ball was signed up. I downed a few pints, had a bite to eat, and got a good night's sleep in the Kash n' Karry parking lot. I haven't looked at this ball in a long time. It will be nice to get it out again and relive those moments.

Keith Hernandez and Darryl Strawberry Autographs

Digging Daphney

I don't know what year it was, possibly some time in the late 80s or early 90s. My daughter, Daphney, was with me that day and she was somewhere between nine and twelve years old. We went down to Ed Smith Stadium in Sarasota for a baseball game, but I don't remember who the White Sox were playing that day.

Before the game, we were sitting in the second level, watching the Sox take some batting practice, when one of the players hit a home run right over the centerfield fence. I told Daphney to run out of the stadium and get that ball! She ran down the stairs, quick as a wink, and disappeared out behind centerfield.

Time passed—where did she go? I had no idea, but she should have headed back by this time, but no sight of her. I kept looking for her out by centerfield. A few moments later, I finally saw Daphney. She popped up inside the field and stood on the warning track holding that ball and waving to me.

All the players who had retrieved balls in the outfield during batting practice were looking at her and laughing—probably wondering where she came from. I quickly waved for her to get out of there, so she turned around, and back under the fence she went.

She made it back to our seats and shared the story. When she went to find the home run ball, she couldn't find it outside the stadium. But she did see a ball under the fence inside the field. She told me she used her hands and dug a hole through all the hard, red clay that was deep enough that she could fit under it.

It was just the funniest thing, remembering her as she stood out on that field, so proud she had the ball. She was waving to me with both hands in the air. Everyone around us had a good laugh, too, and of course, I told her she shouldn't have done that. But she had gotten that ball and she was happy—guess that's all that mattered. That ball went on to have a good life with an autograph of someone in the sweet spot.

Beautiful Daphney, Greg's oldest daughter Daphney the Gopher

You Gotta Do What You Gotta Do

It was the spring of 1986, and my St. Louis Cardinals had been defeated in the 1985 World Series to their cross-state rival, the Kansas City Royals in a four to three series loss.

At that time, there was an ad in the classified section of the local newspaper by someone selling a George Brett autographed ball and a 1985 World Series baseball. What was that all about? I called the number and an elderly woman answered the phone. She told me she had won the ball from a mail-in sweepstakes. I told her I was interested in purchasing the balls. I could use them for autographing with spring training coming up.

I headed over to the lady's house. I opened up the boxes to check out those baseballs. One was an official World Series 1985 ball, but the other ball, signed by George Brett, was a prize promotion ball with a stamped signature rather than an authentic one. She wanted $50 dollars for the pair. I thought it was a fair deal, so I paid her and left.

After the Cardinals defeated the Milwaukee Brewers in the 1982 World Series, 4-3, I had been filling up a couple of baseballs and baseball cards with team signatures. I decided to go after the Kansas City Royals with that 1985 World Series ball and get the entire team to sign it … heck, they were the champions!

The Royals spring training home was Kissimmee, Florida. They usually visited Sarasota to play some games, so in 1986 I went to a game to get the team signatures. I arrived for the game, as the bus pulled up with players—Hal McRae, Willie Wilson, and Dane Iorg, along with coaches, managers, and other players.

The late Dick Howser was the manager at the time. When he got off the bus, I asked him if he'd sign my ball. He signed it right in the sweet spot, the manager's spot between the stiches of the ball.

Nuts! George Brett didn't make the trip. Well, I could get a head start on the team ball and I autographed all day around the dugout and down the left and right field fence line.

In the spring of 1988, I asked my friend from work, Darryl, if he wanted to go to the Royal's spring training camp in Kissimmee with me. I told him I needed George Brett's autograph on my World Series ball. Darryl had been autographing with me before, when I got Nolan Ryan, Harold Baines, Frank Thomas, and Michael Jordan's signatures. So we headed north towards Orlando.

Neither of us had been to the facilities for the Royals, so we're just going to wing it. This was before cell phones hadn't taken over my life—yet. We didn't have a GPS—just road signs and a paper map. I recalled that we pulled into the parking lot around ten in the morning. No players were on the practice fields yet, just what appeared to be maintenance workers.

I wondered if we had we wasted our time and gas. Did the players have the day off? Were they at another stadium? We started to walk around to see who was out on the field. Guess what? Jackpot! When we got closer to the field, no kidding, it was George Brett, taking some infield practice. The field was surrounded by a fence with gates and a small set of bleachers behind home plate. Mr. Brett was working out at third base.

I said to Darryl, "Maybe we're not supposed to be out here." I had my '85 World Series ball and Darryl had an official American League ball. We decided to try until we got tossed out. After watching Mr. Brett work out, the other players left, so it was just a pitching coach and him. He looked over at us a couple of times, which made Darryl nervous, so I knew he was getting cold feet and wanted to leave. However, I convinced him that we were good for now. Just then, a pint-sized bus pulled in.

The adults on the bus guided a group of children up to the practice field gate. It appeared all the kids had some type of special needs. Mr. Brett walked over, opened the gate, and welcomed them by shaking their hands. When Darryl asked me what we were going to do, I told him to follow me—we just walked in with the children.

As they filled the bleachers, we took a position at the bottom portion of the bleachers by the gate. We'd gotten a "look" from Mr. Brett—that he didn't like us being in there and that we didn't belong. He was interacting with the children and adults—maybe friends of his or a foundation he supported. He took a brief moment to step aside and came straight over to Darryl and me.

He yelled, "What are you doing here? What do you want?" (I've left a few choice words out here.)

I said, "I have this 1985 World Series ball and I drove up from Sarasota with my friend to see if you were practicing. We've never been here before and we just wanted an autograph.

Darryl was being quiet. Me? I got that "George Brett look—you know, the look he had when he ran out on the field after the home plate umpire tossed him out for having illegal pine tar on his bat? THAT look. Well, he couldn't beat us up in front of the children or be really mean to us, could he?

I thought he was going to throw us out … and he did, but not before signing my World Series ball and Darryl's, too. We walked back to the car and headed south to Sarasota. It was a good day—mission accomplished!

George Brett autograph next to Dick Houser's on the 1985 World Series Royals Team Ball

You Gotta Do, What you gotta Do

1985 World Series Memorabilia

Over the Wall

It was the spring of 1987 and the Florida Grapefruit League was in full swing. The major league ballplayers reported to camp and I took the day off work.

The St. Louis Cardinals came down from St. Petersburg to play the Pittsburg Pirates in the neighboring city of Bradenton. It had been home to the Pirates since 1969. McKechnie Field, built in 1923, was the oldest stadium in the Grapefruit League. The stadium was named after Hall of Fame manager, Bill McKechnie. He would win a World Series with both the Pirates and the Reds.

That stadium had a lot of history. I've heard rumors that after his retirement, Honus Wagner, would show up at the field and hang out with the players. Many Hall of Famers played at McKechnie Field as well: Roberto Clemente, Bill Mazeroski, Willie Stargell, and Paul Wagner.

I took the day off and loaded my backpack with a couple of baseballs, a few sets of trading cards for both teams, and a couple of Sharpies and ballpoint pens. I thought about getting two team balls signed up and then working on the trading cards.

I had never been to McKechnie Field before. I don't know what it is about Bradenton, but I always got lost—and it happened again. Eventually, I came right up on the stadium, which sat on a city corner. It was old school, like Sarasota Payne Park before it was demolished.

I walked around the stadium to get a feel for where everything was. I started the morning off by getting autographs from the Pirate's players. As the team moved onto the field to do stretching, fielding, and batting, I had my trading cards signed and the ball was filling up with signatures. By now, I'd gotten some All-Star players to sign: Bobby Bonilla, Mike LaValliere, Sid Bream, John Smiley, and Doug Drabek.

There was this rookie I'd been hearing about in the baseball world. His name was Barry Bonds. He was drafted by Pittsburg out of Arizona State; a sixth pick in the first round. It was said that Bonds could tear the cover off a baseball when he hit. Coming out of college at 6'2" and 227 pounds, he moved right into the major leagues.

I could see he was out in the field in the batting cage, but he wasn't coming near the walls or fences, as people called out for him to sign for them. One thing I've learned over the years is not to bother players when they are doing their workouts—it's better to wait until they are done.

The Cardinals arrived next to the visiting team's locker room and I switched gears and started getting signatures on the Cards team ball. I had autographs from Whitey Herzog, Ozzie Smith, Tom Herr, Willy McGee, Terry Pendleton, Tony Pena and George Hendrick. It was a great day!

I was worn out from filling both those team balls, and I had most of the players, but no Barry Bonds. Although he played in the game, he left the field in the eighth inning. When the game officially ended, I scrambled to get as many more autographs as I could. I thought that maybe I could catch Barry Bonds walking out of the stadium to the players' parking lot. At McKechnie Field, there were hardly any fences to separate the fans from the players.

As I came around the back of the home plate seating area (you know, the high-dollar seats), I walked over to a three-foot high, green block wall. It bordered the playing field from the third base line. As the stadium emptied out, I stood at the wall and looked to my left. There I saw an older gentleman, a security volunteer, and another guy down by third base. When I looked to the right corner by the Pirates locker room, I saw no one.

I took one more look at Security (remember, back then it was just volunteers). When no one was looking, I decided to step over the wall and onto the field of green. As I headed for the locker room, after ten steps, I looked around to see the Security guy pointing at me and asking what I'm doing. I remember holding up the backpack and pointing towards the back corner of the stadium. He waved me off, turned around, and left.

My heart was sure beating fast by then and I kept wondering what I was doing. I didn't even really know what Barry Bonds looked like—only what I saw of him on the field that day. I pulled a couple of his trading cards out and got the ball ready. I passed the foul line pole and came up on the side of the locker room. There was an eight-foot fence surrounding it and I saw a crowd of about fifty fans on the other side.

I just stood there, wondering what the hell I was doing. I was twenty-seven years old, trespassing, and I could go to jail if the city police that had been hanging around saw me. Suddenly, the crowd started yelling, "Barry Bonds! Mr. Bonds! Sign my ball!" I looked around the front corner of the building, and there stood a tall, muscular, well-dressed young man. Well, now, I thought, that must be Barry Bonds. Of course, it was him—holy mackerel! Now what do I do?

I stepped out from the side of the building and just stood there. He actually walked near me to get away from the yelling fans. I don't think he had an escape plan to leave the stadium. I got up next to him and asked if he could sign my team ball. He gave me a look, took the ball, and signed it. I then asked if he could sign a couple of trading cards for me and he signed two. My legs were weak. I thanked him, and then turned back towards that short, friendly wall I'd just stepped over and was outta there. What a day it had been!

Side Note

I ended up giving away one of the signed Bonds cards to a collector friend of mine. I still have the Cardinal team ball, but the Pirates team ball (a beautiful one!) loaded with All-Stars, I gave to my friend, Lenny, who was from Pittsburg.

Lenny, in turn, gave the ball to his father when he came to Florida for spring training one year. Lenny told me how that ball would always be sitting on his father's mantle when he went home to Pittsburg to visit him. Years passed and illness came upon Lenny's dad. I told Lenny to grab that ball before someone else did. After seeing his father, Lenny decided to leave the ball where it was. He told me it was still there, over the fireplace.

However, with his father not getting better, Lenny returned to Pittsburg one last time. When he returned from his trip, I asked Lenny if he'd gotten the ball. Lenny told me that it was gone. Someone else had snagged it. Darn!

Part of Barry Bonds Collection

Barry Bonds Autographed Bat Close-up

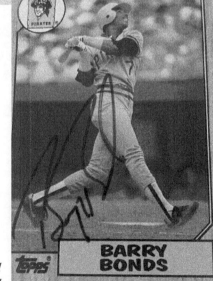

Barry Bonds Autographed
Rookie Baseball Card

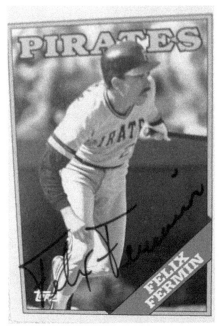

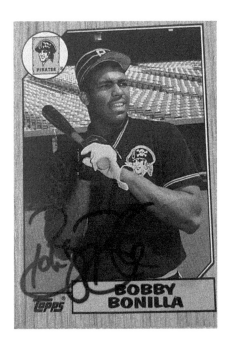

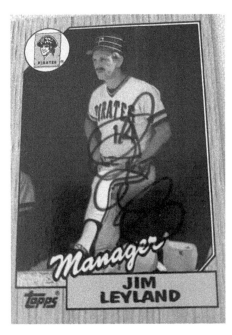

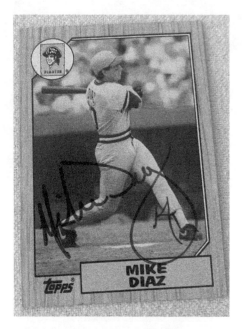

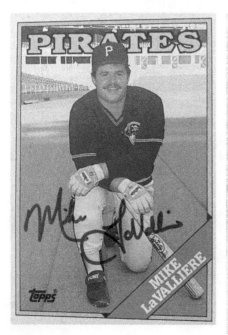

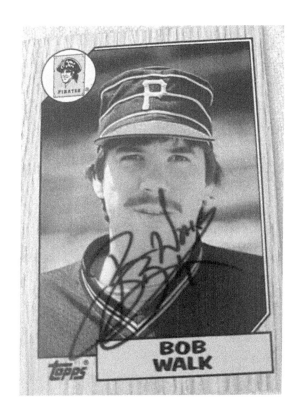

Sold Out—No Seats Available

◆ ◆

It was the spring of 1987, and the NY Mets were scheduled to go into Al Lang Stadium in St. Petersburg, Florida, home of the St. Louis Cardinals from 1947 to 1997. The stadium was built in 1947 by businessman and Mayor Albert Lang—thus given the stadium's name.

The Mets were World Champions, beating the Boston Red Sox in the 1986 World Series four games to three with Ray Knight being named Series MVP. Other players on the roster included Dwight Gooden, Ron Darling, Keith Hernandez, power slugger Darryl Strawberry, Kevin McReynolds, Mookie Wilson, Wally Backman, and a new rookie joining the team this spring, Gregg Jefferies. This runner was the future of the Mets for his on-base percentage hitting and awesome fielding.

I would say the team of the 80s was the St. Louis Cardinals. They were led by head coach, Whitey Herzog, and won the 1982 World Series against the Milwaukee Brewers, but lost in the 1985 Series against the Kansas City Royals, a series clearly decided by bad umpiring. The one call that stood out in my mind was when Twins player, Jorge Orta, pinch-hit a high chopper ground ball to Jack Clark down the first base line. Pitcher Todd Worrell covered first base and caught the toss from Clark with his foot clearly on the bag. Umpire Don Denkinger called Orta safe, which changed the course of the game, costing St. Louis the series … at least in my eyes and my dad's! Also accounting for the series loss was Vince Coleman getting his foot and ankle caught up in the automatic tarp rolling machine that took the infield tarp off the field. Coleman had been announced National League Rookie of the Year and teammate Willie McGee was MVP of the 1985 baseball season.

In the spring of 1987, I was plugging along with my employment career at the Sarasota County School Board as a carpenter/roofer working with eleven other crew members. A guy with whom I was pretty tight was my friend and co-worker, Mark. He was a family man, as I was. He liked NASCAR, football, Hooters, Bush Beer, and Harley Davidsons—not so much baseball. He grew up in the Upper Catskills of NY, and he'd only been to New York City once, but said he didn't care too much for it. He'd never been to see the Mets, Yankees, Islanders, Rangers, Jets, or Giants play. Well, heck, I always thought if you were from New York you were from the city.

I never found any of this out till I asked him if he wanted to go see the Cardinals and the Mets when they played that Saturday morning. I had called up the ticket office at Al Lang and they said they still had plenty of tickets available. That was when Mark told me about his upbringing, and that he had never been to the city for a game. I told him I wanted to go and do some autographing of the Cardinals, Mets, and this future star, Gregg Jefferies. Mark was all in and he even went out and bought a Mets hat for the game.

I told him I would pick him up early Saturday, so we would be there when the ticket window opened at 9 a.m. Since that game was being televised nationally, it most likely would sell out. That morning, I woke before the alarm, dressed quickly, and grabbed my Cardinal hat and my backpack containing 8x10 photos, magazines, and balls. Then I drove a couple of miles across town to get Mark. We headed north, across the Skyway Bridge and into the downtown bayfront of St. Petersburg, about a forty-five-minute drive. It's a beautiful ride, watching the sun come up while crossing the bridge and I knew it would be a nice day for a spring training game.

As we arrived in the stadium parking lot, we passed the front of the stadium. Holy Mackerel! There was a line of people at the ticket window winding down the sidewalk from the foul pole to the left field line. I found a spot to park the car on a grassy area across the street, so we could just get out and see what was going on.

Before we left the car area, Mark insisted we have a cold Bush beer—I'm in on that! After ordering our beverages, we headed up to the ticket windows, but were told the game was already sold out. However, there might be some tickets released from Will Call or Standing Room Only. As we walked back to the car, I could hear people complaining. They also thought plenty of tickets were available. We returned to the car to decide what to do next and decided to have another cold beer.

As we sat in the parking lot, the Mets team buses pulled up to enter the gate to the locker room. The players exited the bus on the street and walked across the sidewalk to the gate. As the players left, security kept fans back from interacting with the players. It seemed like they brought their whole starting lineup from the World Series.

What to do? The stadium was starting to fill up, but the line hadn't moved. I think we had another beer and then I grabbed my backpack and told Mark, we should go check things out and just look around. Mark wanted to go home, but he tagged along anyway.

Walking up again to the ticket windows, the situation really looked grim. We walked down the Cardinal side and first base line. No easy entrance there, as ticket collectors and security had all areas covered. Darn! Following the line of fans waiting for tickets, we stopped at the gate in line with the third base and the foul area. The Mets took the field for batting practice and warmups.

As I was leaning against the gate, I noticed it was locked. Standing next to me was a twelve-year-old kid with his grandmother. He was telling me and Mark to break the gate open. The kid was wearing a Mets hat, so I told Mark to do it. It was getting hot, so chances of our seeing the game were fading fast.

Just then, a huge gentleman wearing his umpire uniform cut through with his son. He grabbed the lock, yelling for someone to unlock it. He yelled once, twice—maybe three times. He waited a minute or two and then proceeded to yank the yoke from around the fence pole, thus gaining entrance to the field. He pushed the gate closed behind him, but didn't secure it.

The wheels started turning in my brain, so I told Mark that I was going in. If I wasn't thrown out in two-minutes, he had better get in there or I'd meet him at the car after the game. He said, "Homes, what if we end up in jail?"

I told him we wouldn't be arrested—they would just throw us out. Since the gate was on the NY Mets side, I removed my Cardinal's hat and placed it into my backpack.

In the gate I went. The Mets locker room door was on the right and straight down the sidewalk. Twenty feet in front of me was a four-foot high fence with an opening as wide as the sidewalk. At the end of the sidewalk, I noticed red clay, green grass, and then third base. On that grass were Keith Hernandez, Dwight Gooden, and Darryl Strawberry, warming up—I was on the field!

What the heck was I doing? It was getting scary and my heart was thumping! Taking a right towards home plate, I noticed a cameraman, so I thought I could blend in—I was just worried about how long I could do this.

While standing in the middle of the players and coaches, I began talking to the cameraman. He told me where he was from, what station he worked for, etc. I told him I was from the *Sarasota Herald Tribune* (big fat lie) and was doing a story on the World Series Champion Mets and their future star, Gregg Jefferies.

Just then, in walked Mark. He made the turn heading right at me; blue jeans, Mets T-shirt, and hat. He was walking like a cowboy with his hands tucked into his pockets. I cracked up, laughing some. I introduced Mark to the cameraman, and Mark told him he was with public relations for the Mets. How the heck did he think that up so fast?

We stayed back along the wall in front of the lower section seats and behind the camera. I told Mark we should try to do some autographing before this all came to an end. We stepped out along the grassy edge of the field. I had an 8x10 photo of Strawberry, some balls, a few Jefferies photos, and a magazine. Mark had his hat, which was easy to hand to a player and get a signature. When he did, then we would move on.

So, that's the way it worked. Players came by and Mark would hold his hat out. Some signed. Some didn't. Strawberry signed the hat and my 8x10. Jefferies signed a ball and my 8x10 photo. I was done. Mark scored big: Strawberry, Hernandez, Dykstra, McReynolds, and a few more I don't recall.

The game was about to start, so Dwight Gooden, who had been working out in the bullpen, came in. By now, Mark and I had moved closer to the dugout. Mark tried to get Gooden to sign his hat, but struck out, since the player was hot, so he went straight to the water cooler at the end of the dugout.

Don't ask me why Mark didn't stop me, but down the three steps into the Mets' dugout we went. We drank from the fountain and stood down at the end. The umpire's son was seated between the players and us. The next thing I knew, we were up at the top of the stairs, hands over our hearts, and singing the National Anthem.

The umpire yelled, "Let's play ball!"

We went back to sit on the dugout bench, and I ended up on the other side of the kid chatting it up with player, Kevin McReynolds. It could have been the cold beers earlier that made me brave. When the Mets were on the field, I guess I moved too far down the bench, and ended up sitting next to the head coach, Dave Johnson. I remember reaching into their canvas ball bags and taking two or three balls. I looked back at Mark. He was waving for me to get back over to where he was at the end of the bench. Just then I realized I was going too far over the limit. I made my way back down to the end of the dugout, where Mark lectured me to stay down here and not to press my luck.

By the middle of the third inning, a younger man had come into the dugout. The entrance was down where the manager, Dave Johnson, was sitting. The young guy was wearing navy blue shorts with a red collared shirt. He stopped for a moment to talk to the coach and then they all glanced our way. The man came down to us and we noticed he was wearing a security badge. He asked us if we had passes to be in the dugout. I said, "No, sir, we don't." He said, "Then what are you doing in here?"

I explained to him that I'd called the ticket booth earlier in the week and they had said there were plenty of tickets, but when we arrived, no seats were available. So we came in with the umpire and his son and sat in here. The security guard asked the umpire's son if he knew us, and he said, "No."

"Well, let's go, you're out of here!"

Needless to say, the Mets were up to bat and the players filled the dugout. Players with whom I had been in friendly conversation with just an inning earlier were now angry. We had invaded their domain. The security guard ushered us past the players and coaches, out the entrance that led to the locker room. Hernandez, McReynolds, and a couple other players stood up to make a stand. McReynolds said we had their balls, so he must have seen me when I took the balls from their bags earlier. I thought a fight was going to break out on national TV.

Both Mark and I stood at 6"1' and about 200 pounds each, so we could carry our own. We moved along without any punches being thrown. Out of the locker room we went, through the door, and into the main lobby of the stadium. At least he didn't throw us out into the street!

It was time for another cold beer anyway, so we got in line for beer and grabbed a hot dog. Mark was worried security was watching us, but no one was. We found a couple of seats. We laughed at what had happened. Mark, a guy, who'd never been to a ballgame in his life, just did what fans dream of doing all their lives. Mark told me how the young kid outside the gate wanted to come in with him after he noticed I was missing. But his grandmother said no to that.

I found out later that the umpire we followed into the stadium was Eric Gregg. He was an umpire from 1975 to 1999 and worked the 1989 World Series. He was a large man—6"3', 350 to 400 pounds. He passed at the age of 55 in Philadelphia. A quote he made before he died went something like, "For a kid coming from the ghetto, I've had a life people only dream about having."

Well, Mark and I never dreamed something like that day would ever happen to us. If not for Mr. Gregg yanking that gate open, it would have been an early ride home.

Cardinals and Mets Teams Autograph Collection

Oquendo game used bat

Bush Stadium Program autographed by
Vince Coleman 1985 Rookie of the Year
and Ozzie Smith H.O.Fer

Whistle Blowers

In 1987, the Minnesota Twins defeated the St. Louis Cardinals in the World Series. I can remember I wasn't too happy with the league, letting the Twins organization pass out whistles to blow at their home games during the series—a practice I have not seen since. After that, I really had no use for anything to do with the Twins.

My longtime friend, Charles, a Mississippi native, for some reason liked the Twins—especially Kirby Puckett, who was a ten-time All-Star, a Golden Glove winner who played right field for the Twins, and a great slugger. Charles and I worked together for a long time before one spring when I asked him if he wanted to head over the Ed Smith Stadium, as the Twins were playing and Kirby Puckett would be there.

I didn't plan on getting anything signed that day. Remember, I was not in any way a fan of the Twins. We left work at 3:30 and headed over to Charles' house to get a baseball. I was worried that by the time we arrived at the stadium, the game would be over, and the players and buses would be long gone. However, when we arrived, the game was still going on, so they no longer were checking tickets at the front booth. The Twins' bus was parked along the curb on 12th Street.

We didn't see Kirby Puckett playing in the game, so we wondered if maybe he just didn't make the trip. We asked the aisle usher, who told us that, yes, Kirby played, but was finished for the day. He was in the locker room by the dugout. I, of course, knew the layout of the locker room and that an exit door came out on the first-level corridor by the gate. It opened right where the visiting team's bus was waiting.

I showed Charles where the exit door was and told him that's where Kirby would come out. I wandered by the bus and noticed someone about halfway back, sitting on the bus, leaning his head against the window. He looked at me and heck, I knew right away it was Kirby Puckett! I yelled to Charles who ran over with his baseball.

Charles and I gave Puckett a smile and wave, and Charles held up his ball. Kirby gives him the "come on" wave with his arm and points to the door at the front of the bus. Kirby yelled to the driver to let Charles on the bus, while I waited off to the side.

That afternoon, Charles came off the team bus with the biggest smile on his face—he'd met one of his heroes! He showed me the signature on the ball, which had a bit of a smudge on the ink. Charles said Mr. Puckett was eating some chicken and the smudge was just Kirby's thumbprint smeared in grease. The last time I saw that baseball, it was sitting on a shelf in Charles' house, the ink of the autograph faded into the leather of the ball.

Kirby Puckett Baseball Weekly

Trip, Slip, and Flip

Thank You, Bernie Williams for Making Me Famous

It was September of 1998, toward the end of the regular baseball season. The New York Yankees were coming to Tropicana Field to take on the Tampa Bay Devil Rays for a two-game middle of the week series. The Yankees were in first place in the American League East, in line to win their second World Series in three years.

It was a Thursday and I had gotten tickets to the game. Tagging along with me were my youngest daughter, Mara (10), my son Greg Jr. (14), and two of his neighborhood friends, Craig and Caleb. My son was a big fan of Derek Jeter, so he was excited to be going. We had seen Jeter in spring training in Sarasota and Tampa. There probably wouldn't be much autographing, since we had to leave after work/school and would be lucky if we made the game in time.

Besides, it's gonna be hard to autograph the visiting team's side, due to the stadium being overloaded with Yankee fans … they are always so polite when autographing—no pushing, shoving, crushing, stepping on toes, spitting, smashing … just being nice.

This next part of the story is dedicated to my brother-in-law, Lou Long, Jr. He said I had to put this story in the book because it was so, so funny (his words).

I remember our seats were down the right field line, just the other side of the foul pole. The Yankees were still out for fielding and batting practicing. We ventured over into fair territory to see if we could snag any incoming home run balls. Tino Martinez was blasting some, as was Darryl Strawberry and Bernie Williams. After practicing, the Yankees went back to the locker room for a cool down, but we didn't get any balls. In fact, none of us thought to even bring a glove. It's always good for the players to see an open glove when you're trying to get them to throw you a ball.

When you have four growing kids with you, they need food. We went to the food court and grabbed some hotdogs, sodas, and a bag of peanuts. No beer for Dad, due to cashflow. As it was, I was sharing a soda with Mara.

We settled into our seats to watch the game, and after the second inning, the kids wanted to go exploring. The stadium had rock climbing, batting cages, speed clock pitching cages, rope climbing—all kinds of stuff for kids. At the ground level was a staircase that ended up to the right side of center field, where there was a touch tank full of harmless stingrays. People would surround the tank with their children and lean in to touch them as the animals swam by. As we were getting ready to check everything out, Mara knocked over the soda we were sharing. Darn!

After I took the kids and we did all the family stuff, Caleb asked me if we could go sit in some seats in right field and maybe grab a home run ball. The other kids wanted to try the batting cage again, so after I told them to watch Mara, Caleb and I headed to the area where we had seen a lot of Yankee players hitting home run balls during practice.

I had five dollars in my pocket, so it was time for ol' Dad to have a beer. They had this in-house lager called "Devil Rays Red" and I bought that. I took one big gulp before heading with Caleb to find some home run seats. We grabbed a row of five seats (for when the other rotten kids showed up). The Yankees had scored two more runs in the top of the 6th, taking a 3-0 lead. I took a few more sips of my Devil Rays Red and tucked it under my seat when Bernie Williams came up to bat.

Williams was leading the American League in batting average and he was in line to win the AL batting title. Just as Bernie enters the batter's box, Mara came up the stairs and out of the tunnel. I told Caleb to get ready—the ball could come our way. As Mara came down the aisle towards me, I reached under my seat to grab my beer. We don't need to spill this nice, cold draft. The six rows below us were mostly vacant, but a couple of Rays' fans were sitting a few rows up and over my right shoulder.

I sat there, holding my beer (still half-full) when with one swing of the bat, Bernie blasted one toward our seats. I yelled to Caleb to get ready because it was coming right towards us. I stood up, still holding my beer, while trying to focus on the whereabouts of the ball against the white-domed ceiling. The ball came out of the shadows like a meteorite, and WHAM, it smacked the empty seats about three rows right in front of us.

As I step over the row of seats in front of us with my right leg and beer still in my hand, the darn ball ricocheted off the seat I was heading to and shot right by in front of me and under the seats. As I turned to my left, and brought my left leg over the seat, I got crossed up and the beer was now in my right hand, high above my head. As I leaned down under the row of seats, the beer streamed out of the cup and was now running down the side of my head, chest, back, and arms. I was soaked.

I spotted the ball and again tried to reach for it, not realizing how close the concrete step was to my head. WHAM! The side of my head met that concrete and about knocked me out. I had dazzled the whole stadium as I could hear their oooo's and ahhhh's. I had to get up because I still had that ball in sight. I reached for the ball, but just then a hand came down from up behind the seat and grabbed it. Darn it!

As I stood up, everyone in the stadium was cheering and laughing for (at?) me. The first thing I heard was Caleb saying, "Mr. Magac! That's the funniest thing I've ever seen in my whole life!!" I felt like everyone in the stadium thought I was the town drunk with that beer dripping off my upper body. My daughter was just sitting there, awestruck.

I looked over my right shoulder just in time to see one of the Rays fans throw the ball back onto the right field playing area. I was going to ask him if I could have that darn ball for my daughter, but everything seemed to happen in slow motion. I looked up at the big screen teletron scoreboard to see the replay and the crowd once again erupted over my crash and burn.

One of the Yankee fans sitting near us told me he would have paid me $500 for that ball! Damn! That was the first and last time I'd ever gotten close to a home run ball. The Yankees won the game, 4-0 and when we left our seats, Caleb had us all laughing. I even got a few laughs and pats on the back from fans as we left the stadium. We drove home to Sarasota and dropped off Craig and Caleb first.

When I came into our house, the phone was ringing (yes, it was on the wall back then) and it was Caleb. He called to let me know that I was on ESPN Sports Center and to turn the TV on quick. I grabbed a VCR tape, shoved it into the machine, and turned on ESPN. It was just the start of the show and they were showing the highlights of the game we attended. Sure enough, there was Bernie Williams at the plate and the ball going into right field. Then there was me, crashing, burning, and spilling that five-dollar beer.

Bernie Williams
on Cover of
Baseball Weekly

Tampa Spring Training
after wining 1996 Al
Champ M.V.P. World Series
(AL) Battling title 1998

The Circus Comes to Town

From 1960 to 1992, the Ringling Brothers Circus had its winter home in Venice, Florida. After touring the country in the spring, summer, and fall, the circus would travel the train rails back to Venice to spend the winters. The train would head south, through Tampa and Sarasota, toward its final destination of Venice. It would unload at the south drawbridge (aka Circus Bridge) and a "circus parade" would travel the city streets to the winter headquarters. Bands sometimes played while residents and winter tourists lined up along the streets to watch.

In 1992, the Seminole Gulf Railroad announced abandonment of the ten miles of track into Venice, so the circus closed its winter home in Venice. Although the circus was gone, you could still find Tito Gaona's "Flying Trapeze Academy" on the grounds.

In 1989, Ringling Brother's Circus was billing the Greatest Show on Earth as the "Gunther Gebel-Williams Farewell Tour." Williams was a famous circus performer and animal trainer, known for his work with big cats (primarily tigers) and elephants. He had 11,697 performances under the big top and was the most celebrated circus performer of his generation. Williams had announced his retirement and the 1989-1990 tour would be his last.

The circus scheduled full dress rehearsal shows in the evening and on weekends before leaving town. I had seen the circus in St. Petersburg and Sarasota, but never traveled down to Venice. I decided that I'd like to see Gunther Gebel-Williams one more time and his Big Cat show was one to see! I loaded up my family (Daphney was twelve and Greg Jr. was five) to go see the circus. At twenty-nine, I didn't always prepare ahead of time to get the best autographs.

We drove south to Venice and there it was—a huge barn-like structure sitting off from the "circus bridge" and behind that was the trapeze academy. The parking lot was filling up for the afternoon show. I hadn't really thought of an autograph and I didn't bring anything to get signed—I was just there to see the show. Just in case, when I locked up the car, I did grab a standard blue ink pen off the console of the car. Always be prepared for the unknown.

We stood in line, purchased the tickets, and walked through the main entrance. When entering the circus tent, there were three rings and wooden bleachers running down one side, while on the other side hung a beautiful circus curtain. This tall entrance was where the elephants, tigers, and performers would enter the ring. I bought a commemorative program, as it had a glossy picture of Gunther Gebel-Williams on the cover with one of his tigers. And all I had was my blue pen!

We went down the left side of the arena about seventy-five feet from where the main event would occur. The large circus curtain was closed, with people going back and forth through it. You could see the elephants in their circus dress costumes and the performers standing around. I remember glimpsing a Venice police officer standing next to the curtain opening.

I started thinking—if that officer would just move down a little way, Daphney and I might be able to slide through that curtain and find Gunther to sign the program. I was not sure if that would work, but people were packing into the arena and the show was starting in less than fifteen minutes. I told Daphney about my plan and she said she was "all in."

Then it happened. The police officer decided to give up his post (must not have wanted to startle the elephants or get stepped on) and headed towards the other end of the building. I nudged Daphney and we scurried down the bleachers to the ground, and behind the curtain we went.

WHOA! Daphney and I were both amazed. I remember two or three brilliantly dressed elephants, beautiful showgirls, clowns, and orange and black tigers. Then it all happened. I could hear the circus Ring Master starting to welcome the crowd to the "Greatest Show on Earth," when no other than Gunther Gebel-Williams came walking up next to us! His hair was golden and wavy, and he was wearing his turquoise blue suit lined with studded diamonds, a long blue majestic cape, and white shoes.

I snapped out of it and asked him if he'd sign our program. I thought he was just going to sign the front, but he took the program, opened it to a specific page and signed it. We thanked him and he patted Daphney right on the top of her head. When he needed assistance to get on an elephant's back, we decided it was time to go before we were stepped on with really big feet!

We got back to our seats and watched a truly great show. You just never know when an autograph moment can happen and the memories they hold. Gunther Gebel-Williams passed away at age 66 from a brain tumor.

Ringling Bros and Barnum Bailey Collection

1980's Clown head garment recovered at Sarasota County Dump, Bee Ridge Road

Gunther Gebel-Williams Autograph

The Yankees Come to Town

◆ ◆

To town (Sarasota) came Don Mattingly, Ricky Henderson, and Dave Winfield. I wanted to go after some ink on one of my wall posters. It was a night game and I had a couple of bucks for tickets, so I took my daughter, Daphney, along as I rode my 550 Honda motorcycle.

We got there early as the gates opened at 5:00 for batting practice—home team first, then the visitors. The Yankees hadn't arrived yet, so we checked on our seats, down the third base side, about twenty-five rows up. We saw a bus tapping to the curb and the visiting team departed the bus, headed to the locker rooms, and then to the dugout. The Yankees brought some big name players—we did see Ricky Henderson, but there was no sign of Don Mattingly.

One of the fans said he heard Mattingly would be driving over to the stadium. I wondered where he would park—down the right field fence where the White Sox players park and close to the clubhouse or in the general parking area behind left field? Sure, it was closer to the locker room for the visiting team, but then we'd have to walk with all the general public attending. This is the stuff that goes through my mind constantly and the decisions that an ink chaser has to make all the time.

So the waiting game began. We stood by the gate. Daphney was ready for some Dippin' Dots when we finally saw Don Mattingly coming right at us with a couple of other teammates. Unfortunately, we weren't the only ones who saw him—another hundred or more fans saw him coming, too, so no Dippin' Dots now! I gave Daphney a baseball and I pulled out my poster.

We were just ahead of the cluster of people forming. Daphney was season trained, so she had the ball and pen, while I was ready with my Sharpie and poster. Mr. Mattingly slowed his pace signing this and that. Daphney and I got right in front him with the locker room door only sixty feet away. Daphney squeezed in there, but I was close behind. Mr. Mattingly slowed up and signed Daphney's ball. My poster was opened up and ready for ink. He took my Sharpie and signed the poster—it's done! It's always a rush when you get your autograph and I was happy, so back we went for some well-deserved Dippin' Dots!

We tried to snag some home run and foul balls down in the left field corner of the bleachers. Daphney leaned over the wall, trying to beg a ball from the players. She told me that all she remembers of her life between five and thirteen years old was her arm stretched out all the way through a fence opening, holding a ball, and asking a baseball player to sign it. Poor kid. I stood watching, happy to have my poster signed.

Ricky Henderson came running out and was shagging pop-ups and grounders, loosening up while New York was taking batting practice. Daphney yelled to Mr. Henderson, "Can you throw me a ball?" He asked if she could catch it, to which she replied, "Yes!" He tossed her a twelve-footer, and she caught it! Oh, yeah … I thought perhaps another autograph from Mr. Henderson on that ball.

One of the things I've learned is it's always easier to get an autograph if you treat that adult with respect. I would say "Mr. Henderson" instead of just calling him "Ricky." One time, I was close to Michael Jordan and I overheard him say to a player next to him, "I'd stop and sign for those kids, if they called me Mr. Jordan, not Michael." So for me and my kids, it was only "Mr." or "Mrs." and "Thank you" and "God bless you."

We went back to our seats to watch the game. I can't recall which team won. What I do remember was that one of the White Sox players—I think was Ozzie Guillen or Robert Ventura—hit a line drive ball that was coming fast and right at us. I moved to protect Daphney since the ball was looking to get us. I got ready to make the catch, when all of a sudden, a hand came up in front of me and the ball slammed into someone else's hand after ricocheting off my chest. Some people two or three seats down ended up with the ball. That was exciting and scary, but a new experience with my daughter.

After the game, Daph and I walked some aisles to recover a few bags of peanuts—heck, we were hungry! You can get some bags that only have a few handfuls gone. You always have to feed the kids.

By then, the New York team bus was loading out in front of the stadium, and we were gonna see if we could catch Mr. Henderson to sign the ball he gave Daphney earlier. People were waiting on players coming out of locker room. Someone at the stadium left the wrong gate open, so lots of people were standing around making contact with the players.

Everybody was hoping Mr. Mattingly might come out this way. I was thinking to myself that no way was that happening. We were looking for Mr. Henderson anyway. The bus was loaded, and the last of the players were mingling through people, signing autographs, with some future stars hoping to make that 45-man roster.

As the driver walked up to the bus, Don Mattingly and Ricky Henderson appeared out of the locker room. Don Mattingly had one thing on his mind—getting on that bus. I can't remember how security was being handled back then, with maybe one or two police officers or perhaps some volunteer stadium people. Mr. Mattingly was in the center of the group, so he was not stopping to sign anything.

Right then, this really tall man with a little girl on his shoulders started to curse Mattingly, saying, "You're a dumb #&$$ for not signing, and you're a *&!" Mr. Mattingly attempted to get this guy, little girl or not. Ricky Henderson and a teammate took control of him, but the tall guy continued to heckle him.

The bus was close, but fans were still wrapped around the front gate area. Mattingly broke loose from his teammates, but they quickly stopped him and put him on the bus. However, the tall guy was still standing alongside the bus, giving it to Mr. Mattingly.

Suddenly, Mattingly came crawling out the bus window about a third of the way from the back of the bus! Wow. He yelled at the tall guy, "I'm gonna kick your ass!"

I'm telling you, he was as mad as a badger. He had made it about halfway out of that bus window before his teammates managed to pull him back inside. They yanked his legs, so the driver was able to move on and head for Tampa.

Well, that was different. I figured it was time to get home, as Daphney was sleepy and had school in the morning. We turned to go, when—what do you know—we see Ricky Henderson, dressed up all fancy. We asked him if he would he sign our ball, which he did. He talked to Daphney for a couple of minutes. I asked why he wasn't on the bus and he told me he was waiting for a limo to do a photo shoot. After fifteen minutes or so, he asked if I had a car and could give him a ride to Tampa.

I told him that all I had that day was my motorcycle. When Daphney and I got to the motorcycle, she had dozed off, having had a long day, so she almost slid off the side of my jacket. It was a long day and night, but we got back to the house in time to eat some leftover peanuts.

Always remember, if a superstar is not signing autographs when you figure it's your turn, it may not *be* your turn. We do not know when they signed last. Sometimes I went three or four days trying to get an autograph.

I've seen Michael Jordan sign fifty to a hundred people at a time. Cal Ripkin Jr.—well, I'd seen him sign a line of people from third base to the left field foul line, six people deep, after playing a full game. So sometimes your turn doesn't happen.

Remember to keep your negative thoughts in your head and treat people as you want to be treated … with respect. Understand that famous people—baseball, hockey, football, movies—they are asked all the time to sign autographs, so they can't enjoy their personal time.

My way to make sure I get my chance is that I get there early and stay late. Who would have thought my daughter and I would see everything we did that day? Man, I wish I would have had my car that night! I would have been buddies with Ricky Henderson for life.

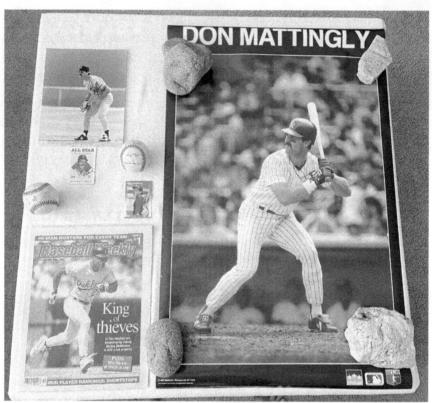

Ricky Henderson and Don Mattingly signed Memorabilia

Don Matting signed photo card and ball   *Close-up of Ricky Henderson Signed Ball and Baseball Cards*

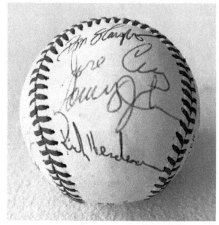

Yankees 1988 Spring Training signed team ball; playing against the White Sox at Old Payne Park Stadium. NY coached by Billy Martin.

49er Joe

My dad, Steve, and his younger brother, Mike, grew up playing sports in East St. Louis, on the east side of the Mississippi River. In high school, my Uncle Mike earned three varsity letters—football, baseball, and basketball. He attended the University of Missouri and became an outstanding lineman, captaining the team his senior year, and was a second team All-American.

Uncle Mike came out of Missouri in 1959 and was drafted by the San Francisco Forty-Niners. He entered the pros in 1960, playing offensive guard, defensive end, and protecting quarterbacks John Brodie and Billy Kilmer. Uncle Mike ended his career in 1967, playing with the Pittsburg Steelers.

When I was growing up, my family would spend Saturdays and Sundays at my grandmother's house, watching Uncle Mike on the black and white television. I remember sitting in front of the TV and my grandmother in her rocking chair yelling, "There's your Uncle Mike! There's your Uncle Mike!" As far as I knew, there were only a few colleges then … Missouri, Illinois (where my Dad went), and Notre Dame (our family was strictly Catholic back then). I am a true '49ers fan because of my Uncle Mike. I share this so you can understand the next part of the story.

My sister, Maggie, and her then fiancé, Steve, moved to San Jose, California, and planned to get married in 1990. My entire family was flying out for the wedding, which just happened to be where the '49ers training camp was. Being that close to the training camp, I knew I would most likely be chasing some ink on the trip.

My wife, daughter Daphney (13), son Greg Jr. (6), and our youngest, Mara (2) made the flight to California. Besides my family, I brought with me a '49ers hat, a Joe Montana wall poster, and an NFL official game football. My plan was to use the ball for just Dwight Clark and Joe Montana autographs. After all, both were famous for "The Catch" that Montana threw to Clark for the touchdown reception that beat the Cowboys in the 1981 NFC Championship game.

After spending the first two days with family, I broke away with the rental car to do some reconnaissance on the training camp. This was before GPS, so I had my paper map with the address written down. The camp was not too far down the interstate from my sister's house. My plan was to get up early in the morning, hang down at the camp, and then make it back for family events in the afternoon. The plan also became to take all three of my children with me every morning.

The first day we made it down, Joe Montana pulled up to the gate, but didn't stop. Neither did Ronnie Lot or Roger Craig. I did get my hat signed by Charles Haley, Brent Jones, Eric Wright, and a few other players. Heck, some signed whom I didn't even know … they wear helmets on TV you know.

On the second morning, we got there so early there wasn't anyone around. We walked through the gate, down the parking lot, and around the huge red brick building onto this big, beautiful green practice field. No one was out for morning drills yet. Should we wait around here? Heck no, I got scared and told the kids we better get out of there. Montana drove right by us on the second day, too.

Day three, he did it again—drove past us. I was getting that hat full of signatures, but I held back on the football because I really, really wanted only Clark and Montana on it.

Day three wasn't a total loss. One of the players to whom we talked (I am pretty sure it was John Taylor) told me that it was Dwight Clark who was just getting out of his car and walking toward the front parking lot. I went over to Mr. Clark and asked for an autograph on the ball—he was happy to sign. Day three also saw autographs by Matt Millen, Jesse Sapolu, and Pierce Holt. I remember this morning clearly, because my son wanted to go home, as he needed to use the bathroom badly. Being Dad of the Year, I told him to just go in the bushes.

Some teenagers who were there told me that Joe Montana only signed in the afternoon. I had afternoon family outings planned each day (Big Ben Forest, Alcatraz—that kind of stuff), so I could only make it one afternoon. Of course, that was the afternoon that Montana stayed longer than I could, and I never encountered him.

You can't say we didn't try. I'd been skunked by Joe Montana! Every. Single. Day. Really? How could you pass up those cute kids of mine? He'd park inside the gate and we'd yell to him to sign, but he was always on the move.

I did have one more Joe Montana sighting before I left California. I took a ride with my sister, Michaelyn, and my mother, Marilyn, to do some quick shopping. I wanted to show them the training camp, so we took that exit. We drove through the parking lot and around the facilities.

As we were headed out to the main highway, there, in front of our car, was an SUV darned similar to the one Joe Montana had been driving that week. I looked closely at the license plate and it read, "49ERJOE." Joe Montana was right there!! All my autograph stuff was back at my sister's house or believe you me, I would have jumped right out at the red light with my football and Sharpie!

My sister, Maggie, had heard that Montana signed items you mailed to him, and she promised to send in a magazine to try and get it signed for me. As for the football, it went back into my closet at home in Sarasota with just Dwight Clark's autograph on it. A few months later, at Christmas, Maggie sent me a magazine she had mailed to Montana for an autograph. What a good sister!

But we are not done yet.

In 1993, the Super Bowl was going to be hosted in Atlanta. My friend, Paul, who is from Atlanta, had heard all about my trip trying to get Mr. Montana's signature on that football with Dwight Clark.

Paul called to tell me that he had gotten VIP passes to the "Super Bowl Experience," an annual event preceding the big game for fans that showcases players, activities, autograph sessions, etc. Paul told me he had heard that Montana might be coming to sign. I wanted to head up there, but hell, I didn't have any money to travel, as Christmas had just ended.

Just in case, I boxed up the football and mailed it to Paul. He called me the night of the Super Bowl Experience and told me that there were a ton of booths that were set up everywhere (NFL sponsors, autographs, sports card companies, book sales, etc.) with hundreds of people milling around and long lines at each booth.

Paul found out that Montana was there and that a long line was already waiting, but he had brought a magazine, a promotional picture of Montana, and of course, my football. Montana would only be signing one autograph per person and only flat items like pictures and posters—no helmets and no balls

WHAT? NO FOOTBALLS?

Yep, that's what the people in the booth kept telling Paul, but he was determined to try. He told everyone around him about my story— going to California, trying for four days to get Montana's autograph, me mailing him the football, etc.

If anyone could get it done (besides me, of course), it would be that smooth-talking Paul. An artist when it comes to making conversation, he will talk you out of your last french fry! Paul was about fifty people back when Mr. Montana arrived—the fans clapped and cheered when he got there. When it was Paul's turn, Montana wouldn't sign the football.

Paul began telling Mr. Montana the same story he told everyone else around him that night—the story about his great friend, Greg, down in Sarasota, his trip to California, and how the football wound up with Paul in Atlanta. Joe Montana signed the football. Hooray!

Since it was only one signature per person, Paul bit the bullet for me that day. He showed everyone in line how he got the football signed just like he said he would.

It was an awesome story and the football now has the autographs of both men who were part of "The Catch." To this day, I still owe Paul a Joe Montana autograph. That's what best friends do for each other.

Signed memorabilia from 49ers training camp

Dwight Clark and Joe Montana Signed Football

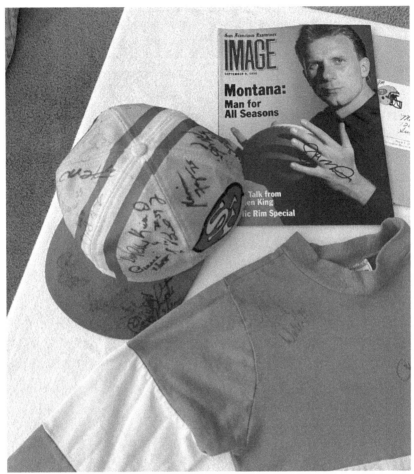

Close ups of memorabilia

Team autographed flyer

Greg's three adorable children Greg Jr., Mara Daye, Dapney

Greg and his son Greg Jr. 1990

Siblings from left to right Greg, Michaelyn,
Maggie down low, Missy up high, and Kelly at the end xoxo

Greg's "Uncle Mike" (his Dad's brother)
Played for the University of Missouri, was an All-American, and
drafted in 1960 by the San Francisco 49ers.

Inking the Great One

◆ ◆

It was a Wednesday, and an exhibition hockey game was to be played between the Los Angeles Kings and the Pittsburgh Penguins. Wayne Gretzky would be in St. Petersburg, at the Florida Sun Coast Dome, now known as Tropicana Field. The game was being played because Phil and Tony Esposito were trying to bring an NHL team to Florida. The dome had been built for baseball, but would also be used for hockey and basketball exhibition games. It would be my best chance to autograph Mr. Gretzky.

I loaded my backpack into my car the night before and brought with me a 2x3 wall poster, the first issue of *Beckett* magazine, *Price Guide for Collectors,* with Wayne on the cover, an 8x10 photo of him, and one hockey puck. Driving to work that morning, I decided to take half a sick day, planning to leave Sarasota at 11:00 and be at the Dome by lunch. I decided to stay in my light blue work uniform, hoping to pass myself off as a worker in the stadium and advance my way into the Dome. My brain and body were in the autograph mode … the high of chasing the signature … would the plan play out or would I be shut out?

When I arrived in St. Pete, I anxiously looked for a parking spot. I found an area where I thought I could leave my car unattended for a long day and possibly, a long night. I grabbed my backpack, locked the doors, and thought to myself, "Here we go."

I parked at the U-Haul dealer directly across the street from the stadium, and I run to the front parking lot. I thought that if any doors were going to be open, it would be the main double doors in the front. I had never tried the front door before … I usually would try sneaking in the back. I quickly open the door to take a look inside.

Doors unlocked! I peered in and saw two ladies at a welcome service window about twelve feet down the hallway. I was kind of nervous and let the door close—damn, what to do? I think to myself, *Just walk in and tell them you're here to work on the bleachers.* Okay, let's do it!

Some delivery guy came up, so I followed right behind him. He went in and stopped at the window, so I'm sidestepping him. I'm almost past the window when I heard, "Sir! Sir! May we help you?" I told them I was there to work on the bleachers. I keep going and heard no more response. I melted in my shoes as I walked behind a curtain. I'm in, and guess what? There happened to be a crew setting up bleachers to fit the oval form for the rink!

Speaking of the rink … there it is—shining, white, frozen water, a centerline, blue lines, face-off circles. I hear them say they are having trouble keeping the ice frozen, with the Dome being built for baseball—the standard hockey buildings are much more compact to cool.

The rink was surrounded by long blue curtains on the back side of the last bleacher row. The curtains help keep the temperature down and give it the feel of a hockey atmosphere. I walked down the stairs to an area where a crew of guys was positioning the last section of bleachers. It's some time after noon and the game starts at 7:00 pm … that's six hours to fill.

I planned on blending in with this crew as long as I could. I talked to a couple of guys like I'm looking for work, just killing time. The day rolled on. I'm hanging around at the end of the bleachers close to the ice and now there were more people around. Local media had been coming in and setting up all day. I've just been trying to stay away from too much activity, security, or front office people.

After five hours of waiting, thinking, hoping, and praying, it all worked out. Not going to get tossed out and I was glad I wasn't arrested when I went through the front doors. I paced back and forth when at about 5 p.m., a group of five businessmen came in and sat about six rows up. The news cameras start rolling in on them, so I walked on down to look. Turned out, it was Phil Esposito! He did some interviews and signed some autographs. I didn't ask for one then because I wanted to wait for what I came for—Gretzky.

The wait was not long. While standing there watching Esposito, two other gentlemen walked down the aisle, shoulder to shoulder with me. Mr. Esposito got up, came forward, and when he shook hands with the man in the brown suit, he said, "How was your trip, Wayne?" The gentleman replied, "It was long."

Holy Moly! It was Wayne Gretzky, standing right next to me!

I stepped back, removed my backpack and waited for a lull in their conversation. I asked Mr. Gretzky for an autograph on an 8x10 picture and my First Edition Hockey *Beckett Collectors* magazine. I was feeling weak in the knees and experiencing the high of it happening! Away went the 8x10 pic, and out came a 2x3 wall poster, which he signed, along with an inside picture in the middle of the magazine.

Gretzky looked at me like, "That's it." Man, I should have gotten a jersey signed! I stepped away till the area cleared, got one more picture signed by a hockey player in the magazine, and at last, I went up to Mr. Esposito and got one of his signatures, too.

It was dinnertime, and I was in the stadium without a ticket, as people were filling up the seats. I never told my wife and children that I was on this adventure, so I figured I'd better call and check in. When I called home, my daughter, Daphney, answered. The first thing she said to me was, "Dad, you're in trouble. Mom said you were on the 6:00 news with Wayne Gretzky." Damn. I'm busted. After telling my daughter that I loved her, I talked to her mom and told her I was staying for the game … I was in trouble again. So much for that.

Game time was coming up, the arena was full, but I don't remember where I sat. It was a new record crowd for hockey, at 25,581 people, plus one more … me. Hockey has made a statement for Florida. At the end of the game, the score was Pittsburg Penguins 5, LA Kings 3. Well, the night was over … or was it?

The stadium emptied out and remember, I still have my work uniform on. As the people were exiting out, I went down to the ice around the player's bench and penalty box. There, in the corner I spotted part of a broken stick of a Penguins player. I asked a guy cleaning up if I could have it. He said, "Sure, why not?"

I continued around the rink to the other player's bench and penalty box. And what do you know—on the floor there lies the broken piece of the stick, the foot or blade. I hold them up together and find a good match up—a clean break. I could glue them together like new!

I hear a lot of commotion, laughing, and talking going on behind the one big blue drop curtain. I snuck a peek and it looked like a VIP guest party was going on! I fluffed myself up, tucked in my shirt, adjusted my belt, and walked on in. It was a party for sure! The Stanley Cup was here in its wooden case, and lo and behold, there was Mr. Gretzky, standing next to it, taking a picture with some people.

A food and drink line was being catered by Hooters, so I helped myself to an ice cold Michelob and popped the top—it was nice and went down smooth—no food though. Next thing on my mind was to try and get the stick signed!

I waited for Wayne to be alone, before asking, so as not to be rude. Two ladies came up to me and asked if I'd show them how to get an autograph. I said, "Sure! I mean, how can Mr. Gretzky say no to such pretty ladies?" They had their game program, so I told them we would just walk up and ask him politely to sign an autograph.

We walked up to Mr. Gretzky, they asked, and he signed for them. I asked him if he could sign the broken stick I found, which he also did, but then told me that was all for me. I guess he remembered me from before game time! Shortly after, a white limo backed into the area for him and he departed.

As I was walking to my car, I meet two autograph guys who happen to be from Sarasota as well. They had a stack of the First Edition *Beckett Vintage Collector* magazines, but they had gotten "skunked" by the great one. I know that feeling and it sucks.

As I'm headed home and nearing the Skyway Bridge that connects that area to the mainland, I thought, *Boom! Yeah! What a day!*

Not really, as the day wasn't over—yet. It was 11:30, but after I paid the bridge toll, there sat a St. Petersburg Deputy Dog. I got the "blue light special," as I was doing 45 mph and the speed limit was 35. I "discussed" with the deputy that I was in a toll area and the fact that St. Petersburg jurisdiction was behind the toll area. After I got my ticket, I showed him the autographed 8x10, the magazine, the poster, and the best of the stick. He asked if I had gone to the game, which I told him I had, so I wasn't going to let a ticket ruin my night! Thank you and good night, officer.

I made it home—I don't remember, but I probably got yelled at.

The next morning, I got up early for work and as I was driving on the interstate, in front of me was a white limo! As I inched up next to it on the highway, I was pretty sure it was them. I think since the Hyatt was a sponsor of the event, Mr. Gretzky stayed at the Sarasota Hyatt and flew out of Tampa that morning.

I made it to work that morning, and as I sat at our break room table, I looked at the local newspaper, and there on the front cover of the Sports section was a full page article about the game. In the newspaper picture, it showed two players coming down the ice—one was the Kings' Steve Kasper and the other was Darren Stokes of the Penguins. Well darned, if that's not the player whose broken stick I'd found and had signed!

What an event! Two full days of chasing the autograph of a Great One! Thanks, Mr. Gretzky! You are one of the Top 5 who takes care of your fans!

Greg with Wayne Gretzky "Down on the ICE!"

Greg with Phil Esposito

*Wayne Gretzky signed Puck
given to Greg from Paul*

Wayne Gretzky Autographed First edition Beckett Card Values

Wayne Gretzky
Collection

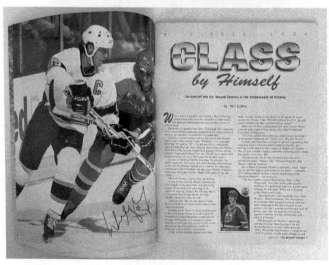

Wayne Gretzky Collection
"signed stick"

Not My Opportunity in Life

It's October 1990 and I'd just turned 30. I was still out there, going after the special autographs. It's like anything in life … it can become addicting. It was preseason for the NBA and the Chicago Bulls were going to take on the Seattle Supersonics in the St. Petersburg Thunderdome. The bulls would be coming to town with an All-Star roster of Michael Jordan, Scottie Pippen, John Paxson, and Bill Cartwright.

I purchased a ticket and was going to the game. I had left directly from work and was wearing my blue-collar work uniform and work boots. This is the same "look" I wore when successfully autographing Wayne Gretzky the month before. In my backpack I had two 8x10 pictures, a major league baseball, a 24x36 wall poster, and a *Baseball Digest* (collector monthly magazine), with Michael Jordan on the cover wearing a Chicago White Sox baseball uniform that came with a free baseball card inside. There was some rumor floating around that he was going to be playing baseball *and* basketball.

I arrived at the stadium early, parked at the "free" U-Haul Rental store, a good long distance to where the buses arrived with the players, and walked to the stadium. No sooner had I gotten there than a bus pulled down to the landing dock where a set of stairs led to a door to the stadium. The bus doors opened and out walked Michael Jordan. He was carrying a duffle bag in each hand and wearing headphones. I was only forty feet away, so I decided to go for it.

I quickly ran down to the bus and yelled Jordan's name, but he couldn't hear me with his headphones on, so he kept going. I saw no other players coming off the bus, so I became scared and headed back down the ramp, away from the gate. Just then, an ice truck was pulling up, so I asked the driver if I could have a ride to the loading dock. The driver said, "Jump on."

The truck backed down the loading dock, and when I jumped off the back of the truck, I thought, "Here goes nothing." I stood in front of the door Michael Jordan had just gone through, the one leading into the stadium. I opened it and walked right through. I had never done this before!

As soon as I walked in the door, I saw Michael Jordan about thirty feet away. He'd just signed autographs for two young children. I walked with a quickened pace, but I couldn't get to him before he vanished into the locker room. Now what? Leave the area? Go outside? Go to the game? Stay here?

The tunnel to the court was across from the locker room door and a good-sized gentleman was sitting in a chair doing security detail. There were different people coming up and down the corridor and I saw reporters entering the locker room. I decided to stay in the back area until game time, or at least until I get thrown out. Remember, I was still in my work uniform and I had my backpack full of stuff to be autographed!

The place was like a beehive. The Seattle Supersonics appeared from the locker room down the hall and hit the court for a warmup. I could see the fans through the tunnel filling the seats of the arena. I always try not to make eye contact with anyone, as I don't want to be questioned as to who I was and what I was doing. I was just trying to wait out Michael Jordan.

I saw that the steady stream of people going into the Bulls locker room were all wearing pink fluorescent passes to get in. I continued hanging around, leaning up against the wall. The Sonics returned from warm-up, so the Bulls were coming out for their turn: Scottie Pippen, John Paxson, and Bill Cartwright, but no Michael Jordan. What the heck?

After the Bulls returned from warmup, I'd found out that Mr. Jordan was pissed off because reporters were in the locker room asking for autographs and that's why he didn't go out to practice. I knew that in the sport's world, that was unprofessional.

I had been hanging around now for about two hours, when suddenly there was this woman standing next to me. She was a real eye-catcher, wearing a fancy blue dress and holding a miniature basketball in each hand. I sparked up a conversation and found she was from the upstairs office, trying to get a few basketballs signed for some special needs children. She was waiting for someone to escort her into the locker room.

I told her how I had snuck in earlier and how Mr. Jordan was upset with reporters asking for autographs. I asked if she would take me in with her or, at least, bring some of my things to be signed. She told me she didn't think that was going to happen. Darn! After she came out of the locker room a bit later, she let me look at the autographs—they were nice! We said our goodbyes and off she went to the elevator.

After seeing those autographed balls, my blood started pumping, my heart rate was fast, and I was all fired up! By now, there were people all over the place: VIPs, reporters, trainers, maintenance, and other personnel. Me? I was still leaning against the wall, waiting, taking short walks back and forth. It was three long hours, but I hadn't seen Michael Jordan since he signed for the little kids. If only I had gotten him then, I'd be in my seat, enjoying a nice cold beer!

All of a sudden, who was leaning against the wall next to me, but Michael Jordan himself! Three feet away, leaning on that wall, with his eyes closed. Most of the players had already left for the court and I just stood there, as quietly as I could. All he had to do was take my Sharpie pen and sign two 8x10 pictures that I had ready to go. How hard was that? Easy as pie.

Jordan started doing to stretches and that's when I decided that it was now or never. I opened the folder, turned to Mr. Jordan, and the conversation went like this:

Me: "Hi, Mr. Jordan, could you possibly sign a couple of pictures for me?"

MJ: (looking at me) "Not right now."

Me: "It will only take a moment of your time."

MJ: "It isn't your opportunity in life right now."

Me: "Well, when will it be?"

MJ: "Not right now."

Me: "I snuck back here when you arrived and I'm probably going to be tossed out, so why not now?"

MJ: (again) "It's not your opportunity in life right now—maybe after the game."

Me: "After the game, there will be 500 VIPs back here and I won't get the chance."

I closed the folder and stepped away as coaches were coming by. It was game time and I got skunked. Damn!

Decision time—he did say "after the game," so did I stay where I was or go to my seat and watch the game? No brainer. I stayed where I was and hoped I didn't get thrown out.

The game got underway and I found a spot behind the portable bleachers. It wasn't the best view, so I couldn't see a lot of the game. I planned on hiding out here until the game was over, when I heard two men's voices and the clanging of keys against a leg as they walked.

There was a cinderblock room, maybe 10x14, with no door on it—some type of electrical room that was very dark inside. I stepped into the room and went to the far corner—it was pitch-black and the men's voices were coming closer. What the heck am I doing? Just then, I saw two silhouettes standing at the doorway, but they didn't have any flashlights and I was trying to be as quiet as a mouse.

One of the guys said, "Don't go in there—I hear someone breathing." Then he announced that he was a Marine and trained to kill with his bare hands.

I quickly said, "It's just me, a guy, trying to get a Michael Jordan autograph." I stepped out into the lighted area and we all kind of laughed. As I moved on down the corridor, I thought to myself, *That was scary!*

I got to talking to the security guy sitting at the entrance. Maybe I was trying to get on the court? Anyway, I don't know what I was thinking, when it came out of my mouth that I had snuck back there that afternoon. I guess we had stood there talking long enough that I could trust the guy. Wrong. What I had done was break the Golden Rule: Kept my head down, made no eye contact, and didn't talk to anyone.

He told me he was going to call somebody to get me out of there. Right away I flipped my folder open and offered him an 8x10 photo, telling him he could get it signed after the game. He told me to get the picture signed and give it to him. I told him that if I got both pictures signed, I'd give him one. There was a pink locker-room pass sitting there and I told him that the pass might help me get the autograph, so he gave it to me.

I drifted away down the hall to get out of that situation. The game was winding down and people were starting to show up in the area. I noticed that everyone going into the locker room was now wearing fluorescent green passes. Damn! The pink pass was for pregame and the green was for after the game. The game ended and the teams headed into the locker rooms.

The Sonics had come back from a second half eighteen-point deficit and defeated the Bulls, 109-103. Dale Elis, for the Sonics, keyed the final surge for the preseason victory. Michael Jordan had twenty-two points with Scottie Pippin adding another twenty.

Meanwhile, the floodgates opened in the corridor—hundreds of people were there. It didn't look promising for me. I stood back about twenty feet, when John Paxton walked past me, heading for the bus. I might as well start letting anybody sign my poster. Phil Jackson, coach of the Bulls was talking with KC Jones, coach of the Sonics, when Paxton started walking my way. I opened up the poster and asked him to sign it, which he did.

Bill Cartwright came walking by me next and he also signed the poster. The crowd was full of excitement, but not out of hand. When Scottie Pippen walked by me, I started walking backwards while he went forward and he also signed the poster. Three other players signed when I heard over the security radio, "We'll be bringing him out soon." No one else heard that but me.

The guards moved down to the open locker room door and I followed and stood right next to them. The people gathered around were talking and not really paying attention. The voice on the radio says, "Ready," and then they were coming out. I saw Michael Jordan come around the corner inside the locker room with another guard. They stepped out into a mass of people.

Jordan takes two steps and I stepped right out in front of him with my poster and said, "Is it my opportunity in life now?"

Giving me a half smirky smile, he took the blue Sharpie and signed the poster! The crowd slowed his pace, so I let him have the Sharpie to sign other people's stuff, too. I started back-peddling, put the poster in my backpack, and then take out the folder with the pictures. I got right up to Jordan again and had one signed before he was out the door and then on the bus.

I wondered where the team was staying, so I head down to the St. Pete Hilton by the bayfront. I hurried to my car and drive to the hotel, as I still had my *Baseball Collector* magazine, another picture, and a baseball to get signed! The hotel is about two miles away from where I was. When I got there, I parked the car, and headed up to the lobby, where I found about 300 people standing around. There were three elevators in the lobby and standing in front of one was Michael Jordan!

As he was waiting for the elevators, he was very accommodating, signing autographs for people. I had my baseball and the magazine out, but decided I needed to get in front of him. Just as I started my move, some young kids jumped up and rubbed his head. Jordan yelled, "That's it!"

He became angry very quickly, so hotel security scurried to move everyone back. The minute the elevator doors opened, he was gone.

I immediately began looking for the stairs. When I found them, I hastily opened the door, and ran to the top floor. I never counted, but it was between seven and twelve floors. When I reached the top floor and opened the door, there was Jordan with a teammate. They stepped out of the elevator and went straight to their rooms.

By then, I was down at the far end of the hallway, by the ice machine and service elevator, and wondered what the hell I should do. A few players were coming down to get ice for their knees and I talked to some of them. I thought that maybe Mr. Jordan might come to get some ice, too.

The service elevator opened, and out stepped a waitress who looked like she was headed straight for Mr. Jordan's door. When she came back, I asked her if that was his room and she said yes. I sat there wondering if I should hit the road or just sit in the lobby until the next morning.

I waited a bit longer, when the service elevator opened again. There was the waitress, back a second time, so I asked her if she would take the ball and have Mr. Jordan sign it. She told me she wasn't allowed to do that, so when she returned from the room, she went back downstairs. The next time the service elevator opened it was Security. I'd been ratted out by room service!

I was dragging when I went downstairs, I was so tired—what a night! The Bulls fans are all still there and I'm still unsure of what to do … go home or hang out until the morning? I had already gotten two Jordan signatures, the coach, and Scottie Pippen, so I decided for home.

The next day the newspaper said it was the largest watched basketball game in Florida with 25,720 in attendance. The Bulls would win the 1991-1992 back-to-back NBA Championship on its way to becoming a basketball dynasty.

Michael Jordan was one of the nicest superstars I'd ever met.

In story Michael tells Greg not his opportunity in life right now!

Game Ticket

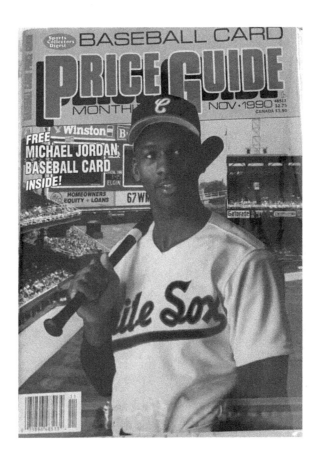

Team Signed Poster

Last Car Going Across!
The Bridge Is Closed!

It's the year 1991 and the winter had been brutal in Florida and Illinois. My three cousins, John, Paul, and Val called to tell me they wanted to head to Florida from St. Louis for some sunshine, the beach, and spring training.

After a 1,100-mile trip the guys finally made it down to my driveway in Sarasota, but darned if they didn't bring the northern winds, rain, and temperatures in the thirties with a windchill factor of twenty-four degrees. After a great dinner at Sarasota's famous Walt's Fish Market with shrimp, oysters, scallops, and grouper, we hit the hay early in order to make an early start to the St. Louis Cardinals spring training game against the Pirates in St. Petersburg.

All through the night, the wind howled outside the house. At one point, I got up and checked on my cousins and there they were, all scared, asking me if it was a hurricane. I told them, hell no, it wasn't a hurricane—the winds would be ten times worse than that, if it was! I told them goodnight and reminded them that morning would come soon enough.

And it did. It seemed weird to dress for a spring training game in winter coats, gloves, and sweat caps. It was cold and windy as we all piled into my big sled of a car—a 1984, four-door, Buick LeSabre, with a V8 engine. I headed north, through Bradenton and over the Skyway Bridge toward St. Petersburg, about a forty-five-minute ride. I stopped for some breakfast at McDonalds, as it's always good to have food in you when chasing the ink—you never know how long you might be waiting for something to unfold.

When I reached the Skyway Bridge to pay the toll, the wind was howling and blowing like no one's business! The toll tender told me, "You're the last car going on the bridge today. We are shutting it down because the wind is blowing too hard."

I asked him how the Pittsburg Pirates were going to get their buses across the bridge, and he told me they might have to cancel the game. I'll tell you one thing. It was good thing that we were driving that big car, as the wind pushed it back and forth across the center line near the top of the bridge, which is 430 feet above the bay! Thankfully, we made it down to the other side of the bridge to the Al Lang Stadium.

We each grabbed a baseball, some trading cards, and pens and headed over to the player's parking lot. Darn, it was still freezing—the stadium's built on the downtown bayfront and that wind was blowing right through our big winter coats! BRRRR! Looking around the parking lot, we didn't see too many players there yet.

The four of us walked over to the front of the stadium to try and find a place that would block the wind. Val and I decided to walk over to the outfield fence to see if there was anyone crazy enough to be out on the field. We saw coach and Hall of Famer, Red Schoendienst, standing on the top of the third base line at the visiting team's dugout, watching the damp, freezing wind blowing. Yup, my cousins definitely brought this from Illinois.

On the first base side stood Ozzie Smith, Tom Pagnozzi, Todd Zeile, Jose Oquendo, and some other players. They weren't doing much—just looking at the weather conditions and trying to stay warm. We stood watching for a while when they all kind of disappeared into the dugout and warm locker room.

Val and I venture back to the front of the stadium to hook back up with Paul and John. That's when we found out the game had been cancelled. This could work out great for us, as the players who showed up early would blaze out of the stadium and with luck, they would sign for us! I remember getting autographs from Bernard Gilkey, Lee Smith, and Rex Hudler as they drove into the stadium that morning. But, when the game was cancelled for good, that's when it was "game on" and time to fill up some National League baseballs! We got Ozzie Smith, Ray Lankford, Tom Pagnozzi, and many other starting team players. They signed our balls, hats, and trading cards.

Things started quieting down, but I could see there were still people here, judging by the cars in the parking lot. Even though the weather made a mess of things by cancelling the game, it made autographing happen in a way I'd never experienced. Next thing you know, it was just me and Val me again hanging out by the main office, when Bob Tewksbury walked by and signed our balls. John and Paul had gone off somewhere, exploring.

As we walked over to the ticket window, Paul and John popped out of some closed metal double doors. They had snuck down into the locker laundry room where all the dirty cleats and uniforms were piled in front of the washing machines. We all had on thick winter coats, so I asked them if they had stuffed a jersey under them! They both became scared, so they didn't do anything but got out quickly. I couldn't believe they didn't grab something!! They said no one was there, so maybe we could all go back in? Maybe we should have, but the opportunity had passed.

Just then, out of the locker room stepped the new coach, Joe Torre, heading to his car. We walked over to Mr. Torre and asked for an autograph, but he told us we would each get one after he got into his car and turned on the heat. He told us we were crazy waiting to get autographs in the cold. However, we told him we thought he was one of the greatest Cardinal players and how we used to watch him while we were growing up in the St. Louis area.

The dirty cleats and uniforms remained behind that day (much to my dismay). However, what we took with us were some great memories that we carry to this day.

Autograph Collection

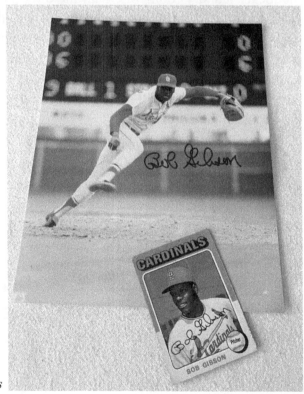

Bob Gibson Autographs

Joe Torre Autograph

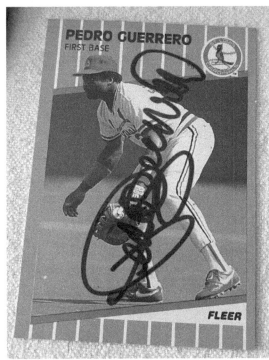

Pedro Guerrero Autograph

One of Greg's oldest newspaper clippings (6/26/1973), highlighting pictures of Joe Torre and Lou Brock, as players.

Super Bowl 25

It was the 25th Anniversary of the Super Bowl and the National Football League would be hosting Super Bowl 25 in Tampa, Florida. The National Football Conference (NFC) New York Giants will be meeting up against the American Football Conference (AFC) Buffalo Bills, so it was Phil Sims against Jim Kelly.

Oh, but no, Phil Sims was injured in a previous game and was going to be replaced by back-up quarterback, Jeff Hostetler.

I had never been to a Super Bowl—never even been in a city where the Super Bowl was being played. So I'm thinking about—what else? Doing some autographing.

A little history about me and the 1990 season. I grew up in East St. Louis, a bus ride away from Busch Stadium. As a youth, my grandmother would take me over to see the St. Louis Cardinals football team play, which now plays in Phoenix. So, I was raised a diehard Cardinals fan.

My Uncle Mike, my dad's brother, played in the NFL for the San Francisco '49ers from 1960 to 1965 and the Pittsburg Steelers from 1965 to 1967. So, I was also raised a Niners and Steelers fan.

Well, in the 1990 season, my work partner, Mark and I, had been getting together for Sunday and Monday night games. He was from the Catskills, so he was a Giants fan.

For the NFC Championship Game, it came down to the '49ers vs. the Giants. The winner would go to the Super Bowl to meet the AFC champs. All said and done, the Giants ousted the '49ers on the leg of field goal kicker, Matt Bahr. They would meet the Buffalo Bills in Tampa.

I was hoping the Niners would be representing the NFC so I could go for some of my team's autographs like Joe Montana, Ronnie Lott, Jerry Rice, Pierce Holt, Roger Craig, Matt Millen, John Taylor, and so on. Being an autograph collector, the Super Bowl coming to Tampa was a great opportunity to chase some ink.

I went to work that following Monday and asked Mark if he wanted to go up to Tampa on the Friday and Saturday to check out the city' We could do some autographing, maybe drink a few beers, and have some fun. He said he'd let me know, since we had two weeks to come up with a plan.

After checking with our wives and making sure family life wouldn't be disturbed with us leaving town, we decided to go after work on Friday the 25th. I had called news networks and hotels in Tampa to find out if the Giants would be staying at the Tampa Hyatt, and the Bills at the Airport Ramada. The day came to run on up to Tampa. Our destination was the Tampa Hyatt, home of the Giants for Super Bowl weekend.

I hadn't put anything together for autographing, just figured I'd find a souvenir stand on a city corner. The evening weather was chilly, and Mark was wearing an NFL Giants jacket and a Giants ball cap. Over the Skyway Bridge we went, arriving in Tampa. I spotted a souvenir stand and purchased a T-shirt with the helmets of both teams facing each other, Giant's blue and Bill's red, with the date and place where it would be played. I also bought a banner flag with the Super Bowl emblem and team helmets for each—one red and one blue.

We ventured on around the city, looking for the Hyatt. This was before cell phones and GPS devices. The sun had set, darkness had filled the night up, and around a corner right there it was, a rounded driveway, with valet parking at the main entrance. Circling around we passed a parking garage and went down the driveway to some public parking spaces.

After parking the Oldsmobile Vista Cruiser 350 rocket station wagon, we got out and headed up to the entrance. Our plan was to just hang around the lobby and entrance, catching any players coming in from dinner, gentlemen's clubs, or sightseeing. It was the place to be!

The players were coming and going, and we each had a blue Sharpie pen. I had put on my new shirt and Mark was sporting his jacket. The first one coming through was backup quarterback, Jeff Hostetler. He signed my shirt, my pennant, and Mark's hat. As the night went on, many players stopped and signed: Jumbo Elliott, Mark Ingram, Matt Bahr, Mark Bavaro, Leonard Marshall, and Pepper Johnson. Some didn't stop, but I remembered one big man coming in later that evening. I told Mark I was going to get in front of him to slow him down. He must have been a lineman, because he knocked me back two doorways and was gone.

It was about time for a beer. We'd been at it two or three hours. Inside the entrance area was a hallway leading to the elevators. It was roped off with a temporary reception desk to the left with the hotel lounge to the right.

As we stood there ready to get a beer, in walked Walter Payton of the Chicago Bears. He was already behind the roped-off area. I said something to the effect of, "Good evening, Mr. Payton. You're one of the greatest running backs I've seen play the game."

He smiled, gave me a wave, and headed for the elevators. Mark said, "Come on, Homes. Let's get a beer."

Into the bar area we went. Just gonna have a couple then head home, as it was getting late. We found a couple open areas at the end of the bar and received nice cold Bud bottles—a well-deserved refreshing way to end the evening.

As we were relaxing, I realized the gentleman standing next to me was Dan Marino, quarterback of the Miami Dolphins. He was talking to a couple of ladies and another gentleman. Mark told me not to bother him. I said I wouldn't bother him until he was done talking.

Some cocktail napkins were sitting there with the Super Bowl 25 emblem on them, so I grabbed a couple of them, sipped my beer, and waited. As soon as he ended his conversation, I popped over and said, "Mr. Marino, would you sign an autograph for me?"

He smiled, grabbed the pen, and signed one. I tried for a second, but he said, "Only one." Mark didn't want to ask him. I wound up giving that autograph to my good friend, Darryl, who worked with us in the shop. Marino was Darryl's favorite quarterback.

Back in the car, heading home, I asked Mark if he had had a good time. He said yes, as he'd gotten Jeff Hostetler and Otis Anderson to sign. We didn't see Lawrence Taylor, Bill Parcells, Phil Simms, or any others. I had a fever that night, so after we were home and grabbed a few winks, I asked Mark if maybe we could come back again.

He said he'd think about it and I could call him in the morning. So I dropped him off at his place, got myself home, and hit the hay.

Waking up early at sunrise, I got the OK to leave the family on Saturday to go chasing more ink and Mark was in for one more day, with the following day being Super Bowl Sunday.

I picked him up about 8:00 a.m. and over the bridge to Tampa we went, arriving back at the hotel around 9:30 a.m. We walked up the sidewalk to the entrance of the hotel. Halfway up the sidewalk, a car pulled up alongside the curb and out stepped a man in a black suit from the front passenger side. Out the back door of the car stepped Bill Parcells, head coach of the Giants, along with two other men. The three of them walked in front of us, not paying us much attention.

The night before, I had grabbed a 12x16 free newspaper called the *Giant's Newspaper*. It had a nice colored action picture of Lawrence Taylor on it, which is a good piece for any autograph.

I looked at Mark and he went for it. I stepped in between Coach Parcells and some guys who seemed to be his bodyguards and asked for an autograph. He took the Sharpie, gave his men a what-the-heck look, and signed the newspaper. Then I quickly went for getting my shirt and pennant signed. He wasn't so happy, but he obliged me.

It seemed we were just in time for some morning activity. We went inside the lobby and looked around. They had a raised-up section for the restaurant, and there was injured starting quarterback, Phil Simms, having breakfast with his son. Chris Simms was around ten or twelve years old at the time, and would later go on to play in the NFL for the Tampa Bay Bucs. I pointed Mr. Simms out to Mark, but knowing the manners of autographing, we did not bother him while he was eating.

We ventured back towards the entrance doors and ended up on the outside sidewalk. Shortly thereafter Lawrence Taylor, Giants MVP defensive end, came walking across the driveway from the parking garage. I had my Sharpie ready. He signed my shirt and the newspaper before Mark stepped in to get his jacket signed—a nice one right on the left shoulder. We wished him good luck in the game and maybe a God bless you.

Mark went inside the hotel, while I stayed outside. I walked maybe twenty-five yards down the sidewalk, and there parked along the curb was an older Lincoln Continental, maybe 1976 or so, with a sky-blue paint scheme. I kind of looked at the passenger in the front seat, who had a curlicue hairdo and glanced at me.

Well, heck! It's Walter Payton, MVP running back for the Chicago Bears. All I had for him to sign was the Lawrence Taylor newspaper. I held it out with the Sharpie toward the window. To my surprise, he put the window down, smiled, and signed. He wrote, "Walter Payton Chicago Bears" (I guess he wrote "bears," because he was signing an item with Giants autographs all over it).

I headed back to the hotel to tell Mark, but when I went into the lobby, I saw he had corralled someone else. Mr. Simms was walking from the restaurant area, so Mark was getting his jacket signed. I asked for my shirt to be signed and Mr. Simms did so before he headed off with his son.

I had this red Sharpie with me, and my shirt was signed up with blue autographs on the mostly blue Giants helmet side. I told Mark I'd like to go over to the Ramada Inn to try and autograph some Buffalo Bills using the red pen to complete the shirt.

Even though Mark did not like the Bills, he agreed to take a ride over. We drove around the Tampa Airport and found the Ramada, standing mostly alone in an open field area. We parked the car and headed in to new turf to see what was going on.

Inside, lots of people were sitting around the lobby. As we were walking the halls, we saw a dining area for the Bills team only. It seemed to be a film room, so we were in the right place. It must have been between 11:00 a.m. and 1:00 p.m. when the team bus finally pulled up at the hotel.

I waited for the bus door to open, while Mark hung back, watching. The door opened and head coach Marv Levy was the first one off the bus. He stood there a couple of minutes, but declined to sign any autographs.

I recognized James Lofton, MVP wide receiver, who signed.

Next was running back, Thurman Thomas. He signed.

Receiver Don Beebe signed. A few other players signed.

Quarterback Jim Kelly stepped off and kept going.

Finally defensive end Bruce Smith stepped off. This was one I really wanted, so I followed him into the lobby. He didn't head for the elevator, but went to the check-in desk. I waited for him to finish his conversation with the receptionist. I had the Bills pennant banner with me. I put it on the counter and handed him the red Sharpie. He signed the pennant.

Then I bowed out my chest to get a nice one on my shirt, too. He looked at me and said, "Only one!" Oh heck. I wished I had known that when we started. I would have gotten the shirt signed first. I asked a couple more times, only to be ignored.

Mark was ready to go, but I wanted to hang out to see if Jim Kelly reappeared. Mark gave me another hour.

I was outside the hotel standing under an overhang. Mark was inside buying a Super Bowl 25 hat at the gift shop. It was starting to drizzle rain and my T-shirt was getting damp! Not good.

Then, as I was standing there, a white limo pulled in and went around to the back of the building. I wondered who it might be coming to pick up—maybe Jim Kelly? I ran in and told Mark about the limo pulling around back. I told him that I was heading back to observe what was going on. Mark said he would wait where he was.

The rain was coming down a little harder, so I tried to keep under the hallways and staircases to keep the rain off my shirt. When I spotted the waiting limo, I hung out in the shadows of a staircase. Every time I heard a noise, I stepped out to look, but nothing so far. My concern about getting my shirt wet made me think it was time to get out of there. Just then, I heard Mark's voice say, "Mr. Kelly, would you sign my hat, please?"

I stepped out from the shadow. Mark was walking about twenty feet behind Jim Kelly, and a huge wide bodyguard. I tried to go straight to Mr. Kelly, as the limo was only fifteen to twenty feet away. Even though I got closer, I couldn't get around this big guy.

When I shouted to him for an autograph, he just kept walking. The big guy told me to stay back, because Mr. Kelly was not signing.

Just then, Mark shouted out, "Greg, I already tried. He's being a jerk."

As Kelly had almost made his way to the limo, I yelled out, "I hope you get your ass kicked tomorrow!"

Mark chimed in, "Yeah, we hope you get your ass kicked tomorrow!"

Shame on us for giving it away: the chase, being over, and not getting the signature. Anyway, it was time to go home. My shirt was getting wetter and dusk was upon us.

Back in Sarasota, I dropped Mark off. It had been a fun-filled two days. Who would win the game? Could the Giants, with their backup quarterback, Jeff Hostetler, defeat Jim Kelly, Bruce Smith, and the Bills?

We would both stay home and watch the game with our families and not see each other until Monday at work. That was Super Bowl Sunday,

January 27, 1991. Whitney Houston sang a memorable performance of *The Star-Spangled Banner*.

By the second quarter, the Bills had taken a demanding 12 to 3 lead. The Giants stayed with their running game, handing the ball off twenty-one times to Ottis Anderson. The Bills' number one AFC defense could not contain him running for one hundred-two yards with one touchdown. The Giants managed to lead the game 20 to 19, with two and a half minutes in the game. With time running out, Jim Kelly moved the ball into Giants' territory for a forty-seven yard field goal attempt by place kicker, Scott Norwood, with seconds on the clock. He just needed to kick the ball between the two uprights of the goal post to become Super Bowl 25 champion. The snap, the kick, and the ball sliced wide, to the right of the post. The Bills lost. The Giants were the Super Bowl champions.

Ottis Anderson was named MVP. The final score was 20 to 19. It was the only Super Bowl to be won by one point, and still is to this day. Jim Kelly took the Bills back to three more Super Bowls, four years in a row. No other quarterback has ever achieved so much and yet come up short of the championship all four times, losing each game just at the very end.

I wonder sometimes if Mark and I put a curse on him that rainy afternoon in Tampa!

Greg (right) and Mark

Super Bowl 25,
The Collection

Super Bowl 25
Autograph Collection

Super Bowl 25
Autograph Collection

Tampa Bay Map & Guide

Bo Knows God

◆ ◆

Bo Jackson was drafted in 1986 by the Kansas City Royals major league baseball team. He was a fourth round pick out of Auburn University. A multi-sports player in college, and a Heisman Trophy winner in 1985, he would decline a first round pick in 1986 by the Tampa Bay Buccaneers football team, turning down a five-year, five-million-dollar contract.

He would again enter the NFL draft in 1987, to be picked up in the seventh round, the 183rd pick by the Oakland Raiders. He entered the NFL in 1987 as a rookie, and in 1990, he made his first pro bowl. In 1991, he helped the Raiders to the AFC divisional playoffs against the Cincinnati Bengals, only to suffer a career-ending hip injury. He ended his short-lived career with eighteen touchdowns and 3,134 yards.

After surgery and rehab, Mr. Jackson signed a contract with the Chicago White Sox baseball team. He was still a crowd pleaser, and everyone was anxious to see him play sports again—considering his towering home runs and his speed in the outfield. Was he back as a professional athlete?

In 1992, Ed Smith Stadium in Sarasota had a promotional poster giveaway. The poster was black and white, maybe 24x36. It had pictures of Carlton Fisk, Tim Raines, Frank Thomas, and Bo Jackson, all full-figures and swinging bats, naturally Frank Thomas and Tim Raines already signed the poster, but I still needed Carlton Fisk and Bo Jackson to complete it.

I tried to get Jackson's autograph at the players' gate and on the practice field out back. No luck at all. I heard he liked to hunt, and I saw that he was driving a jacked-up pickup truck with big ol' mudder tires on it. I thought he'd be hooking up with some redneck Sarasota boys for some hog hunting (if he didn't, he should have).

A night game was coming up. I had discovered a practice field by the fan parking area that was always left open. You could cut across the practice field and end up by the clubhouse and players' parking area. I figured I could bring my son, Greg Jr., and my youngest daughter, Mara, to the game with a couple of balls and the poster. My plan was, when Bo Jackson was removed from the game and headed toward the open gate, we'd make our way over to the locker room area in the dark of the night. We'd wait by Mr. Jackson's truck and get some signatures—scary, but doable.

And that's just what we did on that black spring night under the lights. As soon as Bo Jackson was pulled, we headed towards the gate. Another third of the fans had also left, heading to line up on the sidewalk by the players' parking lot gate, hoping Mr. Jackson would stop there and sign.

We found his truck parked close to the locker room door. Oh boy! Here we go—trespassing again, nerves going. Greg Jr. was eight years old and Mara was four. Each had a ball. Bo Jackson came out the door, stopped, and had a conversation with some people nearby. We were waiting near the back of the truck, as he walked towards us to the driver's side. We asked him if he would sign some autographs, but he said he was tired and wasn't signing tonight.

"OK, thanks anyway. God bless you and your career," I said.

When he heard that, he turned to us, and asked, "What do you want signed?" Then he signed the balls and the poster for kids. I think it reads, "God bless - Bo Jackson!"

So after I had said, "God bless," it changed his whole frame of mind. Not only did he sign for us, but I later saw his brake lights come on at the gate. He was signing for the fans who were waiting on the sidewalk, too. How about that?

We got to the car and drove down the side street, past the players' parking lot. There was Bo, still signing for a good number of fans.

After telling us he was too tired and wasn't signing tonight, I guess blessing him made the difference.

Mr. Jackson would play for the White Sox from 1991 to 1993. He finished his career with the California Angels in 1994, with a batting average of 250, 141 home runs, 415 RBIs, 598 hits, and 694 games.

He was the only professional athlete at that time to be named an All-Star in both baseball and football.

Bo Jackson Collection

Don't Wait Nor Hesitate

It's the year 1992 and the NBA All-Star Game would be hosted in Orlando at the Orlando Arena, home of the Orlando Magic. That year, a new player for the Magic, Shaquille O'Neal, was the first rookie to be voted into the All-Star game since Michael Jordan in the 1984-1985 season. The game would be played on February 9, 1992, which was two days before my 32nd birthday.

At that time, I'd never autographed an NBA player before, but I was a fan of the sport. The players that would be there that weekend were phenomenal: Charles Barkley, Chris Mullin, Michael Jordan, Larry Bird, Magic Johnson, Mark Price, Clyde Drexler, Patrick Ewing, John Stockton, David Robinson ... the list just went on and on. No doubt, this was two of the best-stacked rosters from both the East and West divisions.

The weekend of the All-Star game was a two-day event, having the three-point competition, Legend's game, the slam-dunk contest on Saturday, and then the NBA All Star Game on Sunday. I just knew I had to check it out and had planned to go up on Friday and stay through Sunday. I wanted to get out of town to do some autographing and see some of the MVP's I had watched growing up. How in the world would I do that, while raising a family?

The convenience store at the end of my street had a rack of NBA 8x10 photos for sale. The pictures had the player's stats listed and had been there a while at about four dollars each. I bought them all up and had a good variety (Michael Jordan, Clyde Drexler, Mark Price, etc.).

The big story of the 1991-1992 NBA season was the announcement made by Magic Johnson that he had contracted the HIV virus that causes AIDS and would immediately retire. Even though Magic didn't play that season, the fans still voted him into the All-Star lineup. The fans wanted to see their most beloved player in one more game. The NBA commissioner said he would make that happen, although some of the players were not in agreement with his decision. Isiah Thomas, an All-Star guard for the Detroit Pistons and long-time friend of Magic, stepped in and called a meeting with the players. It was decided that Earvin Magic Johnson would be on the floor in Orlando.

I arrived in Orlando on Saturday February 8, 1992. I really wanted to go up on that Friday, but being a family man, sometimes you just can't get out of town. These are the memories I have of that weekend, thirty years ago.

The parking lot was full on Saturday as the Slam Dunk and the Three-Point competition, along with the Legend's game were going on. I'd never been to the arena before, but I found my way to the back of the building. There were limousines backed up everywhere, as well as a tour bus parked there, too. As I walked to the bus, I could see the lights were on inside. It seemed to be filled with players, their wives, and families.

Just then, John Stockton of the Utah Jazz and his wife walked up. He was dressed like a real cowboy, too. As I flipped through my binder to find his picture, I asked Mr. Stockton if I could have an autograph. At that moment when he was reaching for my pen, his "rootin'-tootin' " wife told me he had a headache. I let him go a few more steps to the bus door and then asked him again. His wife told me, "I told you he had a headache, so leave him alone." As they stepped onto the bus, I was standing there, just holding my pen. One down!

Two college-aged girls came over and asked me who was on the bus and what I was doing. I explained how the bus was transporting the players and their families back to the hotel. The girls were leaving the arena and had purchased some T-shirts of Clyde "the slide" Drexler. Just then, Mr. Drexler came walking out of the arena and he signed my picture and the shirts for the girls. Next to come walking up was Chris Mullin, the shooting guard for the Golden State Warriors. Mr. Mullin was gracious enough to sign both for me and the girls. The girls were having a blast and thought it was great.

For some unknown reason, at that time, I decided to try to get into the arena without a ticket. Bad choice but an interesting story.

There were multiple doors to enter and exit the arena, and at one end, a corner area was roped off for smokers, so they were able to come in and out of the arena easily. Well, I ducked under the rope and entered the doors, went through a hallway tunnel, and found myself in the aisle above the first lower level of the arena.

The Slam Dunk competition was finishing up and fans were starting to leave. I went down the stairs, toward the floor, and took a vacant seat a few rows from the floor. I remember that the Orlando cheerleaders were on the court. When I looked down center court, there at the TNT announcer's booth was Magic Johnson in a suit, commentating with the announcer.

I had Johnson's photo ready to go in my binder and although there was still a good crowd of people, I decided this was my best chance, so I went down the last few stairs. There I was … on the floor of the arena! I walked straight down and stood Magic Johnson's side. His head was turned, as he was speaking to someone. One of the top three rules of autographing is never interrupt when asking for an autograph.

As soon as Magic stopped speaking, I leaned in to get his attention. I had my binder opened and my Sharpie ready to go. When I asked Mr. Johnson if I could please have his autograph for my collection, he glanced at me and at the photos and gave me a smile. Just then, an Orlando police officer came up and tapped me on the shoulder and asked if I should be on the floor. I said no, so he told me to leave the floor and stay in my seat. I said, "Yes, sir," and started walking back up the stairs.

At the top of the aisle, I see Scottie Pippen and David Robinson walking out of the tunnel. Ah, what to do? Go for them? But I'm fixated on Magic Johnson, who just stood up at the announcer's table. When I went back down the stairs, no police officers were visible anywhere.

As Magic walked by, I stepped back down onto the floor, so that I was walking with him for about twelve steps. When I asked him again if he would sign an autograph, it looked like he was going to take the Sharpie!

At that moment, one of Orlando's finest puts me in a choke hold from behind. The officer started to drag me backwards and demands, "Didn't I tell you to stay off the floor?" It was the same officer who had caught me before. He asked me if I wanted to go to jail (I didn't) and to get off and stay off the floor or I would be!

With that, I decided to put my focus back on Pippen and Robinson. I ran up the stairs and through the tunnel to an area that was roped off and guarded by police officers. I made it back to the bus and asked the girls (who were still there) if they had gotten any other autographs. They did: Scottie Pippen, David Robinson, Patrick Ewing, and Karl Malone. Their T-shirts were loaded up! I could only stand there, looking at all those players on that bus as it pulled away.

I went for the big fish and the rest got away. Darn it. But, of course, the night was not over yet.

I walked over to where the limousines were backed in. As I was standing on the curb watching everyone, this tall gentleman was standing a few feet from me. I kept looking at him when he said, "You don't know who I am, do you?"

I told him that I knew he was *somebody,* but I didn't remember who. All I had to do was look in my binder, but it didn't click. As he got into a car, he wished me a good night and was gone.

I opened my binder and suddenly realized I had been standing next to Mark Price, point guard for the Cleveland Cavaliers. Damn, I blew that!

Next, a girl came over to me as another limo was loading up. Out of the arena comes three tall women wearing lace lingerie and black thigh-high boots and they started getting into the limo. I gave the girl who was standing next to me a few 4x6 index cards and told her to get autographs from anybody who got into the limo on the opposite side, and I would try for the other side. She was so excited!

The back-arena door opened again, and in the shadows, stood two tall men, laughing and carrying on. They made their way toward the limousine where we stood. Getting in on the opposite side was Prime-Time Super Bowl champion, Dion Sanders of the Dallas Cowboys. I wasn't quite sure who the other gentleman was entering the car on my side, until I heard him say, "It's hammer time!"

He was wearing ballooned-out bell bottom black pants with a black, sequined, V-neck shirt. Heck! It was MC Hammer, the hip-hop rapper! The girl with my cards was asking Mr. Sanders for an autograph, while at the same time, I asked MC Hammer to sign two note papers, and he did them for me. As the girl and I were moving to our opposite sides, the pair of stars entered the limo and sped away.

That girl was so happy to get an autograph from Dion Sanders, but she didn't get the second autograph … which was for me. Oh, well, foiled again. I did give her my second MC Hammer autograph. That's all I can remember from the eve of the NBA All-Star game.

Since this trip was an "overnighter," I slept in the car to save some cash. When morning came, I threw my binder and backpack into the car and headed across the parking lot. As I neared the stairs in front of the arena, I saw two young boys who were both carrying folders. When I asked if they were there to autograph, they said yes. They had been there Friday and Saturday morning at a small school/church gymnasium at the property next door. They went on to tell me that all the players had been working out every morning in the gym, so the boys had gotten autographs from most of the players. Oh my! Maybe I should have come on Friday!

One of the boys told me that he didn't get his favorite player, Chris Mullin. I told him that I had gotten two autographs from Mr. Mullin and opened by binder to show him. The boys thought they were awesome, and I told him to pick the one he wanted to keep. He was so happy!

Darn! I should have asked if he wanted to trade instead of just giving it away. It's all about karma—what you give will come back to you.

It didn't seem like it was going to be a productive day. Security was tight and the buses with the players hadn't arrived yet. I watched some high-dollar cars being parked in the players' parking lot, while I listened to music being broadcast from some radio booths. There was no way I was going to get close to the buses this time—the police were everywhere, and I didn't want to chance running into Orlando's finest from last night.

I watched as the buses pulled in, so players and coaches could unload. Although some of them acknowledged the screaming fans with some waves, no autographs were given out. I decided to walk around to see what was happening in front of the arena. The All-Star game was sold out, and although there are scalpers everywhere, Greg only had money for a cheeseburger, a drink, and gas to get home. There would be no sneaking in today, as tight security was everywhere.

As the game was winding down, fans started exiting the arena. I asked about ten people if they wanted to get rid of their ticket stub—always good for autographing! One older gentleman came out and was walking down the stairs, when someone asked him for his autograph. I had no idea who he was, but I asked him to sign one of the ticket stubs. He could have been one of the Hall-of-Famers from the Legend's Game the day before.

I was standing around the parking lot, thinking about what to do next, when I noticed a man who was wearing a ball cap and had his hair tied back in a ponytail. As I darted quickly through all the people, I yelled, "Mr. Bolton, can you sign an autograph for me?" I handed him one of the game ticket stubs. Yes, it was Michael Bolton, and the women around us went crazy; taking pictures, giving him hugs, and a couple even asking for autographs. I don't think he was too happy that I had brought attention to him. Oh, well, I got my second autograph of the day. Later, I found out that Michael Bolton sang the National Anthem at the game.

I stopped and purchased a boot-legged T-shirt from a street vendor. It had all the players on the front with the NBA All-Star logo in the center. Man, all those All-Star players I had missed … not too productive for a two-hour drive and an overnighter. As I was walking away from the T-shirt guy, I heard a man say, "Hey, Mr. Erving…would you sign an autograph?" Here, walking right next to me, was Dr. "J", Julius Erving, the small forward for the Philadelphia 76'ers from 1976-1986, winner of a championship in the 1982-1983 season, who would become an All-Star and Hall-of-Famer.

I searched for the last ticket stub, but couldn't find it. Walking at a fast pace, I fumbled for one of the index cards and got it ready just in time, so Dr. J signed it for me. It was my last autograph of the day.

I got back to my car, sat there, and reflected on the two-days. I hardly ever carried a camera, as this was the "stone-age" before cell phones, but I do have the memories in my brain. There were some good things I did, and mistakes I made. I'd left the bus area too early, when I knew players were headed that way. But if Magic Johnson would have signed, that would have been the right move to make. You never know when you are chasing the ink, if you will get the signature or not.

At least I didn't go to jail.

The many autographs collected the weekend of the All-Star Game!

*Dr. "J", Julius Erving
Autograph*

Say It Ain't So, Joe

Joe DiMaggio was going to be signing at a card show at the Omni Civic Center in Orlando, Florida. DiMaggio played with the New York Yankees from 1936 to 1951. He was well known for his batting ability and outfielding. He had a 56-game hitting streak, a record that still stands today. He was briefly married to Marilyn Monroe in 1954 and elected to the Hall of Fame in 1955.

My friend Mike and I headed up for the two-hour drive to Orlando. We had a late start that morning, so when we pulled into the Omni, quite a few cars were already there. We went straight to the ticket booth, because these events were pretty popular and kept selling out. We both wanted to have a ball signed by Mr. DiMaggio, but when we got to the booth, the $50 ball tickets were already sold out. We looked for tickets for bat signing at $100 a ticket, but they were sold out, too. The only thing left that we could have signed were the "flat items" that were $25 each. Mike was very upset that he couldn't get a ticket for a ball signature. I went ahead and purchased a ticket and two 8x10 pictures and told Mike I would see if I could get both pictures signed for the price of one.

We looked around the room at the items for sale or trade at the booths the dealers had set up. This one dealer was always at these shows. He had nice stuff, but always priced his stuffed too high and would never make a deal. I tried to negotiate a couple of times on some items with this dealer, but never had any success.

All of a sudden, the room came alive with a buzz in the air. Mr. DiMaggio had entered the building! They seated him at the table with a gentleman on each side. The people with the highest ticket items would start first, with the $25 tickets (me) bringing up the rear.

I told Mike that I brought one ticket and two photos, so if I was able to have both signed, I'd give him one. I also tell him we should buy a couple of baseballs and put them in our back pockets. Then after the show we could follow Mr. DiMaggio out to his car to have them signed.

Mike didn't think that would work, but he would really like to have a picture with Mr. DiMaggio. For some reason I had a camera with me, a rare occasion. The line was long, but moving at a pretty good pace. I was last in line to drop my pictures and hand off my single ticket, so I was nervous. Yes, I was breaking the rules, but I guess I thought I was autographing, so I should get what I could. Was it stealing? No, maybe not, but cheating—yes, maybe so.

Finally, the line was winding down with me at the end of it. I made it up to the table to the first gentleman receiving the items and tickets to pass on to Joe. I dropped down my pics one of top of the other, I handed the guy my ticket, and as the gentleman pushed the pictures over, they separated. He had already dropped my ticket into the box. He kind of looked at me funny, but let it go. I told Joe he was looking good, shook his hand, wished him well, took a picture or two and exited the area, looking for Mike. I showed him how had the two photos signed, and I handed one to him.

Mr. DiMaggio stood up from the table, talking, shaking hands, and on the move. When he made his way towards the front doors, we followed him across the street to the parking lot. I asked if he'd take a picture with my friend, as he was his number one fan. I had to nudge Mike to get him closer, as he seemed to be pretty awestruck.

I took some pictures, talked for a while, and shook his hand. Then I noticed, stepping from behind the car was that one dealer who always had high prices and would never negotiate with me. He took a baseball out of his back pocket and asked Joe if he would sign it, as the baseball tickets were sold out at the event. I was like, son of a biscuit, not THAT guy! I told Mike I should have gone with my instincts, by not listening to him, and bought an extra ball!

But Mike was happy, because he had his pictures and had gotten two autographs for the price of one. The moral of this story is you should always be prepared for the unexpected moment. Think your thoughts through about the whole adventure. We jumped into the car and headed south.

Joe DiMaggio Collection

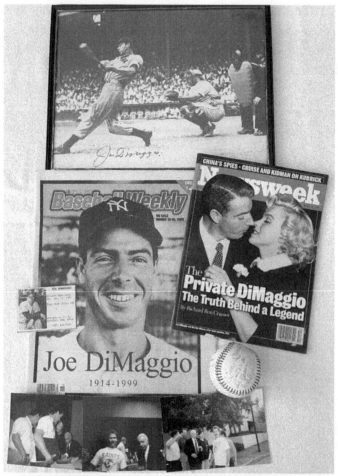

Greg standing with Joe

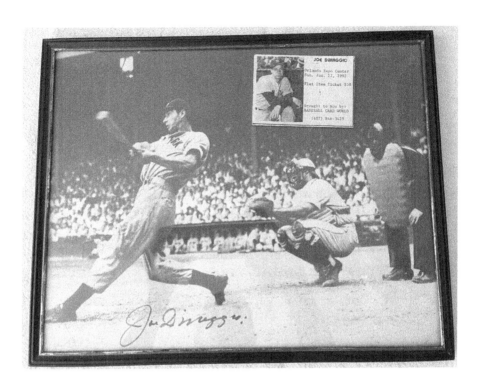

The Big Hurt, Call 911

Frank Thomas was drafted 7th in the first round to the Chicago White Sox right out of Auburn University. Weighing in at 240 pounds, standing 6'5", with a batting average of 359, he would be joining some great sluggers: Harold Baines, Carlton Fisk, and Ozzie Guillen. At that time, the White Sox held spring training right here in my hometown at Ed Smith Stadium.

I couldn't wait to see a man of Thomas' size hit home runs from the northeast practice field, where daily home runs landed on Tuttle Avenue, a busy four-lane road. I've seen many home run balls bouncing with a thud on hoods, trunks, and side door panels. That is a home run danger area for all cars traveling, but it's always hilarious to be there, watching people who don't know what was bombarding their cars.

I spent time out there, retrieving balls and watching carefully while trying to get those ricocheting bouncing balls—competing against other ball chasers trying to get in on the action. I passed the time by sneaking around the practice fields, the main stadium, and the players' parking lot. February of that year, the pitchers reported to camp, then the catchers, and finally all the players were working out there, hitting in the batting cages.

One morning, I was on a road on the west side of the stadium, a small two-lane called North Euclid Road. That area had a gated parking area for the entire organization. But right past the end of the players' parking lot was a small infield practice area for working on infield plays over and over. The team could practice the double play, the pitcher covering first base on a grounder, and plays like covering bunts from the right and left of home plate.

That's where I first saw Frank Thomas, soon to be nicknamed the Big Hurt. Wow, was he was a big man! I don't know if he signed any autographs that day, but I know of a few times he signed there for me and others. My autographing started with small stuff—a ball, pictures, and a hat.

One day I was reading the classified section of the paper, and my eye zoomed in on an ad, and suddenly my heart rate soared up. It was a Frank Thomas bat for sale. I think it was $180. I thought, *I gotta have this, but I don't have enough money. Maybe I can kite a check at Kash n' Karry.* Kiting a check back in the day meant you could cash a check and have two to three days to get the money in the bank, so it wouldn't bounce. This was before the world became flat.

So I called the number in the paper and the guy still had the bat. I told him I wanted to buy it, and asked him how we could meet up. Dave gave me his home address and the next day I was talking with him in his living room. There it was, leaning on the sofa arm, in a clear bat tube. It was a shiny black Worth bat. It had Frank Thomas, Chicago White Sox engraved on the last eight inches on the barrel. It was not game used, but a beautiful gem to me. I decided right then that I would start collecting autographs of baseball players on bats.

As Dave and I talked, we found we both worked for the Sarasota County School Board. He was a teacher at McIntosh Middle School, while I worked in maintenance as a carpentry/cabinet maker. As we talked, I told him I wanted to try and autograph the bat.

Of course, there was a catch. Dave said the bat was stolen from Mr. Thomas' locker, so it might not be a good idea to let him see it too soon. I bought the bat anyway and just waited a while.

One or two years passed, when the White Sox were leaving Sarasota for a new spring training location in Arizona. I had to get that bat signed, but I never even got a jersey signed by Mr. Thomas. However, one year my cousin Val came down and got his signature on a jersey. Val nicknamed his brother John as "smear boy," because one day John accidently smeared that signature.

After work one day, I packed up the bat and went straight to the stadium. I pulled into the parking lot by the practice field and walked in with the bat.

Frank was taking batting practice on the northwest field directly behind centerfield, in the main stadium. A bunch of people were standing along the first base line by a small fence with the higher, standard fence surrounding home plate. There were maybe fifty to a hundred people waiting to see if Mr. Thomas would sign.

Perfect, I thought. I'd fit right in—slip in, slip out. Older folks, young kids, all yelling for the Big Hurt. When he was done, he gathered up his bats, glove, and batting helmet.

"Oh my! He's gonna sign!"

He started at the far end of the line. People were getting anxious, moving here and there. I had a spot about halfway down the line. Frank was hot and sweaty after a long day's workout. He was still carrying the bat he was using for batting practice. He signed one, ten—maybe twenty times.

Somewhere there, he took my bat and people were happy, laughing, talking to Frank, but he was not listening. He stepped back and asked me where I'd gotten that bat. He had since changed to using a Louisville Slugger or a Rawlings. I told him I bought it out of a newspaper For-Sale ad. He said that this was the bat someone stole out of his locker a couple of years back.

I told him I knew nothing of that. However, I would take the bat he had right there, and he could keep the one I had just given him to sign. Meanwhile people thought we were both doing a comedy skit, but I was scared and he was hot. From what I could tell, he was more than a little pissed off. He took my silver Sharpie, signed the bat, and threw it at me like a guided missile. I thanked him and said, "God bless you," and slipped off to open air to breathe.

The bat was signed, so I was happy, but once again, my heart was beating out of my chest. There's a certain high when you accomplish getting the ink on your item of choice.

In 2005, the White Sox won the World Series. The Big Hurt, well, he was really hurt, but I'm sure he was satisfied with a big gold and diamond ring. To this day, that signed bat is one of my prize trophies. Frank Thomas' 521 home runs earned him a place in the Hall of Fame. My heart went to my toes and back that day. I later added a game-used Frank Thomas bat to my collection. It's a Rawlings, as many players change the length and weight of their bats as their swing slows or changes. Frank Thomas was a true gentleman. Thanks, Frank!

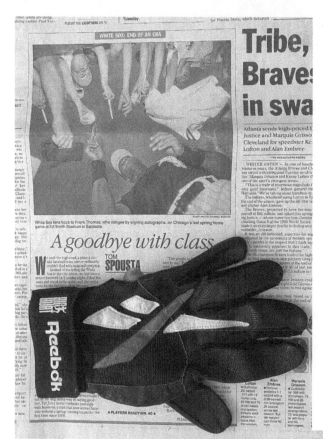

Frank Thomas' Batting Glove

Autographed Frank Thomas Bat

The Infamous Signed Worth Bat, Frank Thomas

The Rookie Comes to Town

The first and last time I saw Michael Jordan was in Sarasota, Florida.

It was February of 1994. There had been reports that Jordan would be leaving the Chicago Bulls to try his skills at baseball, possibly with the Chicago White Sox. In '94, the White Sox spring training home was Ed Smith Stadium, in beautiful Sarasota.

At the time, I was working as a carpenter for the local school board. My co-worker, Mark, and I were at the lumberyard one morning around 6:15 a.m. getting the day's supplies. The yard attendant, Joe, said to us, "Hey, you'll never guess what happened to me last night."

Joe told us that he and his wife were in for the night, when he got a call from a friend with whom he shot pool. His friend was downtown at the Sports Page, a local bar and restaurant. His friend shared that Michael Jordan was at the bar, shooting pool and having cocktails. Joe had jumped back into his clothes, went downtown, and played some pool. By the end of the night, Joe had gotten Jordan's autograph for his grandson. Joe said that Jordan was very nice guy.

Of course, this news had my mind racing and churning, filling up with ideas. It was early, the sun was rising, and Ed Smith Stadium was only nine blocks from the lumberyard. I said to Mark, "How about we first drive over to the stadium one time to see if Jordan's around?"

Mark replied, "Hell, no. We don't have time for that. We have work to do."

But I was driving, so I took a left out of the lumberyard, a right and another right, and we were on 12th Street, which just happens to be the main road leading to the front of Ed Smith Stadium. We passed slowly along the outer stadium on the first base side. There, tucked into the right field corner, just beyond the foul pole, was a portable batting cage. A few older men were standing around the cage in White Sox uniforms, while a couple of women and other men were in business attire. Oh, yes, and in the cage taking hacks at balls being pitched was the newest member of the spring training team for the Chicago White Sox. In a black jersey and high-top black shoes was a tall, lanky man wearing number 45. It was him—Michael Jordan.

Of course, I immediately pulled against the curb and parked. Mark wanted to know what I was doing—he had no feel for autographing. I jumped out of the truck and said. "Come on! We're in county uniforms. We'll just walk through the gate."

Mark followed me into the open side gate. We walked up alongside the cage, just observing, listening to comments and jokes, while watching the awkward swings, balls fouling off the bat, with some hits being smacked past the pitching coach. It wasn't long before a man approached us and asked who we were and what we were about. He told us this was a private event and asked us to leave. We turned and headed back to the truck.

That was the first time I saw Michael Jordan in Sarasota. There were no cell phones back then, and I took no pictures. In hindsight, I should have gone home and gotten my VCR recorder. I could have sold the footage to ESPN, because the news was still asking, "Where is Michael Jordan?"

After spring training, Jordan joined the Birmingham Barons Minor League. But during those weeks of spring training, to Ed Smith Stadium went the baseball fan, the spring breaker, the snowbirds, the autographer, the little kid with the ball and pen, the grandma who wanted an autograph for her grandson, and the one chasing the ink.

So many times I heard grandmothers tell the players they "wanted an autograph for their grandson." Sure—those grandmothers always came back the next day with a new ball to be signed—how many grandsons could they have? The collectors and sports dealers came with their backpacks filled not just with baseballs, but with baseball cards, basketballs, bats, and baseball and basketball jerseys—all wanting signatures.

Jordan would show up for work every morning at 6:45 a.m. You could hear him coming, turning off Tuttle Avenue in his red Corvette or his black Bentley. The line at the gate each morning was long, fifty to a hundred people, maybe more. The first dozen people in line camped there overnight. My cousin, John, decided to drive down from Collinsville, Illinois, after I told him Jordan had been stopping half the morning to sign for most of the line. John stayed seven days.

Every night after dinner, John would go down to the stadium to be one of the first in line the next day, and to my amazement, Jordan didn't stop the whole week. I had had some luck, so before John departed town for the 1,200 mile journey home, I gave him one of my autographed basketballs for his time and effort. But it's still not the same feeling— the high of getting your own item signed by a superstar.

The last time I saw Michael Jordan in Sarasota was the last time to chase some ink for an autograph!

Day 1

Mr. Jordan was playing single A ball for the Birmingham Barons, selling out the stadium during the minor league schedule. I had heard on ESPN that he had twisted his ankle and would need some rehab. The following Monday, I went down to Ed Smith Stadium before the sun rose, about 6:30 a.m. Sure enough, around 6:50, in came Mr. Jordan with a trainer.

As the morning went on, fellow autograph chasers showed up—a gentleman in a wheelchair, a seventeen or eighteen-year-old teenager on a bicycle with a brand new baseball, and one middle-aged gentleman with a baseball, saying he needed an autograph for his son. So, the wait was on. Sometime after noon, out came the car with Jordan and the trainer. One little wave and a smile and he was gone. By then, it was just the man in the wheelchair and me.

Day 2

Tuesday morning found the same four guys at the gate. Word must not have gotten around yet that the superstar was in town. Again, we waited. Again, a morning workout, and Jordan was gone by noon … probably to hit the golf course.

Day 3

Jordan arrived, waved and smiled, and then went in through the gate. We were back to the waiting game, with only three of us—the man in the wheelchair at the front of the line, then me, and finally, the kid on his bike. The kid was a talker. "Will we get an autograph today?" he asked.

I said, "You never know. Just wait and see." That boy's new ball, fresh out of the box on Monday morning, by now had been tossed around and rolled through nine innings of baseball. Ha ha!

Jordan was believed to be in town till Friday

Day 4

Rain was on the horizon, and rain is the enemy to an autograph collector. Teams get wet and players don't sign. Will Michael Jordan even show up? Right on time at 6:50 a.m., he came by the gate. It' was raining by then, but just a slow drizzle (blah). We waited … and, yes, it was still the guy in the wheelchair (never got his name) and myself, but he was a little smarter than me, because he had an umbrella. I hid in the trees covering my items in plastic waiting, waiting, and waiting … no early dismissal.

We saw Jordan and his trainer exit the side locker room door. The car came down the parking lot and pulled to gate … lots of rain coming down. The car stops and my heart rate was picking up! Mr. Jordan was sitting on the passenger side—perfect! He took the item from the wheelchair man, and with raining drizzling down, he signed his stuff and then looked at me and said, "I'll get you tomorrow."

Then he drove off.

There were rumors of a scrimmage game in the main stadium to be played the next day—at least that's what some loose-lipped parking lot guards were talking about. That night, I went home and called my daughter, Daphney, and told her Jordan was in town one last day. I explained that he signed for a guy in a wheelchair and told me he would get me tomorrow.

I asked Daphney if she could come and autograph with me (my daughter and I go way back autographing together) and she agreed to go. Then I called my mom, who laughed at the idea of coming to the ballpark, but I persuaded her by telling her that she'd get to spend the day with her son and favorite granddaughter and that she might even get to meet the handsome Michael Jordan! Surprisingly, she agreed to be there.

It was Friday morning, 6:45, with no rain, but the sun was out with a cool breeze. Joined by my family at the gate, we saw Jordan and his trainer as they drove in, but he didn't even stop for the ladies! Unusual for Jordan, but we waited. I gave them a tour of the stadium, entering the early morning gate that I knew to be open. As the morning moved on, there would be a game in the stadium, so people started showing up. The three of us settle down in the stands, sitting right behind home plate. They had a real umpire and two minor league teams made up of Gulf Coast league players with Jordan in the lineup.

It was a fun time. I think Jordan batted maybe three times that day. I razzed and made cracks at the umpire for any strikes or bad calls he made against Jordan.

Michael Jordan looked back at me, smiled, and laughed a couple of times. Of course, my beautiful daughter had other ideas, flirting and talking with the minor leaguers! My mom was also having a good time. All of a sudden, I noticed Jordan was pulled from the game and gone. I told my mom and daughter to get moving and I'd meet them at the back parking lot gate.

I moved out quickly, running from the front of stadium three blocks down to the back gate. I knew if Jordan didn't see me, he wouldn't stop. When I reached the driveway by the gate, I noticed a big guy about 250 to 300 pounds was now first in line. Oh no, I thought … how will Jordan see me around him?

As I inched closer, Jordan walked across the street to his car. I hurried to the front curve of the driveway and he came back over, as other people from the stadium were gathering behind me. The bigger guy came over and said he was first in line. I told him that I'd been here all week, so Jordan told me yesterday he'd get to me today. I told the big guy if Jordan sees me, he'll stop, and that may be that our only chance! The gentleman agreed to let me be first, and of course, when my mom and daughter came meandering up, I had to tell him they were with me.

I gave my mom a *Sports Illustrated* Michael Jordan—the first ever hologram cover. I had a hardcopy of an *Air Jordan* book and my daughter had a basketball. Jordan was on the move, but hadn't even showered. He and his trainer pulled to the gate and I yelled, "Mr. Jordan you said you'd get me today!"

Oh, yes, he saw me, heard me, and stopped! He signed for me, my mother, and even my daughter.

He wanted to pull away but continued to sign. Then out of the blue, the kid on his bike that I hadn't seen since Wednesday came crashing through the line with his well-worn baseball shouting, "I've got to get him—I waited all week!" as he crashed his bike into the window area of a car where people were lined up.

I was laughing and wondering what the heck was going on. Mr. Jordan laughed, too, but at that moment, he shot through the gate and was gone. The poor kid missed his chance. And that was the last time I ever saw MJ in Sarasota, Florida.

Michael Jordan Collection

Pictures taken at Ed Smith Stadium in Sarasota, Florida

Michael Jordan Framed Autograph

SPORTS

Friday, September 23, 1994

Sarasota saga: Michael's back

Fomer NBA star arrives today to begin work in instructional league.

By John Brockmann
STAFF WRITER

The Chicago White Sox instructional league team, an annual fall gathering, will receive the most attention ever beginning today with the arrival of 31-year-old outfield "prospect" Michael Jordan.

Jordan is one of 47 White Sox minor leaguers brought to Sarasota for some off-season instruction.

But it is Jordan who will stand out at the City of Sarasota Sports Complex.

Jordan is the reason Doug Abel, public relations director for the maj

jor league White Sox, is in town; Jordan is the reason ESPN and various other media outlets have contacted the Sox about schedules for workouts and games.

The overall list of invitees is long and talented.

Included are the White Sox first-round draft choices of the past three years (catcher Mark Johnson, 1994; pitcher Scott Christman, 1993; and first baseman Eddie Pearson, 1992).

Also here are outfielder Jimmy Hurst, who hit 25 home runs for Class A Prince William; first baseman Harold Williams, who hit .303 with 24 homers and 104 RBI for Class A Hickory; and right-handed pitcher Dave Lundquist, a 13-game winner for Hickory.

But the focus of attention from at

PLEASE SEE JORDAN ON 4C

Michael Jordan will be working out with other members the Chicago White Sox farm system at the City of Saras Sports Complex today.

Article from the Sarasota Herald Tribune *(9/23/94), along with a Baseball Signed by Michael Jordan*

Michael Jordan autographed basketball—includes rare #23

Last Chance

It was summertime and the kids were out of school. I received a flyer in the mail that Hank Aaron would be making an appearance at an Orlando mall for autograph signing. Mr. Aaron ended his baseball career in 1976 with 755 career home runs. I never had the chance to see him in person, but I had idolized him my entire life.

I had this nice baseball bat, a "Henry Aaron" model Louisville Slugger. This could be my last chance to meet the all-time home run king! I was so excited, and I started planning how I would get my bat signed. You could purchase as many tickets as you liked, but each ticket was twenty dollars. You would need one ticket to get a picture signed and two tickets for a baseball, but it would cost four tickets to get a baseball bat signed—eighty dollars. At that time, that was the budget for a week of groceries.

It was about two weeks before the autograph show, when my children's mother set a summer family outing date to Adventure Island, a water park in Tampa on the *same* day as the show—oh, boy.

I explained my plan for Orlando for that day, but it looked like it was going to be the waterpark for me—at least in the morning. So I shared with her that I would just take an afternoon ride that day to meet Hank Aaron in Orlando and then I'd zip on back to the waterpark ASAP.

Nope, I was told that was *not* going to happen. It was going to be a fun, *full*, day with the family.

The days passed and the morning of the trip to Adventure Island finally arrived. We loaded the car with the cooler and towels (and my bat!) all safe in the trunk. Off we went and arrived at the water park early—this place had a wave machine, mountain water slides, a beach lagoon, and one of the scariest slides I'd ever been on. It was hot and everyone was having fun, but I had to get to Orlando and it was two hours away.

I got the family all together and told them my plans: go to Orlando, get in line for the meet and greet, have the bat signed and then rush back to pick them up. The children's mother was not happy with me. She couldn't believe I had brought the bat with us and that I was going to leave them there for four to five hours. But, it was my last chance to get the bat signed and I *had* to do it!

I hit the road driving east on I-4 and headed toward Orlando. It wouldn't be early when I got there, so the line would already be formed, but hopefully everything would be moving quickly, and I could get in and out quickly. I found the mall location, went to the entrance, and saw that the line was already out the door. I purchased four twenty-dollar tickets and ventured up towards the front of the line.

There was Mr. Aaron, sitting at a table, signing away! I thought I'd better get in line, as some people were looking at me like I was trying to cut in front of them. When I finally got in line, about seventy-five people were ahead of me. As I was thinking about my family, I hoped they were having fun, but I was also thinking that I probably was in trouble.

Time passed and finally I could see Mr. Aaron—it was my almost my turn! I like to look at a man's hands because they tell me where they've been, the toughness of the person, and their strength. Mr. Aaron's hands had all of that. You could see their power.

I handed my bat to him and told him that I had been following his career throughout my childhood. It was such an honor to meet him. I didn't get any pictures that day—no camera! That's the story of my life.

I got back into my car, but I don't remember returning to Adventure Island or getting home, but I did what I had to do that day. As I think back, that was my last chance for his signature on that bat. Thank you, Mr. Aaron.

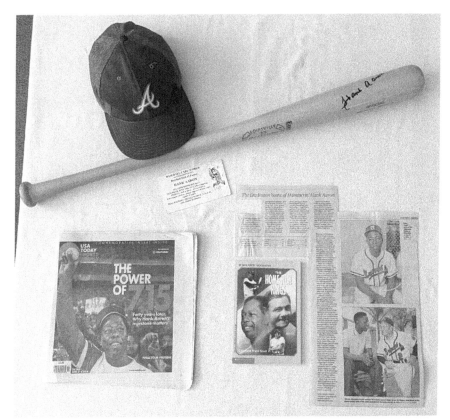

Hank Aaron Collection

Hank Aaron Signed Bat

Homerun king, Hank Aaron...the Legend.

Old school Braves uniform hat.

The Mick #7

I found out that my friend, Mike, was a huge New York Yankees fan. I knew the great ones, of course: Roger Maris, Mickey Mantle, Babe Ruth, Lou Gehrig, and Yogi Berra. However, growing up as a St. Louis Cardinals fan, I was more of a National League guy.

Mike and I were headed to another card show, as Mickey Mantle, maybe the greatest switch hitter of the game, was slated to be at the show. We were up early Saturday morning, headed all the way to Orlando, the home of Mickey Mouse, to get an autograph from Mickey Mantle.

We arrived at our destination, a civic center, which later became the Omni where the Orlando Magic played. We went inside and I purchased a baseball (five dollars) and an autograph ticket (ten dollars). My funds were always tight.

The line was forming, and we were about twenty people back, when in walked Mickey Mantle. He was stocky and had aged, but still had a nice smile. The room filled with excitement. I thought Mike might faint.

As Mantle got ready to sign, the guy in front of me noticed I only had one ball and I could see he had two cases! He told me the balls would be a long-term investment.

Today, when I look back over my collection and see my one Mickey Mantle ball, I often think of that gentleman with the Mantle balls that were now selling for about four hundred dollars each.

Was it the money? The memories? The moment? I think for me, it was watching my friend, Mike, when he shook the hand of one of his boyhood heroes.

Mickey Mantle Collection

Mickey Mantle Collection Signed Baseball & Baseball Magazine

Mickey Mantle Bat, Signed Team Baseball & Picture

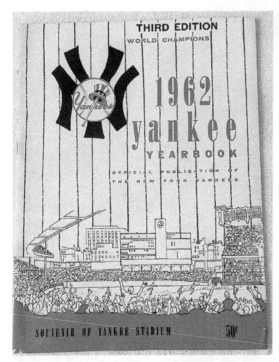

1962 Yankees Team Program found by Greg in a Hiawassee, Georgia thrift store.

Inside look of the 1962 Yankees Team Program

Hollywood Legend

In 1996, someone was headed to the Van Wezel who was one of my favorite actors—Hollywood legend, Gregory Peck. He starred in the film, *To Kill a Mockingbird*, for which he won an Academy Award. However, my most favorite movie was when he played Captain Ahab in *Moby Dick*, hunting down the great white whale. When Mr. Peck came to the Van Wezel that year—he was 79 years old.

The show was called, *Conversation with Gregory Peck*, and he would be talking about his career and life lessons learned, taking questions, and then giving autographs. I thought how cool it would be to have his autograph on a book, maybe even, *To Kill a Mockingbird*. Well, *Amazon*® wasn't available back then, but Sarasota did have Brant's Used Book Store. It had been around forever, so I would go there to hunt for old books. Sarasota also had Main Street Used Books and I loved going there, too.

Between both bookstores, I found one badly worn paperback copy of *To Kill a Mockingbird*, and a book of a western movie featuring pictures of Gregory Peck. It was showtime and I had my books and a Sharpie with me. I waited behind the Van Wezel by the stage doors with about a dozen other fans.

The sun had set on the bay, so the sky was still full of color. It was close to dusk, when coming across the parking lot was a long, black limousine. It came right up to where I was standing. When the driver stepped out and opened the back door, there stood Mr. Peck. He was about four feet away from me!

He promptly told us that he was not signing any autographs. However, when I held out *To Kill a Mockingbird*, he looked at it like it brought back fond memories. He said, "I'll sign *that* book!" He placed his signature on the front cover and presented it to me. Twelve steps later, he was in the building. No one else was given an autograph.

Wow! That happened so fast. I still had another book to get signed. Since I didn't have a ticket to the show, I decided to head home and come back later. My memory is a bit foggy about that part, but I do remember driving back to the Van Wezel later that evening. However, when I arrived, the parking lot was empty. The only vehicle I saw was the black limousine, but this time, it was in the valet area by the front entrance.

I had brought two of my children with me, seven-year-old Mara, and Greg Jr., then thirteen. I can't remember why they were with me, but after we parked, I grabbed my stuff and moved towards the limo. The rear passenger door was open and Gregory Peck was standing there talking to some folks at the main doors to the Van Wezel. When he turned towards us, I asked if he'd sign the other book I had, as well as a newspaper article.

As soon as he started to sign, I heard a voice that resounded from the back of the limo, "Why don't you leave him alone?"

I turned to see this beautiful woman, Veronica Peck, Mr. Peck's wife. She informed us that he was tired. However, he signed for us.

As he signed, I told him that *Moby Dick* was my favorite movie. My favorite scene was when the whale was going back and forth, wrapping the harpoon around his body. Mr. Peck replied, "They damn near drowned me making that scene! Every time I went under water, I prayed I'd come back up."

I shook his hand, thanked him, and introduced him to my children. He looked at Mara, patted her on the head, and told her, "You need to be in bed, young lady." Then he said goodbye, got in the limo, and was gone.

As I drove home that night, I remembered watching his movies with my parents and grandparents. What a rush it was to meet this famous person, hear his voice, share a few words, and shake his hand. What a legend. Thank you for the memories, Mr. Peck.

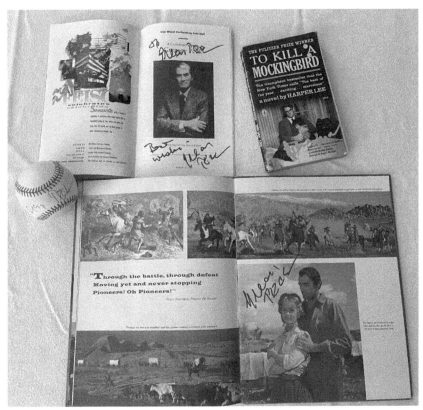

Gregory Peck Collection

Gregory Peck Book & Ball Autograph

Bats, Bats, and MORE Bats

It was the spring of 1997 and the New York Yankees had just won the 96 World Series defeating the Atlanta Braves. Both New York and Atlanta had rosters stacked with All-Star players.

The Yankees had Derek Skyway, Wade Boggs, Bernie Williams, Andy Pettitte, David Cone, and Tino Martinez. The Braves had Chipper Jones, Fred McGriff, Javy Lopez, Tom Glavine, John Smoltz, Greg Maddux, Ryan Klesko, and David Justice. I wanted all of their autographs.

My friend from Atlanta, Paul, called me right before spring training started. He told me he had found a company and met some guy who had a baseball bat business that made bats for major league players. Paul had asked him if he could make him some replica bats of a few of the Braves players. The guy told Paul he could do it—he'd just have to leave off the serial numbers that usually were on the knobs since the bats were technically "unofficial."

Paul called me and told me about the bats. We decided to do a week of spring training and autographing. It wasn't long after that when Paul arrived in Sarasota with bats in-hand: two of Chipper Jones, one of Javy Lopez All-Star, three of Ryan Klesko, and five of rookie prospect, Andruw Jones. There were probably more—I just can't remember. Paul also brought with him four 1996 official World Series balls.

I grabbed my suitcase and picked up my friend, Charles, who also wanted to go. We headed to the other side of the state. Our idea was to drive through the night to the Braves Stadium on the east coast of Florida. We had an address, so we knew it would be a three-hour drive.

We had a dozen bats, but all I could think about was how we were going to get them all signed. However, I figured out a way to carry them all. I used a soft-sided duffle bag with two zippers and big, looping handles. I could slide all the bats at an angle into the bag and zip it halfway up. The bats extended about fourteen inches out of the bag, but it worked great for carrying them.

We arrive at the facilities before sunrise with nobody around and the streetlights still on. We did some exploring of the main stadium and the practice fields to figure out where everything was. Because it was an old-school stadium, only a four-foot fence separated the fans from the players who were walking from the parking lot to the locker room. This place would be autograph friendly.

As the sun started to rise, we grabbed a few hours of sleep in the comfort of the car. Later, office personnel and security started showing up, along with other baseball fans, but no early morning players. One of the guards told us the players were getting physicals that morning and would be showing up between 11:30 and 1:00 that day. Ugh. We'd done the all-night drive when we could have slept at home and made the drive over later. You never know in this game of cat and mouse, so we waited.

I had purchased two Atlanta Braves jerseys on the clearance rack at JC Penny®, so that is what Paul and I were wearing as we walked up to the player's gate (Charles just had on regular clothes). Two security guards were there, but back then, security personnel were just volunteers from the community who wore colored vests. (After 9/11, everything was more closely guarded.)

When we ventured to the player's gate, I was carrying the duffle bag full of bats. Wearing the Braves jerseys and carrying that huge bag full of bats, the security gentlemen thought we were there to drop off the bats for the players. They were just going to let us through the gate and onto the field. WOW! That would be amazing, but we were scared and backed off, telling them we were just fans, looking for the players.

Soon after that, the players *did* show up, along with a ton of fans. That four-foot high barrier ran twenty feet long and was now four people deep all along the fence line. I remember Greg Maddux signing, Chipper Jones, David Justice, John Smoltz, Andruw Jones, Mark Lemke, and Javy Lopez.

The stands were filling up with people and lots of kids, along with their mothers, fathers, and grandmothers, who were yelling out for Chipper Jones to come over and sign for them. You gotta watch these people trying to get autographs—some of them were crazy. Don't get in front of those grandmothers—they won't think twice about punching you in the back—they're ruthless! There is nothing like smashing some kids up against the fences when nobody is looking. Ha, ha—just kidding.

Chipper came over and started signing, making sure he took care of the kids and ladies. He signed for me and Paul that afternoon, as well. I mean, he made sure everyone who asked got a signature or picture. He was a great guy.

We had some pretty good luck getting the bats signed, so then we started working on getting the baseballs signed by the team, too. Our plan was to try to get the World Series balls signed by the entire team in two days. No game was being held that day, just practice, so we went into the stadium and hung around the field. We did fairly well on autographs there, too. However, poor Charles tried twice to get David Justice to sign, but he got skunked.

Speaking of autographs, a backstory accompanied something that happened that day with Ryan Klesko. You'll have to remember this part, because it comes into play during this first day at the Braves spring training camp.

Earlier in 1996, Paul had gone to see a Van Halen concert in Atlanta. When he was there, he noticed Klesko was at the concert, too. Paul said hello to him and mentioned that he was his daughter's favorite baseball player. However, since Paul didn't want to bring attention to Klesko at the concert, so he didn't ask him for an autograph. He told Klesko that he hoped to see him at the stadium someday.

Soon after that encounter, Paul took his two daughters, Stephanie and Jennifer, to Atlanta for a Braves game. While at the game, along the first baseline, Paul yelled to Klesko and reminded him about the concert. Klesko came over to the family, met the girls, and signed some autographs. Paul told him about living in California and spending some time hanging out and partying with Eddie Van Halen and David Lee Roth when they were young musicians playing in LA clubs. Paul told Klesko that the next time he came down to Florida for spring training, he would bring some of the pictures from California for him.

Back to spring training camp. Charles was wandering, while Paul and I were sitting in the stands, watching players taking batting practice and fielding. We were waiting for Mr. Klesko to finish his workout. Finally, he grabbed his glove and bats, and headed to the dugout, which next to us.

We stood up and Paul yells out, "Hey, Ryan! Van Halen!" Then he held up a few 8x10 pictures that he had promised to show Mr. Klesko over a year ago. We each had a Klesko bat for him to sign, but we also wanted his autograph on our World Series balls.

I was pretty sure he was going to blow us off, until Paul held up those pictures! He stopped at the dugout stairs and chatted a little with Paul. Then he took the pictures from his hand and signed a bat for him.

Of course, I stood there, too, but as I tried to hand him the bat, he looked at me like he wondered what I was doing? I asked him politely to sign the bat, and although he seemed reluctant to sign it, he did. Then he was gone.

Just then, David Justice ran past us and Paul yelled out, "Hey! Western Hills High, Cincinnati!" Evidently, Mr. Justice and Paul went to the same high school—you just can't make this stuff up.

We decided to get a hotel room for the night. As we were preparing to leave the stadium, a small car with Mark Lemke, Fred McGriff, and Jeff Blauser in it was leaving, too. I was driving, so of course I followed them.

They noticed we were behind them, so the chase was on! We changed lanes a few times and blew through some yellow lights to keep up, when they pulled into a liquor store. When we pulled in with them, they looked at us and we looked at them. Of course, by then, the three of us were too scared to ask for any autographs.

After freshening up at the hotel and grabbing some dinner, we stopped in a fancy bar for a cocktail and ended the night in a Gentleman's Club. We took a table in the back and ordered some drinks, when Paul noticed some of the Braves players sitting around a table near us.

My friend, Paul, has an uncanny way of knowing people's faces. We didn't bring any attention to them, but as they were leaving, Paul said something to them about being at the game the next day. We followed them out and hit the hotel for the night.

The morning came way too soon, and I guess I kept my friends up all night with my snoring! Oh, my! We headed out early to the stadium and got several autographs while watching the players come in. Paul and I spent some time there and Charles wandered off to see what else was going on. There was a 1:00 game against the Baltimore Orioles.

After a while, we had no idea where Charles was, so Paul and I went to check on the practice field. While we were walking out, I noticed a rookie player from Sarasota High School by the name of Joe Ayrault. I told Joe that I was from Sarasota and knew his high school coach, Clyde Metcalf. I got the opportunity to talk for a while when Joe and Paul wandered away.

I kind of hung out where I was next to the practice field exit, as it was a good spot for autographing. The next thing I knew, Paul came over and told me and our friend Charles and Dave Justice were getting into it over at the practice field and I'd better get over there quick. Paul told me that Charles had told David Justice that he was a racist for not signing his ball yesterday. Mr. Justice had told Charles not to even go there and reminded him that he did sign yesterday. Charles admitted that he had, but told him that he hadn't signed his ball and had skipped over him twice.

Mr. Justice told Charles that he couldn't sign everything and to throw the ball and pen he had over the ten-foot fence. I was on the scene by then and watched as Mr. Justice signed the ball and threw it back over to Charles. Whew—dodged a bullet on that one.

Since the game was about to start, we headed over to our seats. Who did we see, but Ryan Klesko, signing for people over by the dugout. I grabbed the last Klesko bat we needed to get signed and got into the crowd of people. When I ask him for an autograph, he looked at the bat and asked me if didn't he sign for me yesterday. I told him yes, to which he said I was good, then.

So, then I pulled out my World Series ball and asked him to sign that. Again, he reminded me he had signed for me yesterday. Well, that was that. I should have sent Paul to do it. The game started and we were excited to see that Cal Ripken had made the trip. I can remember everything from that game: who won, who got great hits, and who showed spectacular fielding.

Right after the game, Mr. Ripken began signing by the dugout. I kid you not—the line went from home plate and ran all the way down third-base line into the outfield, past the home run foul ball pole. People were against the fence, two to five people deep. That man made sure everyone got an autograph. I hadn't seen anything like it.

After the game I headed over to use the facilities before we left for home. I was by myself, standing on the sidewalk in front of the stadium, when up pulled a car. Who stepped out of it? Ryan Klesko! So, of course, me being me, I pulled out my baseball, stepped over, and asked him to sign it. He didn't give me much of a look this time, just took the ball and signed it for me. As he was closing the door I said, "Van Halen," to which he gave me a strange look and was gone.

We drove back home to Sarasota. By then, you would think, I would have had enough. Nope. Paul, Charles, and I had a good night's rest, because we still had two 1996 World Series balls and some miniature bats we needed signed by the 1996 World Series champion New York

Yankees ... who just happened to train in Tampa. Why not just drive north the next day?

After a good night's sleep, we did just that. I'm not sure what kind of spring training day it was, but it appeared to be an open-stadium workout or perhaps a team family day? The players had their families there, and the media were donig interviews and photos. There were some players on the field, while others were on the practice fields. Mounted police were everywhere, and Wade Boggs rode a Tampa Bay police horse around the field like he had done in New York when they won the championship.

We autographed some players that day, but with a 48-man roster, we couldn't get all of the players in just one or two days. Sometimes you can fill a team ball with players doing morning by the players' parking lot and then afternoons after quitting time. Some of the players we got that day were: Bernie Williams, Wade Boggs, Charlie Hayes, Darryl Strawberry, Cecil Fielder, and others. As hard as we tried, we still hadn't gotten Derek Jeter.

Who would I run into, but Mr. George Steinbrenner, owner of the Yankees. Since I hadn't got head coach, Joe Torre's, autograph on the sweet spot of the baseball, I figured, why not ask the owner to sign—I asked him and he did.

That afternoon, we ventured over to the player's parking lot gate. Somehow, we knew that Jeter was driving an orange, 3000 GT and we saw it, parked way up by the stadium side entrance. No one else who was standing with us knew that was his car. As usual, we waited and we waited, so that eventually all the other autograph seekers had left and went home. We waited the longest.

Finally Derek Jeter appeared and was standing by his car. All we needed was this one guy on our World Series balls. He pulled up to the gate, stopped, and told us that he couldn't believe anybody would wait that long for an autograph (he hadn't met me yet), but he was on his way to do an interview and photoshoot.

However, Mr. Jeter signed our baseballs and on one of the miniature bats, he wrote, ROY (Rookie of the Year) 96, Derek Jeter. I wished I had a couple more things for him to sign that day, but there would be other times. It was a good day ... a good few days. The following day, Paul headed back to Atlanta, while Charles and went back to work.

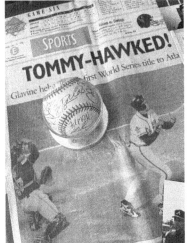

1995 Atlanta Braves W.S. Champs

L. to R. Charles, Paul, Greg

Greg Maddox, Paul

Atlanta Braves 1996 Spring training, West Palm Beach Municipal Stadium

1995 team signed World Series ball

Autographed items

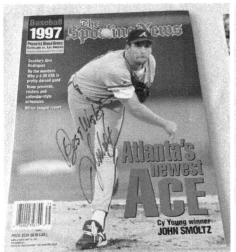

Ace pitcher John Smoltz

3rd Basemen Chipper Jones

Outfielder David Justice

Say Cheese, Please

◆ ◆

In 1997, the Chicago White Sox left Ed Smith Stadium and moved to Arizona to play in the Cactus League. They were no longer in the Grapefruit League.

The Cincinnati Reds left Plant City, Florida, and moved their major and minor league teams to Sarasota in 1999. The team was full of All-Star players, such as Barry Larkin, Greg Vaughn, Michael Tucker, and Aaron Boone. But the upcoming news that year was that the Reds had picked up Ken Griffey Jr. from the American League Seattle Mariners. Griffey was a big home run hitter with lighting speed, who played centerfield and was a designated hitter.

Ken Griffey Jr. was still the favorite player of my daughter, Mara. So, here he was, playing ball in our good ol' hometown.

By the spring of 2000, (the millennium year, an anniversary of one thousand years), my brother-in-law, Thomas, his wife, Lisa, and their three children, Tanisha, Jasmine, and Quintin came down from Alabama for spring break and some fun in the sun. While they were visiting, we were going to take in a game. I had tickets to a game, during which they were going to let children twelve and under come out onto the field to stand paired up with a player for the National Anthem.

Only Mara and her cousin, Tanisha, wanted to go out onto the field. They were both twelve at the time—perfect.

We planned to be at the game when the gates opened at 11 a.m. to make sure the girls had first opportunity to be allowed on the field, not knowing yet how it was going to work. We weren't even sure if they'd even be allowed to ask for an autograph or a picture or two.

When we arrived at the stadium that day, they were also giving out Reds jersey-style T-shirts, white with red pinstripes, and a "C" emblem in the pocket area. They told us to stand by the gate between the home plate backstop and the Reds' dugout.

When the players came out onto the field, they would line up from home plate down to the first baseline and out into the right field foul line. They would be on the playing field, a couple of steps back from the foul line. When the children went out onto the field, they could line up across from the player of their choice, staying a foot or two away from this side of the foul line.

There would be no autographs and no parents were allowed on the field. However, we could take pictures from behind the dugout stands and down the line from the other seat sections.

We told the girls to wait for the National Anthem to finish. Then when it was time to leave the field, they should jump over the foul line and we'd take some quick pictures.

They were worried and said, "But we might get in trouble"

"No, you won't," I said. "It will happen so quick, it'll be funny."

Sixteen or so players and coaches were going to be lined up. As the players entered the right field from the clubhouse, the fans began filling up the stadium. The children were lined up at the gate. I can't remember the first couple of players coming off the batting box area. About a third of the way down the line in front of the dugout were Michael Tucker, Ken Griffey Jr., Barry Larkin, and Sean Casey.

"As soon as the song is over," I told the girls, "one of you stand in between Tucker and Griffey and the other between Griffey and Larkin. Quickly turn around, smile for a picture, and then get off the field. Oh, yeah, and ask them if you can have a bat after the game, if they break one. You never know, unless you ask!"

They opened the gate and Mara got her spot across from Ken Griffey Jr. Tanisha got a spot across from Michael Tucker. The girls said, "Hi," to the players. Michael Tucker interacted mostly with the girls. Sean Casey did, too. Griffey and Larkin stayed to themselves. That was OK. If the girls didn't get scared and stuck to the plan, we would have our surprise.

When the National Anthem ended, everyone yelled, "Play ball!"

The gates opened, so the children could leave the field. As they turned to walk out, the girls quickly jumped over the foul line and in between the players. The players didn't know what was going on. Griffey looked like he had swallowed a bug. But the girls turned and smiled.

"Say cheese!" I yelled. And we got the picture.

The girls came off the field all excited. They had asked about the bats or a ball, too. Tanisha asked Tucker and Mara asked Larkin. Mara said Griffey ignored her.

"Let's get a hot dog, a drink, and some peanuts," I said. It was a hot spring day and luckily our seats were in the shade of the second level.

We had gotten some autographs before the game: Sean Casey, Barry Larkin, Pokey Reese, Mile Bell, and Michael Tucker, but no Ken Griffey Jr. yet. We could try after the game.

I don't remember who they played that day, or who won. Ken Griffey Jr. and some of the other players were pulled after the fifth or sixth inning. Griffey and Larkin walked off the field and out the right field gate, not stopping at the wall or fence to sign anything.

Michael Tucker was still in the game until the end. After the game, we went down by the wall to autograph some more, and beg for anything else. Sometimes you can get some free bags of sunflower seeds or some Double Bubble gum or even a batting glove, a hat, or a cracked bat.

As we were all standing there, who came up but Michael Tucker. He said a few words and handed Tanisha one of his bats. I'll be darned! We were all surprised. What a nice guy, so down to earth.

It made that little girl's day. It was her first major league experience. But the best part of my day was when those girls jumped over the foul line to get that picture. You would have thought those players had seen a ghost or a snake. Funny stuff.

My brother-in-law talks about it all the time. He always says, "Griffey ain't nothing but a punk!"

*Mara and Tanisha
with Griffey Center,
Barry Larkin to left*

All in a Day's Work

In my teenage years and young, adult life, Payne Park was my place to go for baseball. It was the home of the Chicago White Sox until it was demolished in 1990. The White Sox would move to Ed Smith Stadium located on 12th Street and Tuttle Avenue in Sarasota. In 1977, when I was seventeen, the White Sox drafted a Number One pick, a ballplayer by the name of Harold Baines. During his career, I would watch Mr. Baines hit some tape-measure home runs in spring training. He would become one of my favorite players to watch.

He became the designated hitter for the White Sox, and I'd autographed him on some baseball cards and baseballs—he was always nice and soft spoken. I went to the last game played at Payne Park where Mr. Baines hit a home run to center field. I jumped out of my seat, ran around the outside wall, and got the ball! I would later have it signed by Mr. Baines.

Fast forward to 1997—it would be the last time the White Sox would call Sarasota home. They had built a new complex in Tucson, Arizona, and would be moving out west to join the Cactus League. At the time, I had gotten a job with the Sarasota County School Board in the maintenance division. They'd supplied me with a van to go around to all the schools in the area and do remodels, repairs, and such.

Every so often on my lunch break, I would stop by Ed Smith Stadium and slide in the side gate. I'd go sit on the bleachers, and during batting practice, I would scoop up some foul balls. I grabbed foul balls hit by Harold Baines, Frank Thomas, Carlton Fisk, Ozzie Guillen, Craig Grebeck, Robin Ventura, and many others.

Sometimes I would catch an autograph, if someone was leaving the field and walking out close to the wall. I always had on my school board uniform, so I kind of looked like I belonged there as a worker. I can clearly recall being there during my lunch break.

One time, I remember I was a little late getting to the stadium, and the players had already left the field. From the right field bleachers, I walked down the aisle towards home plate, when I noticed, what appeared to be a batting glove. I looked around and up in the press box, but no one was around. I quickly went to the gate, (between the dugout and the backstop), opened it, grabbed the glove, and shoved it into my pocket.

I hurried out of there, but when I got back to my van, I looked at the glove. It was black and red, and on the wrist-strap was a small figure swinging a bat. It said, "The Big Hurt."

That was Frank Thomas' glove! That was his nickname, because he could hurt you with one swing of the bat. My heart had been beating fast since I entered that field. Man, this was awesome!

The next story I recall was when I once again went through the side stadium gate and sat on the bleachers. A few players were working out on the field. I saw a woman sitting with her children a few rows up from behind home plate—a girl, maybe ten years old, and a boy, perhaps thirteen. I noticed the boy had a broken leg and used crutches.

I saw some of the players on the field: Frank Thomas, Ozzie Guillen, Robin Ventura, and Harold Baines. They exited down the right field line and into the clubhouse. I didn't ask for any autographs that time, but I did notice that they had left three bats laying around the infield. Had they left the bats for that family?

I watched as the woman and the two children went through the gate and onto the field. My thought was that they would grab the three bats, but they didn't. Instead, they also walked down the right field line and exited.

You know what I'm thinking—about getting on that field, grabbing those bats, and then rushing back to my van. I walked towards the gate, but I still could not see anyone around yet. My heart was racing as I went down through the gate and out onto the field—I hope no stadium personnel saw me or came to mow the field.

When I reached the nearest bat, which was close to first base, I saw that it was black and cracked—what they call "game-used." I rolled the barrel over with my foot and saw that the barrel had "Chicago White Sox, Frank Thomas" inscribed. Whoa! I quickly grabbed it up and went to the next one.

Once again, I rolled it over with my foot and read, "Craig Grebeck, Chicago White Sox." He was one heck of a utility infielder! I picked it, too and moved on.

The last bat was a beautiful red mahogany with gold lettering. I rolled it over and it was Robin Ventura's bat, the starting third baseman! Of course, I pick that one up, also.

I'm trying to hold all three bats between my legs as I walked. I moved up the stairs and headed to the tunnel. By then, I was about fifty yards away from my van. Through the tunnel I go, past the offices, and out the gate. By the time was back in the van, my body was full of excitement.

Was I wrong for doing this? Maybe.

Or was it my time to collect these? Maybe.

I would go on to get those three bats autographed.

The last time I can recall being at the stadium during my lunch break, I was sitting over on the right field bleachers, collecting a couple of hit balls. Three or four players were finishing up their morning workout. Remember, 1997 would be the last spring training for the White Sox at Ed Smith Stadium.

As the players were leaving the field, I saw that Harold Baines was walking out. I yelled to him, asking if he would sign a ball for me. To my amazement, he headed over to me.

First thing Mr. Baines asked me was if he had signed a ball for me yesterday. I told him, "No, sir. The last time I got an autograph from you was over at Payne Park. You had hit a home run on the last game and you signed that ball for me."

As Mr. Baines started to sign one of the foul balls I had collected, I told him that I had followed him since he was drafted in 1997 and had gotten some autographs from him in the past. I told him that I noticed that he always carried two bats and that maybe in my younger days, he would have handed me one of them.

He looked at me with a half-smile and handed me back the signed ball. Mr. Baines then lifted up his two bats, appeared to be weighing them, when he handed me one and said, "How's that?" Really? Yes, he gave me one of his bats!

I told him thank you, he was the best, and that no player had ever just given me their bat! He laughed and headed for the clubhouse.

Harold Baines—a class act, both on and off the field. Thanks for the wonderful memories and the bat, which down the road you did autograph for me before the White Sox left Sarasota for good.

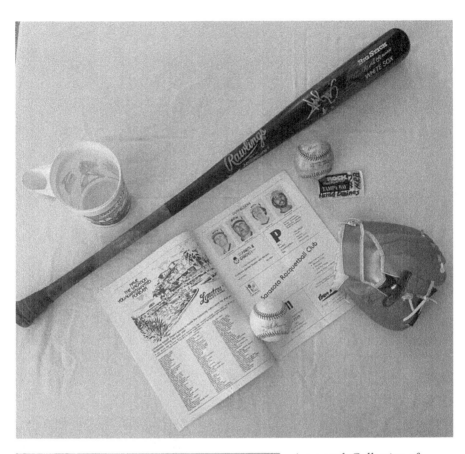

Autograph Collection of Chicago White Sox Harold Baines

ROLAND HEMOND

EDDIE EINHORN

ED SMITH

TONY LARUSSA

JERRY REINSDORF

Score Book: 50¢

ALL*STAR GAME 1983
50th
Anniversary
SOX

1983 Spring
Training Games
White Sox

Sarasota, Florida

Early program from Payne Park

The days when a beer at the ball park was a beer

186

1996 World Series Champion New York Yankees

The Veterans, the Rookie, and the Bat That Got Away

In 1995, I ventured up to the spring training home of the New York Yankees in Tampa, Florida. George Steinbrenner, owner of the team at that time, also owned a good portion of the Tampa Bay shipyard. I headed up there with my daughter, Mara, as she was a Derek Jeter fan. I was a fan of his, too, but I had no love for the Yanks—only in certain situations. On this day, the Yankees were playing an away game against the Blue Jays.

In the early weeks of spring training, not all players rode the bus on game day—some stayed behind to work out on home field with the coaches. We were hoping, as were most fans, to catch Mr. Jeter and maybe Andy Petit and Bernie Williams. Like most of the fans, we were hoping to have a better chance of getting some ink.

We arrived at 9:30 on a cold, but sunny day. The gates to enter the main field were all locked up, so we had to go around to the practice field, down by the left field wall of the main stadium. Pitchers and catchers were in the bullpens, so you could hear the 90 miles-an-hour fast balls slam into the pocket of the catcher's mitt—a well-known sound of spring training. The pedestrian bridge that was usually open to allow fans to watch in the bull pens was also locked, so we walked over to the bleachers along the third base line.

Minor league players came out on the field and started their morning exercise workout, but no big names were out yet. We watched the players split up—some going into the batting cage, while others went to the infield or outfield. I was sure there were some upcoming new star players out there, but I didn't come for any autographs. It must have been about eleven o'clock that morning when they opened the main field, so by this time, more fans had showed up.

Any time I've autographed at this stadium, the crushing that went on between fans getting signatures was some of the heaviest pushing I'd ever encountered. These Yankee fans will crush you, poke you in the eye, and even elbow you like nobody's business. However, when fans start pushing like that, the players just move on down the line or leave altogether. (I have to be honest ... I've done a little crushing in my time). The autograph hounds want that signature really, really, bad—it's a business for some of them, as the right autograph can bring in some pretty good coin.

As Mara and I came out of the tunnel under the second level, #2, Derek Jeter, was swinging a bat in front of the dugout. Tino Martinez was in the batting cage taking some BP (batting practice). Someone was out on second base ... it looked like Wade Boggs. We went down to front row seats by third base. As Martinez hit one, Boggs rounded third base, and zoomed to home plate. Then Martinez jogged to first, as Derek Jeter stepped to home plate and started hitting some nice shots, putting quite a few balls over the outfield walls.

Jeter hit one to the outfield and rounded the bases, stopping at third. Coaches worked with him there, before he ran to home plate. This is one of the days I actually had my camera with me, and so I took one picture of Jeter at third. After the workout, they all exited the field into the dugout and I got a picture of the upcoming rookie, but no autographs. We headed home over the Skyway Bridge.

Another time that same year, I was at Tropicana Field when I met an older Italian gentleman who was doing exactly what I was ... trying to get the ink flowing. His name was John and in his hand he had a game-used black bat that had belonged to Derek Jeter. John received the bat from Derek Jeter the night before and he just had him autograph it. I asked John if it was for sale—he said he'd sell it for $400.

I had about half of that in cash on me and I was seriously thinking of going to the Winn Dixie next to the stadium to get the rest. But doing that would put my account in the hole, so I passed on the bat. That was one of the biggest mistakes I'd ever made in my life (and I've made quite a few).

In 1997, I went to Yankee spring training camp. Derek Jeter and the Yankees had won the 1996 World Series and Derek Jeter won Rookie of the Year and a World Series at just twenty-one years of age with teammates Mario Duncan, Cecil Fielder, Andy Pettitte, Wade Boggs, Tino Martinez, Charlie Haze, Jorge Posada, Bernie Williams, and Paul O'Neal and the whole team of new and experienced talent.

My friends, Paul and Charles (see Bats, Bats, and More Bats), had just spent three days with me autographing the Braves in West Palm Beach and then we drove to Tampa to grab some more signatures. We had some 1996 World Series balls and some mini-bats to have signed.

That elderly Italian man, John—the one with the Jeter game-used signed bat? I'd meet up with him again that year, and but this time, I brought $600 to get the bat I should have bought for $400. However, John now wanted $1,000 for that same bat,because Jeter had won the 1996 Rookie of the Year and the '96 World Series. Then he offered a signed Jose Conseco bat to me for $500. I ended up buying the game-used and signed Conseco bat, but that Jeter bat slipped away again.

I'd see old man John one more time when we were both at Tropicana Field, autographing the Tampa Bay Rays after they had beaten the Red Sox in 2008 to win the American League Championship. We laughed, shook hands, and talked. I asked John if he still had the Derek Jeter bat and when he said yes, I offered him $2,500 for it.

John told me the bat was in the corner of his bedroom closet. However, his grandson had told him not to sell it, because it was worth a lot of money. I often wonder what ever came of that bat and how old man John was doing.

The veteran players who had signed with the Yankees for the 1996 season all had come from the New York Mets 1986 World Series

Championship team. Those vets including included Darryl Strawberry, Dwight Gooden, and David Cone.

My daughter, Mara, and I went on a Tampa trip to Yankees spring training in early 2000—we hadn't been there together since 1995 when we saw Derek Jeter as a rookie. When we arrived at the stadium, the gates were open, so fans were going everywhere. When we first walked into the stadium, not much was happening—we saw mostly media. But there, sitting on the field by third base, was Darryl Strawberry, talking with a reporter.

Mara and I headed down to the wall where several other fans were standing. After Mr. Strawberry finished his interview, he came over and signed some ink. Mara had a ball signed and I gave him a *Baseball Weekly* to sign that pictured him on the cover. I also asked Mr. Strawberry to write something on it before he signed the magazine. He took my pen and signed, "God Bless, Darryl Strawberry." Cool!

No other players were around—there must have been a meeting or maybe perhaps they had physicals that day (you know, bend over and cough). We didn't get a chance with Jeter that day—darn! So Mara and I jumped into the car and headed back over the Skyway Bridge to sunny, Sarasota.

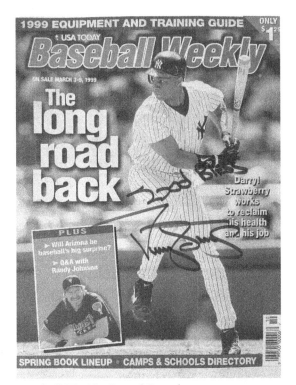

Baseball Weekly *Darryl Strawberry*

Autographed Ball, Derek Jetter standing on 3rd base line, autographed
mini bat signed Derek Jetter R.O.Y. 96

Derek Jeter signed bat

George Steinbrenner signed World Series ball

Yankee /Braves 1995 World Series Signed Balls

Autographed Derek Jeter R.O.Y. 96 "mini bat"

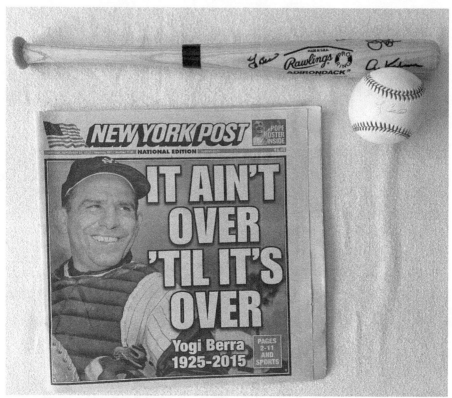

Yogi Berra autographed items

Autographed team ball

I Hope You Like the Show, But I Gots to Go!

It was the fall of 1997 and I remember it well, as the city of Sarasota was trying to tear down the Ringling Hotel—not worth saving they said. My thirteen-year old daughter, Daphney, and I belonged to a group to save the historic hotel. We made signs and protested, but to no avail. It was demolished and replaced with the mighty Ritz Carlton. And so began the transformation of the Sarasota downtown bayfront.

In the fall of 1997, Little Richard would be performing at the Sarasota Van Wezel Performing Arts Center (also known by locals as the Purple Cow). I decided to get tickets to the show, as this was the music of my mother's younger years.

In the weeks before the show, I checked local Goodwill stores and used record shops for any of his albums. I found one, a '33 rpm vinyl— just the record in plastic without a cover sleeve. It did, however, have a full black and white picture of him singing and dancing inlaid into the record itself. I purchased the album. 1997 was not the age of looking up items on the internet or having something overnighted to your house— you had to find stuff locally.

On the day of the show, I told my mom that I wanted to go early and check out the Hyatt Hotel on 6th Street to see if we could catch Mr. Richard in the lobby before the show. She was all good with that, so we hit the road and drove to the Hyatt. When we arrived, we saw a bus and a limo parked in the valet area, so we parked across the street in what used to be the library parking lot.

I grabbed the album and off we went to the lobby. People were at the bar having a good time. We were glancing around, getting all excited about the concert. It was close to show time, so I started to pace, wondering if Mr. Richard would sign or if he was still upstairs. I saw a lot of fancy dressed people coming off the elevator. I was full of anticipation to get this done, so I perched myself right next to the elevator doors.

Someone was headed down from the top floor, so I watched the lighted floor numbers come down—4, 3, 2, 1 and then the doors opened. It was him! I was standing six feet away, face to face. He was surrounded by bodyguards flanking each side.

It was amazing to see him so close up—the makeup on his face made him look fabulously immortal. I asked him for an autograph and he told me not right now, as he had a show to do. I had to step back to avoid being crushed by this bodyguard who was a pretty big dude.

"Wasn't he just gorgeous?" my mother asked. I told her he didn't sign, so she felt bad, as we walked over to the event. We crossed a small bridge over a canal, went up a grassy hill, and finally were there. We found our seats, in the back on the left side—not a bad seat in the house!

The curtain rose and Little Richard was at the piano, his fingers playing and his voice coming alive with rock and roll and the promise of God, filling the building. After his third set, he asked if anyone wanted to come on stage to sing with him—no kidding! I'd jump at any chance at getting close to him.

As I headed down the aisle to the stage, and bounded up the stairs, I was joined by about twenty other fans. Little Richard had us all lined up and ready to sing. I wish I could remember the exact song, but it was probably some gospel or rock music. However, but I do recall he was jamming on the piano and we were singing and dancing at the same time. I looked out in the audience, and saw two friends of mine, Chris and Kathy, sitting about six rows back. They pointed at me and laughed and so did I.

After the song finished, security personnel had us line up. As the line was leaving the stage, I noticed that we each had to walk right by the piano where Little Richard was sitting. I positioned myself toward the back of the line thinking I might be able to get that autograph now (of course, I brought it with me onstage). The line moved, but security was not paying attention, until I was right in front of the piano. As Little Richard began banging another tune on the piano, I stepped over to him, leaned down, and held up the album with the Sharpie.

Mr. Richard looked at me, took the pen, and signed the album. Then he handed me a pocket-sized Bible. By now, security was reaching for my shoulder, telling me I had to move it. I ran off the stage and sat back with my mom. She was so happy for me. What a rush—I had never done that before!

The music and performance that evening was just amazing. When the show was finally winding down, he played another song and then told the crowd, "I hope you liked the show, but I gots to go."

However, he played another song and said the same thing again. After a few more songs, the curtain fell and the show was over. I had the program and the pocket Bible … maybe I could get those signed, too? However, it was late, and Mom was sleepy, so we decided to go home. Looking back, that was the second concert I had attended with my mother. The first was Bob Dylan/Joan Baez in 1976.

Another friend who was at the concert told me he saw my goofy self up on that stage. He said that Little Richard was signing after the show that night. I should have stayed to get a couple more signatures.

As I was working on this book, I heard on the radio that Little Richard had passed away in Nashville (May 9, 2020). It all came back to me … the great time I had seeing Little Richard with my mom and singing and dancing on the stage. A few weeks later, I came across that signed album, and it made me smile one more time.

Little Richard … thanks for the memories. God bless you.

Collection from Little Richard's concert

Close-up of Little Richard's autograph

You Blew It, Dad

It was the NBA 1997–1998 mid-season. The Chicago Bulls won the 1997 NBA Championship, defeating the Utah Jazz in a 4–2 series win on June 13, 1997.

The Bulls, under Coach Phil Jackson, put together an all-star roster led by Michael Jordan, Scottie Pippen, Steve Kerr, Luc Longly, Dennis Rodman, Toni Kukoc, and more.

By 1997, this Bulls team and the 1991 through 1993 team had become a dynasty, with '91, '92, and '93 three-peat championship wins, then rebuilding and winning the '96 and '97 championships. They could win the 1998 championship for another three-peat and collect a sixth championship ring in eight years.

The Bulls were coming to Orlando to play the Magic in their last regular season meeting. I'd always told Greg Jr. and Mara that I'd take them to see Pippen, Jordan, and Rodman before the basketball players retired. That was possibly the last game Michael Jordan would play in Orlando as a Chicago Bull.

The game date was Wednesday, December 10, 1997. I could get tickets on the Internet through a ticket broker or wait until game day and try to buy them off a scalper. Both online and scalpers were selling for high prices.

With Thanksgiving having come and gone, I had to figure out a game plan for buying tickets. December 10th was coming up, and then Santa Claus. I couldn't drain the savings account all at once.

Here's what I came up with:

The day before the game, I'd go to Sports Authority and buy three NBA basketballs. I'd keep the children out of school on game day, and

I'd take a vacation day. We'd leave Sarasota early that morning for Orlando, wait at the arena for the Bulls to arrive for their morning shoot-around, and then follow them to their hotel to try to get autographs. I would let the kids each keep an autographed ball and sell mine to cover the cost of the three balls, the trip, and scalping some tickets to the game that night.

Game day, I put the kids in the car early. Mara wore her Pippen jersey. Greg was wearing his Rodman jersey and his Jordan shoes. We headed up the interstate towards Tampa, and then east towards Orlando. I had been to the Orlando arena before, so at least I knew where I was headed.

When we arrived in Orlando, we exited the interstate near the arena. After the off ramp, there were already people standing with signs saying, "I need tickets." Scalpers were on bicycles, getting tickets further away from the stadium, and then selling them closer to the stadium for big profits.

We arrived at the arena, home of the Orlando Magic. The kids and I hung out at the delivery area entrance to the arena with a handful of other fans too. A twenty-foot wall was on each side and we could look down over the walls at the area where the visiting team's bus pulled in for morning practice. After waiting for about an hour, the Chicago Bulls' bus finally pulled in. The door opened, and out came Phil Jackson, Jon Paxton, Scottie Pippen, Michael Jordan, Toni Kukuc, Steve Kerr, Dennis Rodman, and the rest of the team.

We all yelled down to them. Some waved and others smiled as they entered the building. It didn't look any good autographing could be here with the area blocked off with security. We took a walk around to the front of the arena, but guys were already scalping tickets.

I found one person who just happened to have a pair of tickets for $200. "Best deal of the day," he said. They are "nose-bleed" seats, way up high in the arena. That guy said the prices would just continue to go up, as it might be Michael Jordan's last time playing as a Chicago Bull. I told the guy I wanted them, but that was all the money I had on me. The children could go into the arena with the tickets and I'd sneak in … somehow.

The kids and I got something to eat and waited for the Bulls to leave the arena after the morning practice. My car was close, so when the team loaded the bus, we jumped into our car and followed the bus as it headed for the interstate. Someone had told me they were staying in Disney World.

I don't know what made me do it—the Disney signs or the hotel signs—but as we got off the exit ramp with the bus, I decided I could figure out the rest of the route without staying behind the bus. I got in front of the bus and went on ahead until I saw a Disney hotel sign. I turned left ahead of the bus, trying to check things out and figure where to park.

I remember going down that street and realized that was not a place they would stay. I made a mistake not following that bus. Damn! Now what to do? I went back to the main road where the bus had gone to the left. Just around the bend was a private, gated, residential community golf club. I drove into it and saw a woman at the Security gate.

Greg Jr. was in the front seat with his pillow, blanket, shorts, and Rodman jersey on, while Mara was in the back with her blanket, pillow, shorts, and Pippin jersey on. When I pulled up to the guardhouse, the woman asked if she could help us.

Out of my mouth, from where I don't know, I told her that I was going to the Human Resources office there to apply for a job. She said, "Okay," and opened the gate to let us in. She did give us a good lookin' over, so perhaps she knew we were up to something with those children wearing the sports jerseys.

As we drove down this long, winding road, the bus passed us as it was driving out. I thought, *Oh, man … I blew this one.* We drove past a restaurant and clubhouse and next, nestled among tall pine trees were townhouses and condos that backed up to a golf course.

At the end of the road, we pulled into a parking area with swimming facilities. When we came around by the pool, there was Dennis Rodman, standing on the pool deck with his back to us. He was the only player who hadn't gone straight to his townhouse. I yelled at the kids, "Look! There's Rodman!"

I grabbed my camera and *Sports Illustrated* and jumped out of the car. I began a conversation with Rodman and introduced him to Mara and Greg Jr. Mara was only as tall as his kneecaps! We asked him for some autographs, and he signed Greg Jr.'s jersey and the *Sports Illustrated*.

I asked my son why he wasn't wearing his Rodman shoes (he's wearing his Jordan's). He told me that they were in the trunk of our car, so I ran out to grab them. When I opened the trunk, I saw that Jr. had accidently grabbed his Chuck Taylor's when we left the house that morning. Damn!

I asked Mr. Rodman for a picture of him with the kids, but my camera didn't work. We asked him to sign a basketball, but he was on the move and had to go. There was no one else around, but we were in the right place, so we waited.

The first movement we saw was Steve Kerr with a couple of other players driving out in a red van. Then some other people showed up and walked up to the restaurant to meet with Mr. Rodman.

Well, maybe Jordan would come out to play golf or go swimming? We walked up to the clubhouse/restaurant area and there was Mr. Rodman having lunch with three other guys. Mara was wearing a white T-shirt with the Detroit Pistons Bad Boys picture on it under her Bulls Jersey and she walked over to show him. I don't know why we didn't ask for it to be signed.

I'd spent all my money on those tickets, so we were not going to eat there. Instead, we headed back over to the pool area, but none of us had a bathing suit nor did we want to get our clothes wet! As we stood there, Phil Jackson came out to lounge at the pool. We let him relax, and when he stood up to go, the kids went over with their balls and asked him to sign. He tells them "No, not right now."

The day went on and we waited some more. The kids are groaning and moaning as game time wasn't until 7:30 p.m. It was also a long, hot day and we didn't have anything yet on the basketballs.

A couple of housekeepers were riding around, going in and out of some of the villas. It was about 5:00 by this time, so I asked one of the housekeepers which place Jordan was staying in. I explained that we were trying to have our basketballs signed. She told me she would make me a list of the room numbers the players who were in them. Then she pointed to the room Jordan was staying in.

I could hear the bus arrive back at the parking area, as it pulled up along the poolside. We were waiting for the housekeeper to bring us the list of rooms and she delivered! Now we know which player was staying where.

A group of players and families started to gather at the front of the bus, but I wanted to go after Jordan first, in case we got tossed out quickly. A couple of players showed up for some pictures and autographs. We talked to them and told them we had been there all day, but only had gotten an autograph from Dennis Rodman. The lady tells us that's the autograph she really wants! She tells us she was going to the game and I explained that the kids were going for sure!

That's when it all came crashing down. A trolley loaded with happy-go-lucky, loud drunken people pulled up in the area. Soon, a couple of security vehicles showed up. It was time to step away and hide until the trolley was escorted off the property.

The kids and I stood behind the pool pump house, surrounded by bushes with a large, electrical transformer box. We were about fifteen feet from Michael Jordan's room. Mara wanted to go down to Scottie Pippen's, which was farther away from where Security was, but I didn't listen to her. I wanted Jordan first.

The housekeeper had gone into Jordan's room and came out with a bottle of wine that she told us Jordan had given her. She didn't drink wine, so she asked if I wanted it. Heck, yeah!

Security was still checking the area when, through the bushes, I thought I noticed Luke Longly. For some, stupid reason, I sent Greg Jr. out to get an autograph. Mara said, "No, Dad, that's not him. Don't go, Gregory." But I didn't listen, and I insisted it was Longly. I sent Jr. out, not even thinking about security.

I could hear Greg Jr. talking to someone and they were headed our way. It was a Security guy, who told us we had to leave. I tried to tell him that we were staying at the villas and we'd been here all day. When he asked to see our room key, I told him I left it in the car. He wanted to go to the car and take a look. I came clean. I told him that we really weren't staying here, but were just here for the day, but we did not come on the trolley.

I begged him not to toss us out, but he said we had to go. I wanted to knock him in the head with that bottle of wine. However, I had left it on the transformer and only remembered it as I drove out. Darn! Darn! Darn! I can't believe what I just caused—waiting all day and then blew it again—BAD.

We headed back to the arena—at least we had tickets for the kids to see the game. I told the kids to go on in, buy a program as soon as they got in, and use the rest of the money on themselves. I told them that I would sneak in later, when people took a smoke break at half time. I pointed out a concession stand through the glass doors and told the kids to meet me there at the end of the second period. The kids went in and I walked out front, taking it all in.

As I observed the scalping going on, two police officers were watching things. I hear one officers explain that even though scalping is against the law, these guys make a living from it, so just turn your eye to what was going on. I saw some big money change hands that night for tickets, but the biggest transaction I saw was one guy who paid $8,000 for two center court seats, ten rows up behind the benches.

I tried to sneak in after the first period with no luck. As the smokers came out after the second period, I slipped under the roped off area and bummed a cigarette. I stood close to the door, and when a few people put out their cigarettes, I followed them in.

The kids were right where I told them to be. Mara gave me an update. Greg Jr. didn't buy a program, because they were sold out. My son said the seats were too high and the players looked like ants. Believe it or not, Mara said the couple that was at the condos with us had hidden in the women's pool restroom when Security had arrived. They took pictures and were given autographs from most of the players except for Rodman, who went straight onto the bus.

I blew it. I should've listened to Mara.

The rest of the game we walked around and then went down to the lower level. We looked around the floor and saw some of the players up close. When the game was over, we headed home. In hindsight, I should have followed the Bulls' bus one more time. I thought for sure the bus was going to the airport for a return flight to Chicago, but later heard the Bulls had returned to the condominiums and had the next day off to play golf and visit the theme parks.

On the way home, I admitted to Mara that I blew it in several ways that day—I should have listened to the Chicago Bulls expert. However, we had a lot of fun and this became one of many great memories that we now look back on and laugh.

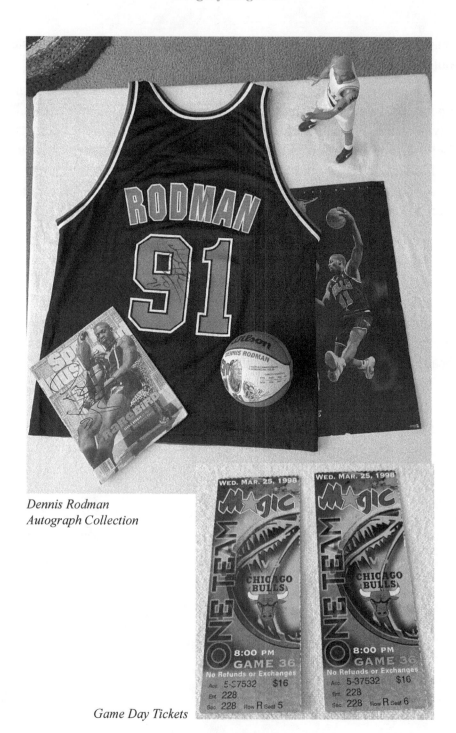

Dennis Rodman
Autograph Collection

Game Day Tickets

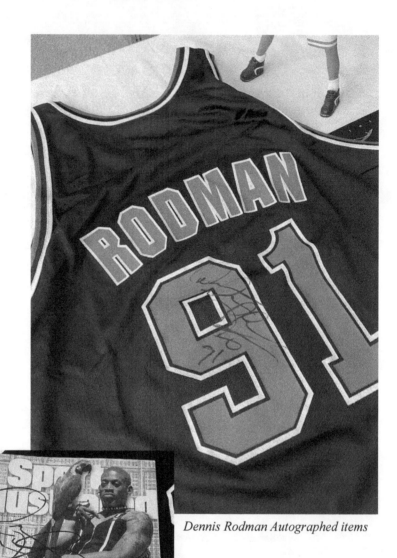

Dennis Rodman Autographed items

Getting Through the Gate

It was the spring of 1998, so spring training camps were opening. The St. Louis Cardinals left St. Petersburg and relocated to Jupiter, Florida. My forty-five-minute ride to St. Pete now was a three-hour ride to see my childhood home team.

But spring training is the best chance to autograph players, and it's an all-day event. You must be there in the early morning, ready to go when the players arrive. You have to be in the stadium during batting practice before game time and you must be there when the players leave the field. Most importantly, you have to be there when they exit through the gate of the players' parking lot.

That spring morning, I was up at 5 a.m. with my daughter, Mara, my son Greg Jr., and his two friends, Craig and Kaleb. We headed across the state to autograph and watch a couple of Cardinals games. Mark McGuire had just broken the home run record in a battle of bats with Chicago Cubs player, Sammy Sosa.

No interstate is available if you're headed directly across the state from Sarasota. That meant we had to drive on two lane roads, cutting through cow towns, pasture lands, and wet grass lands, while riding along the north end of Lake Okeechobee and Indiantown. After that we were in Jupiter.

We made it to the ballpark, purchased tickets to the game, and bought some items at the gift shop. We purchased some 8x10 pictures and a couple of major league baseballs. Then we walked down to the players' parking lot gate. It looked like all the players were in, as the lot was full of cars.

Should we go out to the practice fields or stand in line to get into the stadium? Our tickets that day were for a spot known as the "Grassy Berm." It's the cheapest ticket you can get—find a spot on the lawn and bring a blanket or towel for your family to sit on. The Berm was down the right field line and a prime autograph area. The pitchers sit next to the Berm during the game and warm up there. It's located right where the players enter and exit the field.

Everyone jockeys for place at the Berm. Once that gate is open two hours before game time, the fans are running from the gate to the Berm to stake out their "spot." I've seen people fall, get run over, and argue about who was where first. It's a dog-eat-dog world.

That morning, we claimed our spot on the berm with a blanket. The Cardinals were done with batting practice and were in the clubhouse. The Miami Marlins was the visiting team and was on the field warming up.

The kids were gone somewhere, so I just kicked back and waited for the game to start. The place filled up and it was almost game time. The Cardinals were returning to the field, with a handful of stops here and there to sign some autographs.

Mark McGwire walked on by. I've never seen him sign before a workout or game—only after. Maybe everyone didn't get an autograph, but he made sure he took some time to accommodate the fans.

The game started and the children came and went. I told the kids to make sure they were here at the end of the sixth inning. Big-name players usually left spring training games early. McGwire hit his third home run of the day, so I filmed it all on my VCR camera. It was amazing!

After the crowd sang *Take Me Out to the Ball Game,* McGwire started walking from the dugout with his equipment bag strapped over his shoulder … here we go. Where's he gonna stop? He veered off to the wall just in front of the bull pen and began signing. Should I move near him or wait to see if he got closer? The fans were already swarming in, like bees on honey.

You've got to see it to believe it—hundreds of attendees: kids, old and young people, fat and skinny, twenty rows deep, all asking players for autographs. When people started getting crazier, player moved along.

McGwire made his way to where the wall angled out in front of us—looks like we had a chance ... he reached the berm!! We all have something to be signed!

After all the pushing, shoving, and crushing, McGwire was gone. We grouped back together at the blanket. Mara had a ball signed, Craig got an 8x10 signed, and I had a bat signed, but Kaleb got skunked— nothing for him. My son, Greg Jr., was nowhere to be found. He told me earlier he was going to try and get a bat from a Marlin's player.

The crowd returned to being laid back. Some people were leaving, but I was waiting for my son. It was the bottom of the ninth inning before he came—I'll be darned, he's got a bat! The player's name on it is Rondell White. He was a home run hitter who floated around Major League teams, but never really settled in anywhere—still it was a pretty good experience for Greg Jr.

I promised the kids we were getting a hotel room with a pool and would be watching another game tomorrow. After checking in, we went to an all-you-can-eat Chinese restaurant with crab legs. What a mistake that was! Three fourteen-year-old boys filled their plates with a variety of food and a ton of crab legs. Well, no one was eating, just goofing around, horse playing, and I wanted to knock them all in the head. The place was small and eventually the owner came over and said, "You waste food, no go back for more!"

We requested a 6 a.m. wake-up call from the front desk and ate early at the complimentary breakfast buffet. Then we headed over to the stadium. All I could think about was getting Kaleb an autograph on his ball. Oh my! We're waiting at the player's parking lot at the gate as the coaches and players drove in, but no one was stopping. The Security Guard, an older gentleman, told us McGwire was already inside. Strike one.

We walked back to the practice fields. McGwire and the team were taking batting practice, working on infielding, while outfielders were shagging fly balls. We sat on the bleachers watching and waiting. Some players ran off to the other field, while some rookie minor leaguers came over to the fence and signed. Soon McGwire and the remaining players headed back to the clubhouse. Strike two. It's gonna be a long day. I bought five tickets as we waited for the gate to open.

At 11:00 a.m. as soon as that gate is unlocked, we run and claim a spot on the berm. At 1 p.m., both teams were on the field, the National Anthem was played, and it was time to play ball. The pitchers were good and shutting down the bats on the team. A fast-paced game would be good, as I still had a three-hour ride home. The innings passed and McGwire was no longer playing first base. He'd been pulled and was just sitting in the dugout. After another inning or so, he came walking out towards us carrying his equipment bag.

He stopped about twenty steps from the dugout and started signing. Just like yesterday, people started pushing and shoving. McGwire picked up his bats and bag and ducked out the back gate to the clubhouse. Darn, was it done? Kaleb was still without a signature. I'm thinking of going home, but we watched the end of the game.

Then we hiked over to the players' parking lot gates, and waited while most of the players left. We knew McGwire was still there, because we still can see his car, but I was ready to go.

We headed to my car, but on the way, I saw a newspaper metal stand—one of those old fashioned ones that you put a quarter in to get a daily newspaper. I noticed it had a 14x16 advertisement in a slot on front with McGwire signing a bat on it. I slid it out the back—it was black and white cardboard.

When we got to the car, I started it and cranked up the air conditioning. Then I took my blue Sharpie, and on that cardboard I wrote "McGwire," in big blue letters with a big number "25" and then wrote the word, "Pass." As a joke, I told the gang I was going drive into the players' gate, so Kaleb could get his ball signed. They were like, "Awesome, cool, let's do it."

I told them, "No," as I might be arrested. Driving down the street, I put the pass sign in the driver's side front window. I told Greg Jr. to keep the VCR camera going, and we were all laughing, bouncing around, and freaking out. I don't know why I did it, but I turned in the gate with fans on both sides seeking autographs. The older Security guy standing on the driver's side looks at the fake pass and waved me in!

I parked in the back row about 65 spaces from McGwire's car. Greg Jr. had been filming the whole time and still was. The side door coming out of the locker room was right there, and by the door was a lady with two or three young children standing with her. We all got out of the car and I thought to myself that this was crazy. McGwire was probably going to knock me in the head.

Kaleb asked where the best place to wait would be. I told him that would probably be up by the door with those younger children. Greg Jr. went about halfway to the door and stood off the sidewalk, still playing cameraman. Mara and I stood by the car, but she had an 8x10 picture and a magazine ready to be signed.

There he was—McGwire was coming out of the clubhouse! He stopped and talked to the lady and the kids, signed some stuff, and then he signed Kaleb's ball—Yes! He walked by Craig next and then went by the camera man, Greg Jr. When he was ten steps away, I told Mara to ask, but she told me to do it. Neither one of us asked him, until he was about two car spaces away. Then I finally asked, "Mr. McGwire, will you sign an autograph for her?"

McGwire turned around and said, "What the *%^#$! Why didn't you ask when I was right here passing you, you son of a &^%#%&? Why did you wait for me to get this $%#^& away from you?"

I told him we had hesitated, because we were nervous. He asked if we were supposed to be in the players' parking lot. Thinking quickly,

I told him we were waiting on a minor leaguer who was on the forty-five-man roster. After I said that, McGwire asked us what we wanted signed.

While he was signing for us, I showed him a Hooters hat I had bought for him in Sarasota. It was Hooters orange with a rippled American Flag on the front. I asked if he wanted it and he smiled and said he'd take it. That was it. He was in his car and was gone.

We all piled back into my car, filled with a rush of excitement. We were laughing all the way as I drove my car out the gate. People were yelling at me, "Mr. McGwire, please sign for us!"

Back then, I looked very similar to him—with my mustache and beard shaped like his, especially when I was wearing my Cardinals hat, which I had on. As for cameraman, Greg Jr., he got scared and shut the VCR off when McGwire walked by him, missing the entire encounter with Mara and me.

Mark McGwire Collections

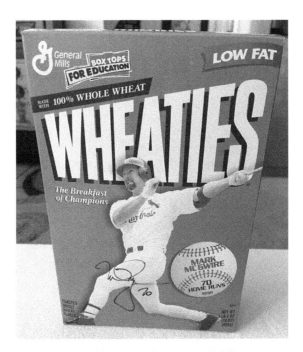

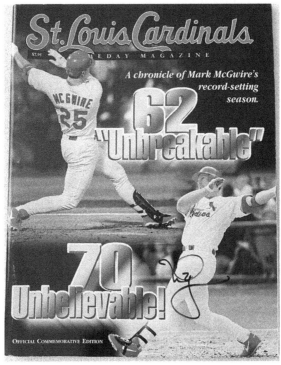

Gregory Magac Sr.

The Birdie in the Hat

Well, this autograph would end up being one of the most difficult, peculiar, and argumentative moments of my chasing the ink years. At the time, my youngest daughter, Mara, was a Ken Griffey Jr. fan. She had a jersey hanging on her bedroom wall and always said he was #1. I came home one day after work and told Mara we were headed to see the Tampa Bay Devil Rays play Ken Griffey Jr. and the Seattle Mariners. Hopefully, we might get her jersey signed. She was so excited.

We loaded up the car and were off, with the jersey folded around some cardboard to give the surface some strength for the autograph. We arrived at the stadium early (of course). Most stadiums open the gates two hours before game time and allow you to sit down by the dugouts before game time. We kept an eye out for Griffey Jr., but even though the Mariners were on the field, #24 was nowhere to be found.

The stadium started to fill as game time was getting closer. The group of players hitting balls at home plate were finishing up, when Ken Griffey finally popped out of the dugout and headed towards home plate. The crowd erupted with cheers, with seemingly everyone yelling at once, "Go Griffey! Sign my ball! Hit it over the wall!" There was a new buzz in the stands as Griffey launched home run balls over the right, left, and centerfield walls.

We remained along the left field wall, right past the dugout, but by now people contending for an autograph went from the wall by the batter's box all the way out to the Mariner's bullpen. After Griffey crushed a few more balls, he ran the bases and exited back into the dugout. He grabbed his glove and ran past us to the outfield to shag some balls, even though we (and the rest of his fans) yelled for him to sign some autographs. However, he showed no interest, and it didn't look good.

People were showing up for their seats, so the ushers were telling us it was time to go! No luck before the game. I told Mara the night was not over yet. I told her, "Let's get a hot dog and a Coke and find our seats."

As the years have passed, I don't recall much of the game, and I don't know if I could find the ticket stub among all the boxes I have. What I do remember was going out to the team bus that had backed into the unloading dock behind the stadium after the game.

I thought that maybe we could call to him to sign while he was getting on the bus, but if not, I had backed my car onto the grass across the street as my contingency plan. I intended to follow the bus in my car to the Vinoy, a historic hotel in downtown St. Petersburg. It was a few miles from the stadium, down by the bayfront where the players were staying.

Other fans seeking autographs started showing up at the gate. Time passed, players started loading the bus, and people yelled at some players, but no one came to the fence to sign. Then out of the shadow and into the night light, there was Mr. Griffey, talking with some people. The fans at the fence yelled to him, but he took no notice—he just got on the bus and it departed.

Mara and I ran across the street and jumped into our car. We got rolling immediately, so I could see the taillights of the bus turning a few blocks down. I tried to turn onto a street that would allow me to arrive at the hotel before the bus. Needless to say, St. Pete has a lot of one-way streets, so I had to backtrack a little bit. By the time we were parked in front of the hotel, the bus had already emptied and was pulling away.

Now the Vinoy is where visiting teams usually stay when they play in St. Petersburg. Signs are posted stating no asking for autographs or pictures from players or you'll be asked to leave the premises. Decision time—do we call it a night or go inside? About that time, a white-topped, dusty blue Lincoln Continental pulled up in the u-shaped front drive of the hotel. Next, the chauffeur opened the car door and stood next to the car. I said, "Come on, Mara, let's take a chance."

As we're getting into the driveway, Mr. Griffey came walking down the stairs, side-by-side with another man. Mara was wearing the jersey. I had nothing to be signed, because tonight was all about Mara being his #1 fan. We went straight to Mr. Griffey before anyone could ask us to leave.

Mara asked him to sign her jersey, but Mr. Griffey refused. I asked him why he couldn't sign it, as she just wanted to hang the jersey in her bedroom. We weren't going to sell it or anything like that, but he still said no.

Here's where the title of this chapter came from. When my sister, Kellybird, was living in Washington State, she was invited to a Seattle Mariners game and sat up in a VIP box. While there, she was talking with a woman at the game whose name was Birdie Griffey … the mother of Ken Griffey Jr.

Kellybird was a Doctor of Oriental Medicine, but who probably had not been to a pro sporting event since her childhood. She asked Mrs. Griffey to sign her Mariners hat. Griffey's mom agreed and signed, "Kellybird, Best Wishes, Birdie Griffey." Kelly had given me that hat. I, in turn, gave the hat to Mara, who was wearing it that night.

I asked Mr. Griffey why he couldn't sign her jersey, as his mother had already signed the hat my daughter was wearing. Mr. Griffey asked to see the hat, so Mara handed it to him. After looking it over, he told her he'd sign the hat.

I told him that Mara would really like the jersey signed. At that moment, Mr. Griffey handed me back the hat, took the jersey from Mara, and signed it. He told her not to sell it, as he doesn't sign very often.

Me being me, I tried to hand him back the hat, as I said, "I thought you were gonna sign the hat." He told me to go away. I am pretty sure he wanted to knock me in the head.

We thanked Mr. Griffey and headed home across the Skyway Bridge. Time moved on and now Mara has her own house and family. The jersey and the hat are stored under her bed … waiting to be hung up again someday.

Ken Griffey Jr. Collection

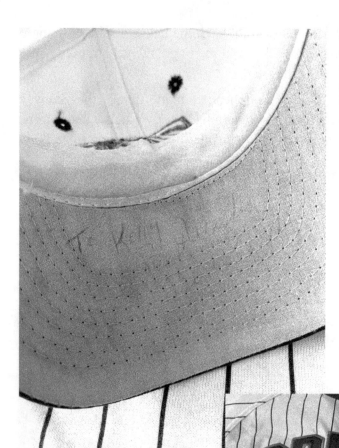

*Ken Griffey
Autographed Jersey
and Hat His
Mother Signed*

*Inscription reads:
"To Kelly—Best Wishes,
Birdie Griffey"*

2000 Presidential Run

The election was underway, with President Bill Clinton wrapping up a second term in the White House and the Republicans nominating then Governor George Bush of Texas to run against Democratic pick, Vice President, Al Gore.

I'd read in the newspaper that Governor Bush would be making a campaign stop at the Sarasota/Bradenton Airport. The event was being held at the southwest tarmac. For the first time, I thought, maybe I'll go after a politician's signature! Hey, he could be President of the United States some day! I could have him sign a book or maybe a baseball. I went down to the Main Street Used Bookstore the following day and found a book by Governor George Bush about life's lessons. It was a hard copy book with a nice jacket—this might do the trick.

I was working that day, so I had planned to take my school board truck over to the airport during my lunch break. I had the book with me, but decided at the last minute to run by the house and grab an older baseball I had sitting in a box. While I was there, I remembered I had a Dallas Cowboys baseball hat my brother-in-law, Mark, had brought back for me from a family trip. I put the hat on and headed out the door.

When I get to the airport, there was an open field filling up with vehicles. I pulled in, parked the van, and grabbed my stuff, including my Sharpie pen. I stepped inside a gate where some other people were gathered, but I had arrived right on time. A small stage area with a podium was set up in front. The people had formed a half-circle around the stage. I tried to picture which way Bush would come down to interact with the crowd, so got myself into a possibly good position.

A black SUV came down the tarmac and stopped right where everyone was gathered. Out a couple of doors came some well-dressed bodyguards (Secret Service?), and then Governor Bush appeared. Everyone clapped as he walked to the podium and started speaking. I noticed a teacher with some younger students standing next to me. They had this white Teddy Bear about two feet high with red, white, and blue stars and a striped bow tie. When Governor Bush ended his speech, everyone clapped, as he came down from the stage. By now, there were between two to three hundred people there.

Bush shook hands and took some pictures. I don't think he signed any autographs until he walked up to the teacher and her kids, who wanted to have him sign, "Republicans," on the bear.

After them, guess who was standing right there—yup—me! It was pretty amazing, shaking the hand of someone who could be the next president of the United States.

I asked him if he could sign something about the millennium. He gave me a goofy grin and signed, "Best Wishes, 2000—George Bush," in the book. I quickly asked if he could sign the ball (dirty old thing). As he was signing the ball he said, "Nice hat you have on."

I had forgotten I was wearing the Dallas Cowboy's hat! I asked him if he could sign that, too, and took it off my head. I could tell he was trying to move along—he grabbed the hat, signed it, and said, "That's all for you, Buddy."

As he left the area, a gentleman behind me said that he had gotten some good pictures of me and Governor Bush. I gave the guy my phone number, so we met later, and he gave me some nice photos.

As everyone knows, George Walker Bush would later become the 43rd President of the United States. Florida's vote was too close to call and had to be recounted.

I have a nice autograph now, and President George Bush called me his buddy.

*2000 President
George Bush
Collection*

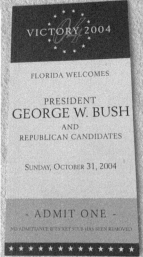

Workin' at the Carwash

◆ ◆

In the year 2000, the Cincinnati Reds made Ed Smith Stadium in Sarasota their spring training home. The Chicago White Sox left for Arizona and the Cactus League. This was the same year that the Reds acquired Ken Griffey Jr. from the Seattle Mariners.

When Griffey Jr. was originally drafted in 1987, he went as a first-round pick to the Mariners and quickly became known as a fierce home run hitter. When he was traded to the Reds, he'd received the Golden Glove Award, had a batting average of .284, and had a total of 309 home runs. His father, Ken Griffey Sr. had been a coach for the Reds since 1997.

I went to a couple baseball games that year and, of course, I autographed the players. I was trying to get a Reds team ball and a nice black Louisville team bat signed by everyone. I asked the players and coaches to sign while I stood by the dugout during the games, during warmups and when they were driving in and out of the gate.

I saw Ken Griffey Jr. sign just a couple of times for some kids, but he drove right by the entrance coming and going and never signed then. All I needed was one more signature for a full team—it was Ken Griffey Jr.'s.

I was at the old Kmart department store in town, looking at sporting equipment, when I came across a jet-black Franklin ball glove. The writing on the glove was in silver and the autograph signature, in the mitt of the glove was—who else, but Ken Griffey, Jr.

The glove was right-handed, but Griffey Jr. wears a left-hander's glove. However, it was on clearance … a sixty-dollar glove on sale for twenty. It sure would be a nice signed piece, using a silver Sharpie to match the other print on the glove.

I bought the glove and now it was game on to get it signed. I'd autographed Griffey Jr. in the past, so I knew he was a hard one to get!

I took a sick day off from work and arrived at the stadium early. I was at the players' gate when Griffey Jr. arrived, but he didn't stop. All the players were in when I noticed that no security guard was at the gate yet. In the row of vehicles parked at the gate corner was a twelve-foot open space leading from the lot to the stadium field. On the other side was a double-wide sidewalk leading to the locker rooms.

Don't ask me why, but I decided to go stand by the cars parked near the right field gate. No one was around, but my heart was pumping, as I'm always thinking about being arrested for trespassing or something else. Hopefully, Mr. Griffey would come walking by, sign, and everything would all be right—wishful thinking.

Security finally showed up for sitting duty by the gate. I was leaning on the hood of a car that was blocked by a truck. I can remember it was early in camp, so teams weren't traveling to play ball yet. Most of the starting rosters would be taking batting and fielding practice in the stadium, while the pitchers and catchers would be practicing on the back fields.

It was around 9:30 a.m. when players started coming out of the locker room, most of them running by me at a small trot. No Griffey Jr. yet, but I hadn't blown my cover ... yet. Next, in comes about six players who are walking, talking, and laughing and finally, there was Griffey Jr. in the center of that group. I was on the left side, too far away, so I started to cut across and make adjustments, when there, right in my path, was Ken Griffey _Sr_.

I looked at Senior and, well, he's a man of men. He gave me a scowl—a look that said, "Who are you? What are you doing here? Don't even think about bothering my son."

I read all of this in one mean, kick-your-ass look. So what did I do? I got scared and got the hell out of there—yes, sir!

However, I still wanted to get my glove signed. How many days would it take? Would it be a waste of time? I told my friend, Tommy J., that I was going to take off work the next day to try again.

When morning came, Tommy J. had joined me at the gate. Ken Griffey Jr. drove in, but didn't stop to sign. We hung out through the morning workouts—Griffey was in the batting cage first and then went into the stadium. He finished his workout and left the parking lot around noon. A few cars filled with people seem to follow him. I'm parked too far away, so no following for me.

I ask Tommy J. if he wants to try again tomorrow—third time's a charm. I tell him we can park my car close to the gate and follow him after workouts. I'd heard that people had been following him to lunch or dinner and had gotten autographs on his way out of restaurants.

When morning came, Tommy J. and I got to the gate early and parked the car across the street from the gate. As the players arrived, so did the Cincinnati fans, who were trying to get autographs. When Ken Griffey Jr. drove in, he was close to being the last player to arrive, but he didn't stop. Ah, shoot—now we wait again.

It's not even noon when we see him walking to his car. I go over, start my car, and get ready. He passed the gate without stopping and we automatically run to the car when some twelve-year old kid with a bat asks if he can come with us, so I told him to jump in.

Mr. Griffey was headed north on Euclid Ave., towards 12th street, but then turned left on Highway 301. Even though the light was red, we didn't see him in traffic. Tommy J. looked over to the left where there was a small strip mall with a car wash.

Tommy yells, "He's at the car wash!" I looked over and he sure was—standing outside his car, waiting for service. Getting in the left-hand lane at 17th Street, we make a U-turn, pulled in the front of the lot, and parked.

Tommy asks, "What are we going to do?"

I said, "Hell, if I know! Let's go get an autograph." We all got out of the car—me with my glove, Tommy with his jersey, and this kid with the bat. I told the kid to ask first 'cause he's a youngster and how could Griffey say no? The kid seemed reluctant to go first, so I said. "To hell with it," and I told them I would do it.

At that moment, a lady along with her young daughter was getting her car washed. She went up and was talking with him. As she retrieved a pen and paper for an autograph, I told Tommy that this was the time to go. *Griffey couldn't be mean to us in front of a little girl, could he?*

We walked up to the detail area and became part of the group. As Mr. Griffey finishing signing for the little girl, he lifted up his eyes to take a look. Of course, I'm first, with Tommy, shadowed next to me, and the kid in the back. I asked him if he could sign the glove. The conversation went like this:

Me: Can you sign this glove, Mr. Griffey?

KG: I'm not signing it.

Me: If you sign this glove, I'll never ask you for another autograph in my entire life.

KG: Did you follow me over here from the stadium?

Me: Yes.

KG: That's a bunch of bullshit!

Me: Well, if you'd just signed over at the stadium or by the gate, we wouldn't have followed you. I missed three days of work hoping you would stop and sign. I've been to home games last season and you never signed then either. If you sign this glove, I'll never ask again.

KG: Right, I'll bet you'll be back at the stadium gate tomorrow.

During this conversation, he called up some pretty choice names for us … the ones you'd get soap put in your mouth for using from your mother.

To him, we weren't nice guys. However, he finally took the Sharpie and signed the glove for me and then the jersey for Tommy (who was shaking like a leaf—not sure if he was nervous or just needed a drink).

When it was the kid's turn, he looked at him and then at the bat. Finally, he asked him, "Did you follow me to the restaurant yesterday? Didn't I sign a ball for you?"

The kid, (coming clean) finally said, "Yes, sir, you did."

Mr. Griffey signed his bat and we all thanked him and went to the car. I said to the kid, "What's wrong with you? You followed him yesterday? You could have screwed it all up for us!"

Before leaving, I called my friend, Charles. He had a *Baseball Weekly* with Griffey on the cover that he wanted to have signed, but hadn't had any luck. I let him know where Griffey was, because I knew Charles could drive that company truck like no other, so he could make it in time before Griffey was done. Well, Charles made it in time and Mr. Griffey signed his magazine. Cool!

I should have knocked that kid in the head and took his bat, but we took him back to the stadium and dropped him off.

I never asked Ken Griffey Jr. for an autograph again.

Ken Griffey Jr.
Autograph Collection

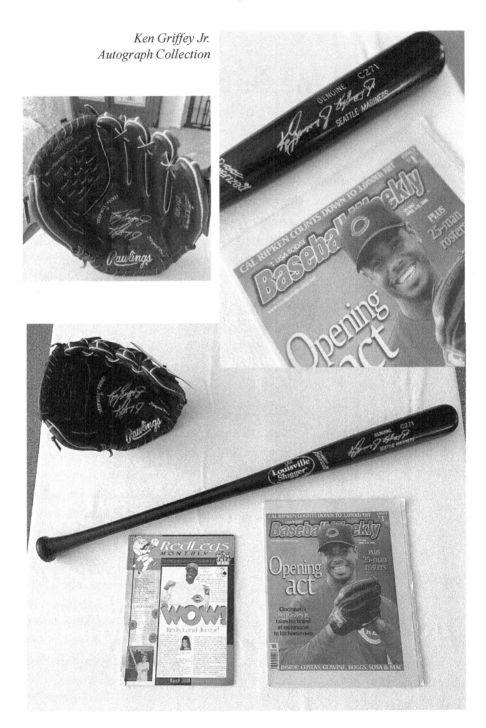

Get Me Outta Here!

◆ ◆

It was during the summer of 2003 that I met my future wife, Robin. At the time, she was an assistant principal at an elementary school. The relationship seemed to be going well, as we'd made it past July and August, so the school year had begun. By now, Robin knew that my hobby (obsession?) was collecting autographs. I was slowing down a bit, but was still active if the right circumstances came along.

In October, the local newspaper said President Jimmy Carter would be making an appearance on Monday, November 24th to sign his new book at the Sarasota News and Books Store on Main Street. This was something for me, because I could add a second US President to my collection.

We purchased the tickets that would allow us to receive an autograph and a copy of his book. But you know me, always thinking. I ventured over to the used bookstores in town and found a small book in a plastic sleeve about Jimmy Carter's youth and upbringing. I'm thinking that since I paid for one autograph, perhaps I could get an extra signature by bringing another book—just kind of slide it over to President Carter when no one is looking.

The evening of the event arrived, so we drove Robin's white Highlander to the bookstore. Not only did I have an extra book with me, but I also had the front page of the local section of our newspaper, which had an article about the event. This would be the first time Robin was with me when I autographed.

I thought it would be a basic night of autographing—standing in line, getting the books signed, and then heading home. Who would have thought … ?

We arrived at the bookstore on Main Street and Palm Avenue. I told Robin to drive around to the back of the building, where I knew there was an alley in the parking lot next to it. It was dark out, so I could barely see the President's black limousine, along with some black SUVs. Several Secret Service agents standing around the vehicles as we parked in the alley.

A long line had formed outside the bookstore, but we could see President Carter, standing about twenty-five feet from the doorway at a table. After we checked in, we each received a ticket and a book. Additional Secret Service agents were inside watching over everything.

Robin was in front of me, so she could get her signature first, while I took a couple of pictures of her and the President. After Robin was done, I handed her the camera. Then I put down the new book and had it signed. However, when I lifted it up, I had the small book right there, too. I asked President Carter if he could also sign the one I had purchased from the used book store—sure enough, he signed it!

Quickly, I laid the newspaper down for his signature, when a woman approached me. She told me that he was only signing his new book. I picked up the little book and Robin and I moved over to the back of the store. I was thinking that I could have the newspaper signed as he was leaving, but Robin didn't think that was a good idea.

The store owner asked everyone to leave, as the employees were going to have pictures taken with the President. When we went out to the alley, I was hoping that I might have a chance by the limo. However, the agents in black suits told us we had to go.

The article in the newspaper had mentioned a private party was being held for the President at the Bird Key Yacht Club, an exclusive enclave, not far from the bookstore. I told Robin that we should follow them. I'm pretty sure she wanted to go home, but she was willing to go along.

The motorcade, with the President in the limo, pulled out from the bookstore and guess who was following in a white Highlander? Me! As we crossed the John Ringling Bridge, I drove alongside the limousine and the three black SUVs.

I told Robin to grab the camera and take a picture … totally forgetting about the flash! It went off and lit up the road. I yelled to Robin, asking her what she was thinking, but she yelled at me, saying it was my idea! By now, one of the black SUVs had pulled up behind us. I sped up and moved to the outside lane, thinking that maybe I should just turn around and head home.

The motorcade makes a U-turn into the Bird Key Yacht Club, so I drove a little further and then make the turn as well. The motorcade stopped directly in front of the restaurant, but I drove to the parking lot and parked in the dark. I ask Robin if she thought I should walk up and ask the President for an autograph. Now she was getting a little upset, and probably scared, so she wanted to leave.

All of a sudden, one of the black SUVs pulled up alongside the passenger side of the car where Robin was and another one comes rolling up behind us, effectively blocking us in. Right then, Robin yells, "Get me outta here!" Of course, I couldn't because we were blocked in!

One of the agents stood next to my window, suit jacket open, so I could see what looks like the butt of a 9mm Glock. He asks me what I was doing, and could he help me with anything.

I told him that I was trying to get an autograph from the President. However, he told me this area was closed to the public so I had to leave. The agent told me to have a nice evening and I told him to do the same. Before you knew it, we were headed back across the bridge to our house.

Robin wasn't too happy about the outcome of the latter part of the evening, but she did have fun (as did I) when we met President Carter and shook his hand. By the way, the picture she took when we went over the bridge did come out pretty good—ha, ha!

Remembering the evening with Robin, she said she thought President Carter had the nicest smile and the prettiest blue eyes she had ever seen. Unfortunately, this would not be the last time I had a run-in with the Secret Service.

President Carter Collection

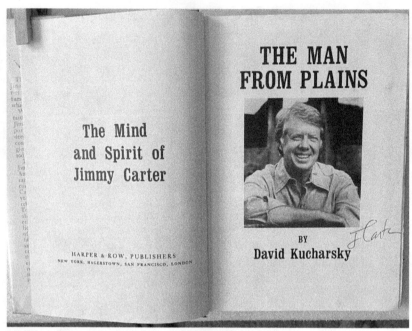

President Carter Signed Book - The Man from Plains

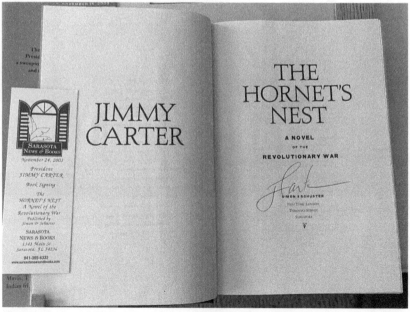

President Carter Signed Book - The Hornet's Nest

By 2003, I'd become a follower of Tony Stewart, driving the #20 car for Home Depot. I had met my wife, Robin, that year and she didn't know anything about the sport. When I told her I rooted for the Home Depot car, she decided that her driver would be Jimmie Johnson, who drove the Lowes car. I don't know if she picked him because he was a driver of a rival lumber company or because she thought he was cute.

My friend, "Beer Can Bob," was a Dale Earnhardt Jr. fan, as was my daughter, Daphney, who lived in Birmingham, near the Talladega Raceway, home of the Dale Earnhardt team. Beer Can, his brother-in-law, and a couple of other friends had been going to Martinsville Speedway for the past fifteen to twenty years. Beer Can invited us to go to their cabin in the mountains of Wilson, Virginia, ride over to the race, and then come back home.

I passed his suggestion on to Robin, but she didn't like the idea of going up in the mountains with a bunch of men. Instead, she found a package deal for the two of us. It included a two-night stay at a hotel in North Carolina with bus transportation to Martinsville racetrack for qualifying races on Saturday and the race on Sunday. The plan was to meet Beer Can and friends at the track.

In the meantime, I made contact with my friend, Bobby, who was living in North Carolina, and still working for the Chip Ganassi Racing team. I told him we were coming up for the race and we talked some about the old times and what we were both up to now. Bobby wanted me to come to his facility to see all the cars, the motor department, and everything it took to put a racecar on the track on Sunday. He would also be at the track at Martinsville.

Driving from Sarasota to our destination in North Carolina, we made a short detour to stop off and see Bobby at Chip Ganassi Headquarters. When we walked into the building, we immediately saw the trophies from the races won by the drivers. Bobby was called up to the front and it was great to see him! We took a tour of the garage department and saw dozens of chasses and car bodies ready for motors and paint jobs.

Bobby showed us the motor department (his expertise area) and we saw several work benches with a few guys working on specific areas. They could tear down a motor, find a problem, and have it rebuilt in a very short time. The use of technology was everywhere, even to determine if a certain motor would work at a specific racetrack. The place was immaculate with every area clean as a whistle. After the tour, we promised to meet Bobby at the track.

On Saturday morning, there were two buses waiting outside the hotel to take us to the track for qualifying. It was a cold October morning— highs in the '30s. Arriving at the track was a whole new experience for both of us. The drivers had semitrailers selling merchandise; and semi-trucks were parked in rows all along the hillside heading into the track. Robin was freezing, so she bought a Jimmy Johnson hoodie.

We ventured inside the track to watch the drivers speed around. Martinsville is a short track, where a driver can have lap speeds as high as 100 mph. The engines roared as they rounded the track, while some cars crashed off the walls during time trials. I was just taking it all in, and although the sun was out, we headed back to hotel, where it was warmer.

The forecast for race day on Sunday called for rain or maybe even snow. We had planned to meet up with Beer Can at the track and then call Bobby—maybe he'd take us into the pits to meet the drivers. Every time we went into the hotel bar that weekend, we noticed it was full of women with blonde hair who were wearing Dale Earnhardt Jr. Budweiser jackets. Beer Can sure would have loved to have been there!

Morning came and we awoke to a cold, wet drizzle, but when we loaded the bus for the race, it started to rain even harder. As we drove through the rolling hills and mountains, the rain turned to snow. Now we worried if there would even be a race! After two hours, we arrived at the track and the first thing I did was head over to the semitrailers to see if any drivers were signing autographs. They had long lines for some drivers, but Jimmie Johnson and Tony Stewart weren't there. Can NASCAR even race in the snow? I think not!

We meet up with Bobby and he told me he thought I would have been the first one to come visit him after he moved. He told me that back in the day, he could have taken me anywhere I wanted to go in the pits, meet the drivers, and get autographs and wrecked metal from the cars. Darn. I really blew that. Raising a family takes up time, I guess.

I asked about going into the pits that day, but Bobby said that since 9/11, security was very tight. He also said there had been some incidents with drivers and their fans, so there was limited access to them now.

After saying goodbye to Bobby, I knew what I wanted to do. Martinsville's racetrack is known for its fried bologna and onion sandwiches and I wanted one! I stood in line with a hundred other people and purchased a few that I put into my jacket. They were nice and hot, so they also kept my hands warm. Then I had to find my vegetarian wife a hot pretzel to eat before we could finally head for our seats.

The snow had stopped, so the track was being dried by a big blower truck. Our seats were up high, so we could see the entire track and watch the drivers coming into turn three and out of turn four. Soon came the National Anthem and then, "Drivers, start your engines!" The roar of the engines filled my body with nothing but excitement.

Remember, this was our first, live race and I was rooting for Tony Stewart and Robin was cheering for Jimmie Johnson, so we had Home Depot vs. Lowes throughout the whole race! We saw some great driving and a few big crashes.

When I took out my first bologna sandwich, some gals in front of us offered to buy one. However, they were wearing Earnhardt jackets and had been calling Jimmie Johnson some pretty bad words in front of my wife, so I chose not to listen to them.

Jimmie Johnson, who'd led 245 laps of the race, was challenged at the end by Denny Hamlin, a hometown favorite. However, Johnson would wind up in the winner's circle that chilly day in 2006. There was Robin, cheering and clapping for her driver (the one she only started watching a few years ago), as he won the first live race she'd ever attended.

As we were leaving, Robin told me she had seen autographed posters by Jimmie Johnson at the merchant trailer. I had to have one—

after all, he'd won the race. I would keep it next to the 6x8 Jeff Gordon trading card that I purchased at Service Merchandise Department Store in their sporting goods section years ago. As of now, I had two NASCAR autographs. The story would continue.

I did return to Martinsville a few times, not with Robin, but with Beer Can Bob and his crew. The cabin was way up in the Virginia mountains, where they plant and grow Christmas trees each year. The cabin was about seventeen to twenty hours from Florida, so I became the "driver" and would pick up the guys along the way.

We'd stay at the cabin for a few days and then shoot down the mountain early Sunday morning to watch the race in Martinsville. We'd always pay to park at this one gas station across the highway, a little way down from the track. We'd tailgate before the race and Beer Can and I would walk the rows of driver's merchandise, looking for good deals or even a driver who was signing.

We did catch Joey Logano one morning and had him sign a diecast car. Then another year, we caught up with Brad Keselowski, who also signed one of his #2 Miller diecast cars. Beer Can and I were always trying to have a run-in with his favorite driver, Dale Earnhardt Jr., but it never happened.

The last time we went to Martinsville, we paid extra for a "meet and greet" with a few drivers. Earnhardt was supposed to be one, but we had the time wrong and didn't get to meet him. Both Beer Can and I did take the opportunity to sign a white and black checkered start/finish line flag I had bought. I wrote, "Greg Magac Sr./Dale Earnhardt Jr. will win this race today." Beer Can wrote, "Beer Can Bob was here," and dated it.

After a lifetime of smoking cigarettes, Beer Can was not doing so well by that time. His lungs were weak, he could hardly breathe, and we had a heck of a time walking him to the track and to our seats. I couldn't help but think that this would be Beer Can's last ride to the big show. As we headed to our seats, we came across a legend— Richard Petty. He stopped and chatted with us for a moment, signed an autograph, and then moved on.

The last twenty-five laps, Dale Earnhardt Jr. was leading with Jeff Gordon hot on his heels. But in the end, as the checkered flag flew, it was Dale Earnhardt Jr. who won Martinsville. My dear friend, Beer Can, had been coming to Martinsville for over twenty years, waiting for this day. I cried with happiness and sadness, knowing this would most likely be Beer Can's last race. It was.

I caught up with Tony Stewart before he retired from driving the #20 Home Depot car. I read somewhere that he would be signing autographs at a Home Depot in Daytona. My youngest daughter, Mara, made the ride with me across the state.

When we got there, the line had already started forming. Even though the event coordinators told us "one autograph per person," Mara, pregnant at the time with my granddaughter, Arianna, received two each! (Like father, like daughter.) On the ride over, I had told Mara that Mr. Stewart's nickname was "Smoke." When we got up to the front of the line, she asked him to sign "Smoke" on one of the diecast cars we had—and he did.

Of course, I'm always hunting more things to collect. I really wanted the cardboard standee likeness of Mr. Stewart that he had signed that day. It was right behind the signing table. At the end of the signing, Mr. Stewart left the area with some Home Depot employees for a special "Meet and Greet." I stood there, wasting several minutes contemplating whether to take it or not, but I finally grabbed it. The silliest manager of the bunch busted me and told me to put that back where I'd found it. Darn it—I waited too long thinking!

Tony Stewart was the nicest guy to talk to and it's a memory my daughter and I have together that I hold dearly.

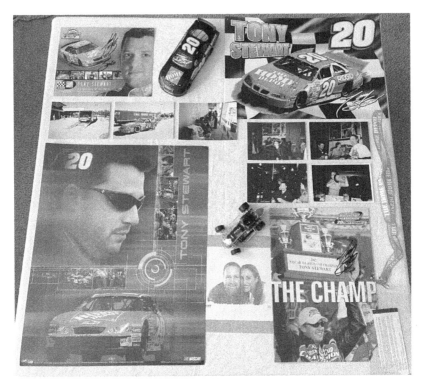

Tony Stewart Collection

5 x7 Rookie Card Signed
#203/1500

Greg with his friend, Bobby Fisher
NASCAR motor builder

The Martinsville Crew (Beer Can (front), Buddy (left) and Greg, Dan and Vern

On the left; Cale Yarborough, car owner, Center; Bobby Fisher, engine builder, R.C.A. pitcrew, Right; John Andretti driver and winner of 1997 Pepsi 400

Greg's Homemade Signed Tony Stewart Helmet

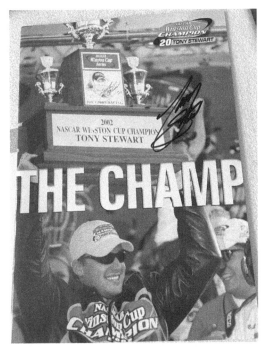

*Authographs Tony Stewart
Nascar*

*Autographed "Smoke" Tony's
nickname on open wheel dirt*

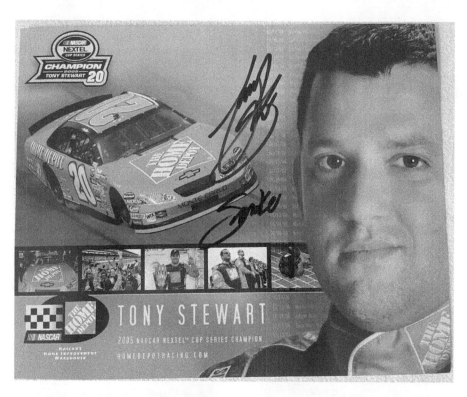

A Night on the Town

◆ ◆

It was the summer of 2004 and Robin and I had been dating for a year. I had just read that former President Bill Clinton was going to be holding a book signing of his new book in the city of Coral Gables, Florida, near Miami. I could add yet another Presidential autograph to my collection.

After work on July 21ˢᵗ, Robin met me at the house with an overnight bag. It was a three-hour drive to Miami, and the event wasn't scheduled until the afternoon of the next day. I added my overnight bag, too, and unbeknownst to Robin, I also loaded two full-sized lawn chairs, cushions, blankets, and pillows. We drive down to Miami and I told Robin we were going to drive to Coral Gables, Florida, to find the Books and Books location where the event would take place.

I wanted to go straight to the bookstore to see if anyone was camping out for the night ahead of the event. I told Robin that if there was already a line forming, we would be adding our chairs and sleeping under the stars. Wait—Robin thought we were getting a hotel room in Coral Gables, where we would get up early, take a shower, grab some breakfast, and *then* head over to the bookstore—little did she know.

We drove to the location and sure enough, there was a line forming with about eight people already there that evening, each with chairs and sleeping bags. I pulled over and started to unload our stuff. Robin was like—really?

"Of course, Robin," I said, "where else would you want to spend a hot July evening in Florida, but out on the sidewalk in Coral Gables in front of a bookstore?"

I found a parking spot for our car and we settled into our portable beds for the night. For sure, the stars were out. During the night, people were talking, cars were driving by (some drivers stopped to ask what we were all doing there), and we heard sirens and horns, but we slept on and off. A wonderful alarm clock woke us early the next morning—right across the street was a very tall high-rise going up. The construction workers started their hammers way before the sun came up. Robin was so happy … I think.

Downtown was coming alive, so we left our chairs holding our spot, while we walked to a coffee house, grabbed a coffee and danish, and headed back to our "campsite" to wait for the doors to open at 2 p.m. When we got returned, we could see the line that had formed was already two blocks long.

During the night, we had gotten to know the other people crazy enough to camp out like we were. There was a father with his teenage daughter (I can't recall their names, but he wanted her to meet a US President and experience it together.) Her father would later that afternoon become known to me as Batman. It was only 9 a.m., so we still had five hours until the event began.

When the bookstore opened that morning, we all received wrist bands, a ticket to the event, and a copy of Bill Clinton's book, *My Life*. I got to thinking that perhaps I could try to get an extra autograph, so I went into the bookstore—it was open for regular business all day. In the children's section, I found two paperback books, one on President Clinton and the other on his wife, Hillary Clinton. *This will work*, I thought, so I purchased the books and walked back to Robin.

I had packed some drinks and snacks and every now and then, Robin headed into the bookstore for a little air conditioning. It was after noon, 95 degrees, and the line had grown to ten city blocks long—weaving up one street and down the other. Damn. Helicopters were flying overhead to get a view of the large, large crowd.

For some reason, I told Robin I was going to take a walk around to the back of the store (a city block) just to "see" what was happening. (I am going to preface this by telling you that I did not have a cell phone in 2004, so I couldn't communicate with Robin once I left our spot.) I walked along the huge lines, turning this way and that way to find the parking lot in the back of the store. I thought perhaps I could just hang out in back and get my small books autographed when Clinton drove in. I think the sun must have gotten to me by this time.

However, I rethought the situation and decided to go back out front with Robin. As I was walking back, I noticed that the line seemed to be starting further up the street than I remembered. Did the line move? No way—the booksellers had told us that they would not let anyone in until 2 p.m. on the nose—it was only 1 p.m. When I reached the front of the line, I saw that Robin wasn't there, nor were any of the people we had hung out with all night.

The doors opened early and the line was now zig-zagging through the store! When I started to walk in and take my rightful place up front, two men in black suits (oh, no … Secret Service agents … again) stopped me. They asked me where I thought I was going, so I told them my story of being out on the sidewalk all night. Then I told them that I just walked from around back, saw the doors had opened early, and that my wife was in there somewhere!

The Secret Service agent looked at me and said, "Oh! You're the asshole! They're looking for you, so you're not going anywhere." I didn't know what they were talking about, so when I tried, once again to go inside, the agent said again, "I told you, you're not going in there shi**^ head." That's when I knew I was in trouble. Why didn't I just stay with Robin? What was going on?

The agent led me to another part of the store, and there was Robin, sitting on a stool crying, with icepacks on her neck. Turns out, when the doors opened early, a mob rushed through the doors, pushing and shoving their way in ahead of others, crushing Robin and a few other people. One of the agents had sat Robin down in the air conditioning and got her an ice pack. I got the evil eye from a few of the other agents close by, but Robin pulled it together. I'm a shmuck. Now, we had to figure out how to get our rightful place back in the front of the line.

Just then, the father (my new hero, Batman) of the teenage girl, found us both, told the Secret Service guys the story, and said we needed to be up front with them. We didn't get any pushback when we followed Batman towards the front of the line. I could tell there were people inside who weren't even close to us that morning!

In came President Clinton, who sat at a large wooden desk in the middle of the room. People were to enter from the left, get their book signed, and then exit on the right. I had my extra book under President Clinton's, and the line was moving quickly—place your book down, have a word (or two) with the President, get the signature, and you're done. Robin was first, and then me.

President Clinton signed his book for me. However, when I asked him to sign the second book, one of the employees told me that wasn't allowed. He was too late—President Clinton had already signed it.

To this day I regret getting out of line and going around back. I should have been there to protect Robin. The line for meeting the President went block after block after block—longer than any line I had ever seen … even at Disney World. Little did Robin know what a night on the town with me really meant.

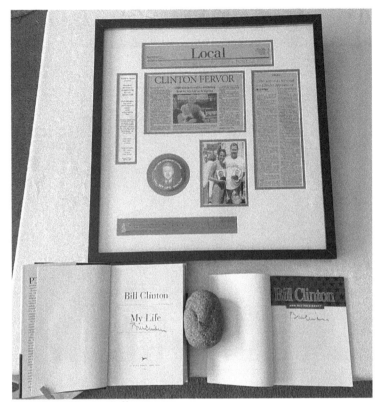

President Clinton Collection

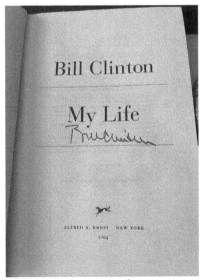

Clinton Book Autograph

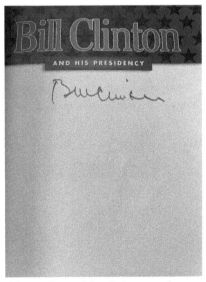

Clinton Second Book Autographs

Robin waiting for bookstore to open

Overnight sidewalk encounters father/daughter from Miami nice/friendly

Waiting overnight on sidewalk for first ten in line for Bill Clinton

If You Don't Ask,
You Don't Know

◆◆

The year was 2005. It was summertime, June, and my son, Greg, was turning 21 on the 20th. It was also Father's Day weekend. My wife, Robin, had gotten us tickets for a baseball game at Tropicana Field as a surprise Father's Day gift. Tropicana Field is in St. Petersburg, the home of the Tampa Bay Devil Rays.

On June 18th, my old hometown team, the St. Louis Cardinals, were coming into town for a three-game series. The Cardinals had made it to the 2004 World Series, losing to the Boston Red Sox in a disheartening 4 to 0 sweep. Ugh!

Anyway, I recall Greg and I both had to work on game day. We got together after work, and rushed out of town, running late. When we arrived at the stadium, we grabbed cold beers and headed for our seats. Robin had said she'd gotten tickets behind the Cardinals' dugout. I was thinking somewhere a few rows back in that section.

The game had already started, and we walked down the steps of the lower level. Boy, were these seats behind the dugout! Row A, seats one and two, right behind the corner of the home plate side, right by the batter's box, right where the players enter and exit the playing field. Boy did I screw up! I should have been there two hours before the game for batting practice and autographing. Best seat I have ever had and the latest I had ever arrived for a game. "Son of a biscuit!"

We settled into our seats. The Cardinals were wearing their retro sky-blue uniforms from the 1980s. I found out later that after the game, the uniforms were going to be auctioned off for charity.

The game was going along very well. Some good hitting and pitching made for an exciting game. Plus, we were kind of keeping the beer guy busy. Remember, we were celebrating Greg turning 21 and Father's Day!

Being that close to home plate and me being pretty boisterous, I was doing some heckling to both teams. One player for the Cardinals was a first baseman and power hitter named Albert Pujols. There were a few times that day when he'd come up to the plate, with runners in scoring position. I would yell stuff like, "Come on, Pujols! Drive 'em in! Albert blast a home run! Come on Pujols, show us what ya' got! Come on, Pujols, this guy can't pitch. Knock the leather off the ball."

Greg and I cheered him on the whole day. He ended the day with one hit, one run scored and two RBIs. He looked up at us a couple of times during the game to see who was making all the noise. Wasn't us. Or was it? This was one of the few times I hadn't brought anything to have signed—not even a Sharpie or pen. It was just a relaxing night at the game with my son. The outcome of the game was a 5 to 2 victory for the Cardinals.

As we were standing there overlooking the dugout and cheering, the Cardinals celebrated their win out near second base and the pitcher's mound. Mr. Pujols came down into the dugout, so I yelled to him, "Could we have a bat?" He ran back onto the field to high five with more of the players.

By this time, some people had gathered around us waiting to see if they could get a ball or some autographs. Pujols was headed back towards us, and as he got a few feet from the dugout steps, I yelled, "Hey Mr. Pujols, if not your bat, how about your hat?"

Right then, just as Pujols was stepping down into the dugout, this goofball next to me said loudly "You really think he's gonna give you his bat or his hat?"

I think Pujols heard that, because the next thing I knew he stepped back up out of the dugout and smiled, flipping his hat up at us. I snatched it up and handed it to Greg. He was flabbergasted. "Is that Pujols hat?" he asked.

"Yes, he just tossed it up here," I replied.

"Was it really him?" Greg asked again.

I told him that it was, but he said, "Nutuh. No way!" The guy next to me was amazed, too.

I've always told my children, "If you don't ask, you don't know. Ask for a bat, a ball, a hat, or a batting glove." Hell, these guys give their shoes away sometimes.

Albert Pujols is still an active player. He left the Cardinals in 2011 to play for the California Angels. He currently plays for the Los Angeles Dodgers, #55, first baseman. So far, his lifetime batting average is 297. He's played 2,955 games and has two World Series rings, ten All-Star games, three MVP awards, and was Rookie of the Year in 2001. As an active player with 678 home runs, he is fifth on the career home run list, chasing Alex Rodriguez with 696, Babe Ruth with 714, Henry Aaron with 755, and Barry Bonds with 762.

Keep it going, Albert! Thanks for the hat!

Pujols Collection – game used hat

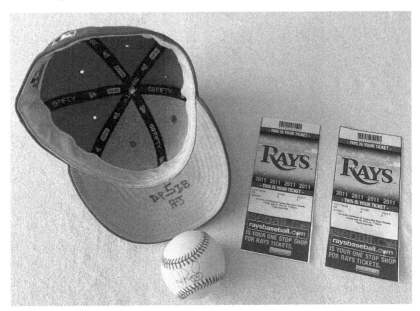

Underside of Pujols Hat

Greg Sr., Greg Jr. and grandson, Mason

Greg and his Dad at a Cardinal's game.

M.V.P. Albert Pujols

Let's Go Fishing

It took me four tries … yes, four performances to get one signature on that one guitar. Willie Nelson is a hard one to get.

The first timeI tried was when I was with a friend of mine, Sammy Jo, who was the morning DJ for 106.5 Country, a local radio station. Mr. Nelson was performing at the Sarasota Van Wezel, and Sammy was supposed to introduce Mr. Nelson on stage. I was with her when we headed towards the stage door, me with a guitar in hand. She opened the door to go into the building, but I hesitated. She looked back and asked, "You coming?"

I said no that day and chickened out. Probably could have met the legend. So, no autograph. Strike one.

Next stop was the Florida Strawberry Festival. Good concert. No autograph. Strike two.

Next stop was Weeki Wachee Springs, a small venue with a good show. I drove up with my niece, Serene, and took a CD to get autographed. We sat near the stage during the concert, and I showed Mr. Nelson the CD a couple of times, but after the show he was gone, so no autograph again. Strike three.

Now, for the fourth try, I wanted to get a guitar signed. Willie Nelson and the band were coming to sunny Sarasota, so it was time for my "A" game. It was the day of the show, so I took a day off from work. My wife, Robin, was off, too.

First thing in the morning I was already looking at the clock. Time for coffee and cocktail—that's the way it worked back then. I couldn't decide—should I go early? Wait until the afternoon?

It was a no brainer—I'd just take a ride down there and see if any buses or Security were around. Off I went to the Van Wezel parking lot, but found no buses. The Performing Arts Hall was right on the water's edge of Sarasota Bay and behind the building was a small 10 by 12 wooden dock.

I'm like, why waste the day? I headed home to get my fishing poles, made some peanut butter and jelly sandwiches, and got a few Cokes and some water. The guitar was still in the back seat, so I added my tackle box and bait bucket next to it. The show was not till 7:00 p.m., but I feel if I wasn't there, you might miss an opportunity. I made one stop at the local neighborhood bar, The Red Barn. I went in for a cocktail that I hope would calm me down (not).

The day bartender, Kathy, had just started her shift. She laughed and said, "What are you doing, Magac?" She brought me my usual Smirnoff and cranberry over. I told her I was going fishing, so she asked me where.

I told her that I was spending the day fishing down behind the Van Wezel, but I wasn't going to the show. I was just trying to get Mr. Nelson's autograph—I'd been trying for ten years.

Kathy knew I collected autographs, so she laughed and said, "You should write a book."

I told her that other people have told me that, but what would I title the book? Kathy said, *"Chasing the Ink,"*

This book is one thing I have to do before heading out to the Milky Way!

After the cocktail, I picked up a twelve-pack of water, a five-gallon bucket of shrimp, and added them to the poles, guitar, and Sharpie pens already on the back seat. Then I was off to the bayfront to fish and wait. When I arrived, there was a bus backed right along the curb, thirty feet from the dock. I parked out in the lot, gathered up my stuff, and headed out to the dock.

I set up against the handrail and threw my line out as far as it could go. No bites, but the beer was cold. I was there by myself, when the bus doors opened and out walked this guy. He went around the bus and opened the equipment storage area, down low behind the front driver's side tire.

"What are you fishing for?" he asked. I told him, "Trout, redfish, or really whatever is biting."

He came over to the dock and checked out the water. I said, "There's some poles right there, if you want to fish." He said no thanks, because he has a pole on the bus. When their runner gets here, he might ask him to take him to get bait

When he asked me where he could get bait, I recommended Hart's Landing. It was so close to the Van Wezel, you could almost see it, right next to the Ringling Bridge. I told him to go south on US 41, take Ocean Boulevard, and then a right. Don't go across the bridge, but veer off to the right, go under bridge, and the bait stand is right there.

"Or," I said, "you can just use my shrimp. I have plenty!" Then I offered him a cold beer, which he declined.

I think by the time I was reeling in a grunt or pinfish, he was heading to get his pole. I showed him how to hook up a shrimp. He introduced himself as "B" and told me he loved fishing. He always kept his pole with him if the chance to use it pops up while touring. While we were fishing, a couple more gentlemen and a lady joined us on the dock. B introduced me to them, but I've forgotten their names. One guy was the harmonica player and the other was the drummer, while the lady was the band masseuse.

We kept getting bites, but weren't catching many fish. The harmonica player asked to use my five-gallon bucket as a seat, while he got a massage and, of course, I said, "Sure."

The drummer was just taking in the beautiful day. We'd run out of shrimp by then, but I told the guys I could get more in a short time, if they wanted to keep fishing. B offered to buy it, but would ride along with me.

When we went to the truck, he noticed my guitar. He asked if I played, but I told him no. However, I had been trying to get Mr. Nelson to autograph that guitar for about ten years. I told him I had taken the whole day off work to go fishing and make a day out of it.

On the way to the bait stand, he told me he was the bass player, and had been for twenty something years. I thought that was pretty cool. I had the biggest celebrity I'd ever had in my truck! I was big-timing it!

I parked, hopped out, and jumped back in with the shrimp. Then I gave him a short tour of the bayfront. He told me not to worry about that guitar. He'd take it on the bus before the show and have it signed. I said, "Really? That'd be great!"

We returned to the dock and went back to fishing or drowning shrimp. The masseuse went for a jog, and I showed the harmonica player how to hold and throw the pole. B asked me if I had tickets to the show, I told him no, so he said he would leave two tickets at Will Call for Greg.

I was still fishing and drinking a beer when four or five younger men showed up. B introduced me to the guys. One was Willie Nelson's son and the rest were his band. They called their group, "Lukas Nelson and Promise of the Real." By that time, the day was moving toward evening, somewhere around four or five o'clock. I gave more fishing lessons to some of the others, while B caught a trout. Everyone was amazed. I told them it was a speckled trout.

Fishing started to wrap up, so B told me to be ready with the guitar when he came off his bus. He said Willie's bus wouldn't be nearby until about fifteen minutes before the show. I assured him I would be ready.

I was out on the dock gathering stuff up. Then I called my wife to see if she wanted to go to the show, but she said, "No thanks."

I called a couple of other friends, but no one wanted the second ticket. Then I dropped my phone into the water, where it met its end. No more calls. Oh, well.

I had everything put away, when a bus with a beautiful paint job of eagles and wolves backed into the lot. About five minutes later, B came off the bus, and I handed him the guitar. I asked if I could come aboard the bus, but he said that wouldn't be a good idea. Willie didn't like people he had not met before coming on his bus. I understood.

B got back on the bus and five minutes later, he returned. The guitar had a nice autograph right over the strings. Then B said thanks for the fishing and told me to have a good day. He said the next time they came to town, I should book a fishing guide for us and he would pay for it. I said, "Sure thing!" He told me my tickets would be at Will Call, but if I was ever in a city where they were playing, I should look him up for tickets.

We said our goodbyes, and he headed for the stage door. I put the guitar into my truck and locked it. I thought if I went to the lobby and bought a tour poster, I might have a chance for one more autograph of my own, when Willie came off the bus.

I bought a "Willie Nelson for President" poster and came back to the stage door. A few other autograph seekers were waiting. Willie came off the bus with his manager, and sure enough, he stopped and signed for us, as he made his way inside. Another autograph! Wow—what a day! You never know what each new day will hold. With no phone to call home, I went to check Will Call for my tickets. The woman looked under Greg Magac and then just Magac, but no tickets. Darn!

So I just went around and back up the stairs to listen. I snuck in once, but with no ticket, the usher told me I couldn't stay. I just listened, but I wanted to catch B to tell him what happened at Will Call. When the concert ended, I was hanging out by the stage door, as B and the other band members came out. I told B that no ticket had been left for me, so he was bewildered. I had heard him make the call while we were on the dock.

I told him that I had a great day, so it was all good. He told me to remember that any time I needed some tickets, any place, any time, I should just get a hold of him. Then he gave me his number.

When I headed back to the truck, I noticed that Willie's son and his band members were skateboarding in the parking lot. I got the poster out and asked him if he would sign his dad's poster. He said, "Sure," and signed it. I asked him if he had any spare guitar picks. He searched his pockets and found one with his dad's name on it. Cool! It would go with the guitar. He thanked me for the fishing lesson. I didn't even think he knew it was me.

It was time to head home, but what a story to tell!

The next time the band came to town, I was vacationing out of town, so I wasn't able to surprise B with a fishing trip. Since I'd lost his phone number by then, the next time the band was coming to Sarasota or nearby, I called my daughter, Daphney. I was hoping she could check online to see if she could contact B and somehow get some tickets.

Well, as not all stories have happy endings, Daphney found out that B had fallen at home in Nashville and died. Rest in peace, B. May your line always be tight, the sun on your face, and the wind in your sail. Thanks for the memories.

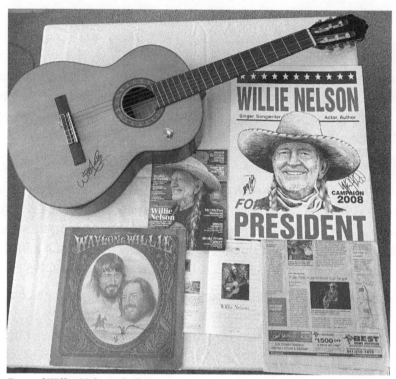

Part of Willie Nelson Collection

Willie Nelson in Concert

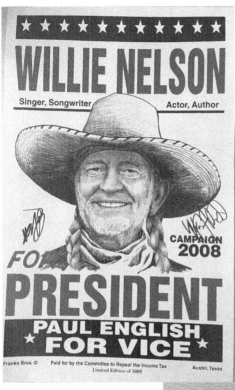

Willie Nelson & Son, Lukas,
Autographed Poster

Willie Nelson Signed
Guitar Closeup

Gramps, with his Grandkids
Left to right-Owen, London, Maxwell Maddox, Mason, Arianna
Everybody loves fishing!

I'll Meet You in Jupiter, Florida

I was raised as a St. Louis Cardinal fan by family, mostly by my grandma, Stella. She would get a couple of tickets from here or there and we'd go down to the bus stop and catch the Red Bird Express. It was the bus with the Red Cardinal flag flying, and it would take us straight to the ballpark.

In 1997, the Cardinals moved their spring training facilities from St. Petersburg to Jupiter, Florida, on the east coast, right above West Palm Beach. To autograph the Cardinals now, I had to make a three-hour drive.

My cousin, Jon, has made more trips from Illinois to Florida than anyone I know. He'd come down for fishing, baseball, Walt Disney, and space shuttle launches. He would drive all night for spring training—1200 miles in twenty-three hours. In 1998, Jon showed up for the Cardinals spring training on Opening Day in Jupiter with his two oldest daughters, Angie and Christine; his wife, Debbie; and his father-in-law, Frank.

The plan was (always!) to be there early, buy our tickets, go to the right field gate, and be the first in line to grab a good spot on the grassy berm, because this was the best spot to get an autograph. That year we collected many, many autographs: Mark McGwire, Ron Gant, Ray Lankford, John Mabry, Willie McGee, Gary Gaetti, and a new rookie the Cardinals had just signed, a right-fielder named JD Drew. Mr. Drew was a nice, young man, who made Angie and Christine giggle and laugh when he was talking to them.

Spring training at Rodger Dean Stadium in Jupiter would become a ritual for my cousin, John, and me. I would leave at four in the morning to head to Jupiter and we'd meet up at the right field gate. I'd bring anyone who wanted to come along—John's family would always be there, the first in line. John's girls would be there, too—all five of them: Angie, Christine, Ellen, Grace, and Joni. They would lay their blankets and lawn chairs at the gate before the sun came up, as the gate didn't open until 11am—two hours before game time. When they finally opened, it would be a mad dash for the grassy berm in right field (the cheap seats), but it was the better place to autograph.

During spring training in 1999 and 2000, it was a McGuire frenzy to get an autograph, but John's girls had become known as the "Drew Crew," the first fan club of JD Crew. The girls would hold up Drew Crew signs and he would always come over, carry on a conversation, and make them laugh. He'd sign pictures and balls and even a bat for *them.*

JD Drew left the Cardinals in 2003 and went on to play for the Braves and then the Dodgers, eventually settling with the Red Sox. In 2007, I'd cross paths with him one more time in his career. I was autographing at the old downtown Fort Myers stadium, home of the Boston Red Sox. I had some old *Sports Illustrated* magazines from the 2007 World Series and a ball I was trying to get signed.

I made it to the stadium early that morning, standing at the entrance gate to the players' parking lot, getting a few autographs before the game. After spending the morning at the gate, I moved into the stadium for batting practice and then stayed for the game, hoping to get signatures after the game, too. During the game, at a charity event table, they were auctioning off a game-used JD Drew bat! You had to be the highest bidder for the silent auction at the end of the seventh inning to win it.

The bids on the bat were at $125 with no less than $25 per bid. I put down $150, as the bat was not autographed. I checked on the bat throughout the game, but I figured the highest I could go was $250 or $300. I went back around the sixth inning and someone had bumped the bid up to $175! I put the bid up to $200 and kept an eye on it. No one came back, so at the bottom of the seventh inning, the bat was mine!

In the morning hours, before the game, I had seen JD Drew pulling into the players' parking area in an olive, hunter-green, jacked-up Ford truck. He had backed it along the fence line. When it was the eighth inning, I noticed that Drew had left the game, so I exited the stadium to stand by his truck, in case he blazed out early. When the game ended, people were exiting and players were leaving, so a much bigger crowd formed around the players' gate.

I decide to just hang out where I was, by Drew's truck. So I waited. The players' parking lot emptied, the fans on the sidewalk were gone, but I knew this green truck was the one. Did he leave with another player to grab a meal and I missed him? The sun was setting, but I decided to hang out until it was dark. And it damn near was dark when a man's figure showed up coming from the locker room toward the truck.

It was Mr. Drew ... finally!! As he walked over, looking like a guy ready to go hunting, I told him that I had won his bat in the silent auction and asked if he would sign it for me.

Mr. Drew asked, "What's the matter with the bat now? Isn't it nice just the way it is?"

I replied that I thought it was very nice, but it'd be even *nicer* with his signature on it. When he asked me to throw the bat over the fence, I did so immediately. As he was signing, he inquired what I had paid for it. I could have lied and said $500, but I stuck with the truth of $200. Mr. Drew said that I didn't pay enough for it, and he tossed my bat back over the fence. As I thanked him, he climbed into his truck and sped off.

As I walked to my truck and looked back on the long, hot day, I reflected on all the autographs I had gotten that day: David Ortiz, Mike Lowell, Jason Varitek, and JD Drew. I should have asked him if he remembered the Drew Crew, my cousin's daughters, but I didn't think of it at the time.

Then one year, my cousin quit coming down. All of our children had grown up and we'd aged some. However, if he called now and asked me to meet him in Jupiter on opening day at the right field gate, I'd be there.

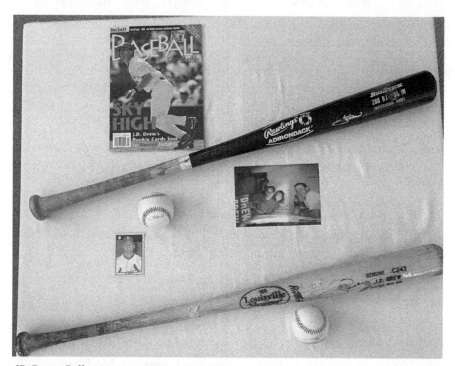

JD Drew Collection

JD Drew Signed Bat and Ball

Christine doing what Uncle Greg taught her

Greg with his mom, Marilyn, flashing the #1 sign

Two of Jon's girl's Christine, Angie with Greg's daughter, Mara on the left

Jon, Greg's Cousin, Jon's Mom Carol, and Greg on right

Jon's wife Debbie (left), the "Road Gang," and Greg (on right)

The Magac/Rukavina Spring Training Gang

Greg with daughter Mara, on berm in Jupiter, Florida

Greg talking with H.O.F. Cardinal Lou Brock during a Spring training game in Jupiter

The Rukavina family

J.D. Drew meet and greet with the Drew Crew Angie,
Christine with their Dad in the Shadow

Here Comes Swifty

Sometimes things just rock and roll with the music. It was a Thursday when I received a call from a local county DJ, who asked if I would like two tickets to a concert on Friday, September 21, 2007, starring Rodney Atkins, Taylor Swift, and Brad Paisley. Of course, I said I would take the tickets.

I called up my cowboy buck-a-roo line-dancing fool, Buddy Bucster, to see if he wanted to join me. We joined a party bus that afternoon … free food and beers on board, and headed up the interstate. We attended a meet and greet with Rodney Adkins, where I purchased a Taylor Swift CD. It was her first, the one with Tim McGraw's song on it, so possibly we could get an autograph, if we bumped into her.

When we met Rodney Atkins, we talked to him about his songs *(Watching You, These Are My People)* and he signed some 8x10 pictures. I also asked him to sign a Budweiser hat, but Buddy lost that later in life. Rodney was a great guy!

After coming off the Atkins bus (we were a little bit intoxicated), we decided to see if we could locate that young, curly-haired blonde country singer. I was the one who knew what he was doing, and didn't want to bring attention to myself, while Buddy was talking to everyone and we ended up losing our group. No worries—sure enough, Buddy found out what bus Taylor was on.

We headed over to her bus, but were met by some pretty big guys, who told us that Taylor was not having her meet-and-greet any more. Time had run out and the concert was about to begin. We asked if we could wait and see Taylor come off the bus, but were met with a big, fat NO.

Rodney Atkins came out on stage and did his song and then Taylor Swift was introduced. Rodney fired up the crowd by playing his new song, *If You're Going Through Hell,* and then Taylor came out with *Lose Yourself,* followed by *Teardrops on My Guitar.*

Somewhere during her set, she sang the Tim McGraw song and then she sang, *Picture to Burn.* She brought the house down! First, Taylor apologized to the crowd for having to cancel her meet-and-greet. Then she told the crowd that she had signed a bunch of CDs that could be purchased at her booth.

I told Buddy I would be back, so don't fall over (sometimes Buddy falls over), and I raced to Taylor's booth. A box of twenty or thirty CDs was fifteen dollars each, so I purchased two of them thinking, *What the heck, I knew this singer was the next big thing!* All the girls in my family already knew every one of her songs! Looking back, I should have bought more than two.

I got back to Buddy just in time to see Brad Paisley come onstage. He sang some great ones about the south: *Whiskey Mud on the Tires, Check You for Ticks,* and *I'm Gonna Miss Her.* As we were leaving the amphitheater, I decided to buy a few more autographed CDs. I went over to the booth, only to find out they were all sold out. Well, at least I got two.

On the way home, Buddy started whining about wanting to give one of the CDs to his daughter, so I passed it over and was now down to one CD. At last report, Buddy's adult daughter didn't know if she still has that CD or not.

In 2006, my first granddaughter, Arianna, was born. By the time she was two years old, she could sing to all of Taylor Swift's songs. *Picture to Burn* was her go-to song, and we have a video of her singing it from her car seat. My autographed CD went from Arianna's mom's car, to Nana's car, and from this house to that house, and all over.

After Taylor Swift's great achievements and popularity, I decided to track down that CD and store it away for safekeeping. And I did find it, in Nana's car, and yes, it is stored away with my most prized autographs! Thank you, Taylor Swift, for "keeping it real" with your fans and for leaving me with a wonderful memory of my granddaughter singing along to your song.

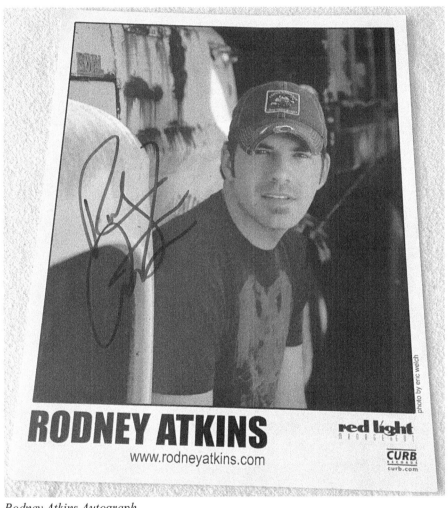

Rodney Atkins Autograph

Taylor Swift Collection

Taylor Swift Signed CD

You Shook Me All Night Long

Being a teenager during the 70's and growing up listening to my older brother, Steve, play the guitar, we heard lots of rock and roll. Bands like Aerosmith, AC/DC, Van Halen, Led Zeppelin, Boston, the Beatles, the Allman Brothers, and Lynyrd Skynyrd of the Sarasota area. We attended a lot of concerts in the Tampa area.

One of the hardest of groups to autograph seems to be rock and roll bands. I could never break the barrier of getting backstage. I'd research where the bands would stay before a concert and find out they'd be in a hotel in a city away from where they were playing.

One of my favorite bands was AC/DC, a band that formed in 1973 in Sydney, Australia, by two brothers, Malcom and Angus Young. The main vocalist was Dave Evan and the first year the band cut two singles. When Dave Evans left the band, the members turned to their chauffer, singer songwriter, Bon Scott, to become the lead singer. Scott sang on the first six studio albums and became a legend himself. After Scott's death in 1980 due to alcohol poisoning, Malcom and Angus were ready to fold it up. However, Scott's family told the brothers that he had told them to make sure the band continued after his death.

Malcom Young and the band started auditions for a new front man, but after a long search, came up empty. Robert Lange, who produced the album, *Highway to Hell,* recommended they consider Brian Johnson from a small band called, Geordie. Johnson had left the band at age 32 thinking he wasn't going to make it. He moved back to his parents' house and worked for a vinyl repair shop for collectible cars. Johnson auditioned twice, but finally on April 19, 1980, he received a ticket to the Bahamas to join the group. The band recorded their masterpiece album, *Back in Black,* which became the band's best-selling album of all time.

When the band wasn't touring or recording, Brian could be found relaxing by the pool, as he was a Sarasota resident of Bird Key, one of the first waterfront neighborhoods located after crossing the John Ringling Bridge. This historic bridge was demolished after the higher-ups of the city tore down Ringling's historic hotel. Once you cross the bridge and pass Bird Key on your left, you come to an area known as St. Armand's Circle. It's a historic business area that has clothing stores, unique boutiques, and wonderful restaurants. Many locals and tourists visit the area.

On St. Armand's Key in 1994 was a restaurant called Bananas. I was out with some friends at Bananas having some drinks, when I noticed two gentlemen wearing black leather AC/DC jackets. To me, they looked like Malcom Young and his brother, Angus. I asked them if they were members of the band, but they told me they wore the jackets because they were "fans." Fans? I didn't believe it for a second. I went back over to my friends and I told them that I thought Brian Johnson was in the building with his entire AC/DC band.

I was wearing a white collared golf shirt, but I wanted to have the two men sign my shirt, so I walked back to the bar to get an ink pen. All of a sudden, the local bar band that was on stage took off and up jumped AC/DC! They played *Highway to Hell* and *You Shook Me All Night Long*. The whole place was rocking out!

I grabbed the pen and tried to make my way up near the stage. Suddenly the back door opened. As I looked outside, backed up to the door, was a black limousine with four or five women in it. The band immediately headed for the open door and dove into the limo. I was able only to reach Brian Johnson, so he signed the front of my shirt. When I tried to get out to the limo, I was stopped by the bouncer.

Fast forward to December 8, 2007. Brian Johnson and Cliff Williams of AC/DC were going to hold a gig at the Irish Rover Pub in the Sarasota Gulf Gate area—more bars, restaurants, and shopping stores. The Irish Rover was celebrating their second anniversary. I can't remember when the show time was, but I grabbed my AC/DC album and my blue Sharpie and then headed out around 3:30. I made it to the Irish Rover in about ten minutes—remember, the early bird gets the worm (sometimes).

The album I had grabbed from my collection was *For Those about to Rock* and was the first album to reach number one in the United States. The first song written by Brian Johnson was on the *Back in Black* album and the song was *You Shook Me All Night Long*. In an interview, Brian had said he was trying to impress his friends, as the lyrics were inspired by girls and cars.

I drove to the pub and I could tell by the way things were set up that it was going to be a large bash. I called it right, getting there early. Only one other person I saw there was looking to autograph. He was a twelve-year-old boy with his father, who was holding an electric guitar. I just hung around the outside, while the pub owners and the boy and his father went inside.

It wasn't there more than an hour when an SUV pulled in with a woman driving and a gentleman in the passenger seat. He was wearing the iconic newsboy cap, a symbol of the working class in the north of England. I gave them some space and let them do their thing.

Then, as Brian Johnson turned toward the pub, I approached him and asked for an autograph. They were both really nice, so we chatted for a bit while he signed, "All the Best, Brian Johnson AC/DC."

Sometimes it's so easy. The pub wasn't open to the public yet, so I put the signed album in my truck and went across the street to have a couple of pints of New Castle in the bar to celebrate my success.

By the time I finished my second pint, the parking lot and tent area were full of people—it was party on! The band started the show with a bang and played all their hits. After playing *A Whole Lot of Rosie*, Brian introduced Scotti Hill, the guitarist for *Skid Row*," who sat in for one song.

So many great hits were played that night: *Back in Black, Hells Bells, TNT*, and *You Shook Me All Night Long*. To think it was only five dollars to get in! As the show ended, I went to my truck to get the album thinking that maybe I could get Cliff Williams to sign, too.

A black limousine was parked out front with a couple of Sarasota County Sheriff's officers standing near it. I waited by the limo, so when Cliff came out, he had no problem signing the album.

Scotti Hill was hanging around outside too, so I pulled the record out of the album cover and asked him to sign on the paper sleeve that covered the record (which he did). I watched and waited again for Brian Johnson to appear. When he came out, a crowd was trying to get a signature on whatever they had.

While he was signing, I said to him, "Hey Mr. Johnson—can I have your hat?" (You never know unless you ask).

For a second, I thought he was going to hand it to me, but he just adjusted it and said, "It's the only one I have, mate." I thanked him for putting on a great show and signing my album. He smiled and crawled into the limo.

It was an awesome night! I headed to my truck, then home to my wife and dog. Oh, how I love the home life and my pillow! Thanks again, Mr. Brian Johnson … you rock!

Brian Johnson on his
Harley Davidson

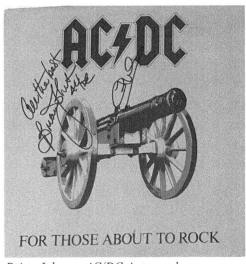

Brian Johnson AC/DC Autograph

2008: American League Champs, Tampa Bay Rays

◆ ◆

In 2006, Lou Piniella, the manager for the Tampa Bay Rays baseball team, was replaced by Joe Madden. With the change of coaches, a change came in uniforms and a new 2008 roster of All-Star players: Carlos Pena, Evan Longoria, David Price, Jonny Gomes, Scott Kazmir, Carl Crawford, and Jason Bartlett to name a few.

In 2008, the Rays would have their first winning season going into the American League Series Championship with a 97-65 record. They would be taking on their archrival, the Boston Red Sox. Boston would travel to Tampa with head coach, Terry Francona, and their lineup was full of All-Star players as well: David Ortiz, JD Drew, Mike Lowell, Jason Varitek, Matsuzaka Daisuke, Manny Ramirez, and more.

Boston would take game one in Tropicana Field and Tampa would win games two, three, and four. But that darn Boston fought back, winning games five and six. This made game seven a showdown back in Tampa.

Let's get some tickets! My daughters (Mara and Daphney) and my sister (Michaelyn) all put our money together and got four seats about twenty rows back in the lower level behind Boston's dugout. Should they win, it would be the first time in the Rays' history to claim the American League Championship since the city was awarded a major league team in 1998.

Entering the stadium that night was what you would expect— totally electrifying, and what a game it was! Dustin Pedroia got the Red Sox off to a good start with a first inning home run off of starting pitcher for the Rays, Matt Garza. Garza would settle in and have an

MVP performance that night. The Rays tied the game in the fourth inning with an Evan Longoria RBI double. Then they went ahead in the fifth on an RBI single by Rocco Baldelli. Rookie David Price, who'd only made a Major League debut a couple of months earlier, came in to pitch to JD Drew in the top of the eighth inning, with bases loaded. He struck him out on a check swing to end the bottom of the inning. Willy Aybar, the Rays' utility infielder and sometimes DH, hit an insurance home run to lead the game three to one.

At the top of the ninth, as Price returned to the mound, the stadium went crazy! A trip to the World Series was only three outs away! Price recorded his first Major League save by getting Jed Lowrie to ground into a forced play at second base to win the game. The Rays players swarmed out of the dugout to the second base area for a grand celebration of joy! My daughters, sister, and I were celebrating with all the other fans—what a game!

The next day's newspaper had all the details of the game. The Rays would be facing the Philadelphia Phillies in the 2008 World Series. I decided to take a few days off, as there might be some good days to chase some ink! I grabbed a baseball and a black pro model bat from my closet and headed across the Skyway Bridge towards Tropicana Field, arriving in the area outside the fence of the players' parking lot.

There were still a lot of news media trucks there, covering the series and teams. At the players' parking lot, the only opening to get autographs was about a 14x16 rectangle to hand items to players to sign if they came over. It was late in the morning, so I figured the players would have been celebrating most of the night and would be arriving a little later in the day. A few other autograph fans showed up and we coaxed some of the players and coaches to walk over to the opening and sign.

I was going back and forth between handing the baseball in the fence hole and handing the bat in: blue ball point pen for the ball and a silver Sharpie for the bat. While I was standing there, I noticed a lot of players were pulling into the main gate and getting out at the security booth, allowing a valet to park their cars. I asked the others why no one stood over by that gate, as it seemed like the spot would have better access to the players. They said that no one has ever tried it there. Well, I was done for the day, but I would try again tomorrow.

The ball and bat were looking good, but there were more players I needed on them before they would be considered "team items." I asked my daughter, Daphney, if she wanted to come along and she told me it would be like old-times and would love to. I also found out that I would be babysitting my two-year-old granddaughter, Arianna, but I wasn't going to let that cancel my plans!

I decided I'd make a couple of signs, then take some folding chairs and post up at the main gate with my beautiful daughter and granddaughter! This would certainly grab the attention of the players!

We made the forty-five-minute drive arriving early at the stadium. We set up the chairs and had our signs ready. While I was watching Arianna, Daphney was already buddying up to the Security guy at the booth. No one else was there—just us. It couldn't have gone any better.

All the players from whom I needed autographs either stopped for us, or if they drove past, got out and walked back! Daphney had buttered up the security guard so much that _he_ was asking the players if they could sign for us.

Carlos Pena, Evan Longoria, Jonny Gomes, Carl Crawford, Jason Bartlett, and even Coach Joe Maddon signed for us! Everyone signed Daphney's Rays hat, but forgot to have Longoria sign—she was too busy getting a hug … or two! Arianna was just sitting in the chair, looking all cute. It was a great day—the ball and bat were loaded up with the team's autographs. It was time to head home.

We'd done great autographing the American League Champs. Now all we needed was for the Rays to win the World Series! Unfortunately, it wasn't meant to be.

Greg with two daughters left to right; Mara, Daphney, Dad

*Granddaughter Arianna autographing
outside players parking lot with
Gramps at Tropicana field after
Winning A.L.C.*

Greg Celebrating game 7 win with sister Michaelyn

The King of the Blues

Every year the Van Wezel Performing Arts Center in Sarasota put out its schedule for upcoming shows. Starting in 1980, legendary blues performer, BB King began doing shows there and sometime in the 1990s, I decided I was going to see BB King's show. The first show I tried to go to was sold out. That was okay, but maybe I could do some "stage door" autographing out back.

The night of the show, I took a couple of albums and went to the Van Wezel after the concert started. You can hear the music pretty good, if you head up the stairs to the back of the Center, but that night the bus was parked right up there, blocking most of the access.

After the concert, people started coming out of the back doors, where a few other people were waiting for an autograph. I had heard that Mr. King nearly always signs, but that night, a gentleman came out and told us that he wouldn't be signing that night, because they had to get on the road. I wouldn't need my Sharpie tonight. Darn!

Another time, the Van Wezel was in the middle of a big renovation, so Mr. King would perform under a huge white tent outside the Center. I didn't have a ticket then either, but I was able to see and hear through the openings around the tent. When the show ended, as Mr. King went toward his bus, a few people yelled for him to sign, but again—not that night.

Another ten years went by, so I was now fifty years old. BB King was coming back to Sarasota. It was time to try again for his autograph. The date of the concert arrived and the items I carried with me were a guitar, an album, and the *Ticket Magazine* from the *Sarasota Herald Tribune*. I asked my wife, Robin, if she wanted to come along.

I drove down early to get there a couple of hours before the show. When their bus backed in, I was the only one there. I walk over to the door of the bus and a gentleman was standing there and asked me what I wanted. I told him I was trying to get Mr. King's autograph, but I was told that he doesn't sign until after the show. However, he also said that he still doesn't sign guitars, unless you purchased one of his Gibson BB King Lucille guitars.

I put my guitar into my car and headed back to the bus. Soon a few other autograph seekers showed up. The doors to the bus opened, and there stood BB King—he was going to sign one autograph for each person, as long as nobody got overexcited. I was the first to go and I smiled at the guy who had told me that Mr. King only signs after the show. He signed my album! I was good to go … for now.

Robin showed up a little bit later and I told her the story of how I got the album signed. Since we didn't have tickets for the show, we went to have a cocktail and dinner. When we returned to the concert hall, a line of people was waiting for the show to end to meet Mr. King. My friend, Tommy J, and his son, Kyle, had come down to see if they could get an autograph, too.

I walked up to the bus to talk to the driver. He told me that he had driven Mr. King all over "these United States," so they have ridden thousands of miles together. He asked me about the fishing in the area and I promised him that the next time they came to town, I'd have some seafood for them to eat.

After the concert, Mr. King allowed fans on his bus, a few at a time. I told Robin to move to the end of the line, so we could take our time talking to him. We climbed on the bus, along with Tommy and Kyle. It's always a rush for me to meet and shake the hand of a person I listened to growing up.

As we all gathered in the back room on the sofa, one of his staff took some group pictures. We talked about family, faith, God, and how to treat women. He told us that he'd been in eighteen bus crashes, as sometimes drivers fall asleep at the wheel or have other mishaps. Mr.

King told us that everybody gets the blues—maybe over a breakup, the loss of a loved one, or even your dog dying or having no money—it will all give you the blues.

Mr. King told us that the blues were meant to be played on the front porch at sunset after a hard day working the fields. He said he learned the blues from his great-grandmother who had been enslaved. She told him to sing about sadness, and how it unburdens the soul.

I told him how sorry I was that people had to come to this country as slaves, since this country was built on freedom and justice for all. But I guess we are still working on that. He handed us some guitar picks and little BB King lapel pins. The bus driver told us it was time to go.

The following year, our paths crossed again. I have a friend who is a stone crab fisherman and I asked him to get me a five-pound bag for Mr. King. My plan was just to drop them off at the bus, say hello, and then leave. I put the crab in the bottom of my refrigerator and totally forgot about the concert. After dinner with Robin, I was ready to kick my shoes off when it hit me. I forgot about the concert! It was late, so I had no idea if the buses would still be there, but I put my shoes back on and headed out the door.

I arrived at the Van Wezel in record time, but when I got there, I didn't see any buses or even a semi-truck. Mr. King was gone. However, I knew that the Hyatt, three blocks south, was usually where stars stayed when they were in town. If they were going to spend the night in Sarasota, they would park the bus in the back. I circled around, back by the Hyatt and sure enough, there was a bus and someone sitting out front smoking a cigarette. I got out of the car with the crab and asked the guy if this was Mr. King's bus. He told me it was one of his buses, but that Mr. King was already gone.

So, I left the bag of claws with the gentleman, explained how to crack them open and dip them in sauce, and to either eat them now or put them on ice for when he met up with Mr. King. Of course, Mr. King could have been on that bus—those drivers lie to you all the time! Ha, ha. I hope that guy enjoyed the crab and didn't just throw them away because he thought I was crazy.

The next year came along. I still remember that I had promised that driver I'd bring him some fried seafood and that last year I had messed up with the stone crabs! I wanted to cook up some good seafood and make people smile. This time I stayed focused on the calendar. I wanted to get the picture of us with BB King signed, too.

A few days before the concert, I got ahold of one of my fishing buddies and he hooked me up with some grouper filets. Then I headed over to Walt's Fish Market—an icon in Sarasota—he's been here since 1920 and has some *good* stuff. I bought up some nice-sized shrimp and scallops.

I was in my kitchen, flour and seasoning all over the counters, three cast iron pans going and spitting grease, when in walked my wife, Robin. She could see I was on a mission, as I had lined a commercial cookie sheet with paper towels and was placing some nicely browned, crunchy looking seafood on it and BOY did it smell good!

I finished up so I could get on the road, when in walked my daughter, Daphney, who wanted to know what the hell I was doing! I said that I was taking seafood down to BB King and his crew and how I had promised the bus driver. Daphney sampled the food, she asked if I really thought they would eat food brought to them by a stranger. I told her that if they didn't want it, I'd bring it back to our house and we would eat it.

I loaded up my truck and stopped at Walt's again to pick up some hush puppies, lemons, and cocktail sauce. Time was ticking, so I headed over to the Van Wezel. When I arrived, the sun was just starting to set over Sarasota Bay. When I pulled around back and a bus was parked in the area by the stage door entrance. It had been about four years since I had promised that bus driver I would bring him some seafood, so I was really hoping he'd be there.

I walked over to the bus and there he was—the same driver. He looked at me and this was the conversation:

Driver: "You again? What do you want now?"

Me: "I brought you all some fried fish, shrimp, and hushpuppies."

Driver: "Where's it at?"

Me: "Over in that red truck."

Driver: "Well, go get it and bring it on the bus!"

I ran back to the truck to grab the food, the 8x10 photo, and a Sharpie and then hurried back to the bus. The driver opened the doors and told me to come on in and I thought … it's happening!

As I climbed the steps, I could see that a gentleman was in the driver's seat and a young woman was standing in the aisle next to a counter. I caught her off guard when I arrived with all that food. I remember placing it on the counter, and just standing there.

When I looked around, there was Mr. King, sitting in a chair in the next room. A felt rope was hanging across the hall where he was sitting.

I said hello to Mr. King and told him I had brought him some really good southern seafood. He asked me if I had any gumbo, as he'd really enjoy some good gumbo, but I told him I didn't bring any gumbo.

Right then, that lady had picked up a piece of fish and tried it out. She told BB that it was some of the best fried fish she'd ever tasted. She said, "Young man, you know how to fry fish!"

Then, she gave me a piece of costume jewelry, a gold 2014 tour necklace medallion, and a guitar pin. Mr. King asked if I wanted my photo signed. He had seen Robin in the picture, and remembered that night, as he never forgets a pretty lady.

From somewhere on the bus, he pulled out a 2013-2014 tour poster, autographed it, and gave it to me. I didn't hang out too much longer, so that they could eat and rest before the concert. I know those drivers were ready to go at it!

What a great moment in my life. It was a good feeling!

It would be the last visit to Sarasota for BB King. The following year, May 14, 2015, he died in his sleep at age 89 in Las Vegas. After hearing of his death, I went home and played some blues on my harmonica, singing *The Thrill's Gone*—but it's always in my memories.

BB King Collection

Autographed Ticket Magazine, Sarasota Herald Tribune

Van Wezel Performing Art hall signed program

Greg and Wife Robin with BB King on his tour bus

Greg   Robin   BB King

Finding the Right Spot

◆ ◆

It was the spring of 2011 and I was fifty-one years old. In 2008, when I married my wife, Robin, I married into a family of college football fans. My new father-in-law, Lou Long, was an avid Florida Gators fan, who bled orange and blue. He invited me to go on a trip to Gainesville, home of the University of Florida, to watch the spring Orange and Blue game, when fans are invited into the stadium to see the team scrimmage.

I told Lou Sr. that I would like to go and took both of Robin's brothers (Lou Jr. and Kyle), along with our nephews (Matt and Jake). After a three-hour drive, we arrived at the stadium early, so we would be able to see the team buses pull up and unload the players on the city street. The Gator fans would line both sides of the sidewalk from the street to the stadium locker room entrance, high fiving and cheering on the players and coaches.

It was awesome. The whole stadium area was abuzz with fans and residential areas around the campus were splattered with orange and blue. Flags flew from sorority and fraternity houses—this was definitely Gator Country! I'd never been to a college football game before. Heck, I'd only been on a couple of smaller college campuses in my day. Each of my sisters had graduated from the University of Florida, but I'd never been there before.

After tailgating a while, we went along the sidewalk, lining up with the other fans as the buses showed up. Upon their arrival, it *really* got loud, as everyone cheered the team on. In front of the stadium there were three new bronze statues recognizing former players who were Heisman Trophy Winner (HTW): Steve Spurrier HTW 1966, Danny Wuerffel HTW 1996, and Tim Tebow 2007 HTW. So where were these guys?

I have a blue Sharpie with me in my pocket. Just in case.

The sun is up and it was going to be hot. As we made our way into the stadium, I noticed there wasn't much shade. Sure was thankful I was wearing a Gator hat. Our seats were about a third of the way up the stadium, directly on the 45-yard line. The players were out on the field, loosening up, getting ready for the game. The stadium then started erupting, so I was wondering what was going on. Turns out, Tim Tebow was out on the field shaking hands and talking with some of the players.

By the start of the second half, people were looking for shade and the only place you could find it was three quarters up in the stadium in the nose-bleed section. There was talk of leaving for home as the heat was taking its toll on Lou Sr. and the kids. However, being the avid Gator fan that he was, Lou Sr. walked up past a hundred seats before reaching the shade with all of us following him. That walk about killed me, but there was Lou Sr., over seventy years old and with health issues, determined to make the trek and continue with his day.

Early into the fourth quarter, we decided to head out. As we were exiting the stadium, a small crowd was forming over near the new bronze statues. I told Lou Jr. to come check it out with me. Here I go … in autograph mode with my Gator hat and shirt.

My nephews, Jake and Matt, and Lou Jr., and I head out. Jake asks me, "What we do if *they* (Tebow, Spurrier, or Wuerffel) are there?

I told him that we would pick a spot and see if we could get an autograph. Sure enough, Tim Tebow, in a coat and tie, was talking to some other gentlemen. We went right up there as he started thanking the fans, his teammates, coaches, family, and God.

Well, I picked my spot and Jake and Lou Jr. were about twelve feet to my right—they were in the perfect spot! When Mr. Tebow was done speaking, he stepped right into the area where I was standing. He started signing autographs, so when I reached out with my hat, he signed it. He was moving to my right, heading toward Jake and Lou Jr.

I looked down the line and saw Mr. Tebow sign right where Jake and Lou Jr. were standing.

I made my way around the crowd to get another good spot by a door that he could use to return to the building. I still had my Gator shirt on, but I still needed one more signature for the day!

Poor Jake was overlooked—Mr. Tebow just missed the kid. He was still signing here and there, as he made his way towards me, when suddenly he stopped to pray with some people.

For a big guy, he was very soft-spoken and had the bluest eyes. I was hoping that the boys would pop around by me, but I couldn't see them. When I asked Mr. Tebow if he could sign my shirt, he told me only one autograph per person. I told him to have a blessed life and he wished me the same.

I met up with the boys and showed Jake the hat with the autograph and gave it to him. When we got to the car, he told his grandpa, Lou Sr. that Uncle Greg had gotten Tim Tebow's autograph on the hat! My father-in-law couldn't believe it and asked how I had done it. I told him it was years of practice and finding the right spot in the crowd. Lou Sr. held the hat in his hands and said reverently, "That's his signature."

I replied, "Yes, sir!"

Lou Sr. then said, "That's one of the greatest quarterbacks in Gator history. It's been a grand day. Let's go home."

Tim Tebow Collection

National Champion Gator Football

North Touchdown Terrace Tickets

Tim Tebow Signed Newspaper

Tim Tebow Signed Hat

Kid Dynamite

◆ ◆

As a youngster, I loved listening to boxing matches on the radio while I was lying in bed: Frazier vs. Ali; Ali vs. Foreman; Marvelous Marvin Hagler vs. Sugar Ray Leonard.

There was a young boxer who was born on June 30, 1966 in Brooklyn, New York. His mother passed away when he was sixteen years old. At that time, he was taken into the home of veteran boxing trainer, Cus D'Amato. Before becoming a professional boxer, he held a record 13-2 with eleven knockouts. He was the fighter of the Decade during the 1980s when he won five world titles in five different weight classes. Some called him the "Baddest Man on the Planet." His name was Mike Tyson and he became the youngest Heavyweight Boxing Champion at twenty years of age.

On February 11, 1990, I wanted to celebrate my birthday with a party, while watching Mike Tyson knock out a boxer named Buster Douglas. My brother-in-law had arrived from a long-time service in the Army and had heard all about this "Iron Mike" Tyson. As we settled in for the fight, right away we could sense that Iron Mike was not going to knock out Douglas in the first round.

After a few rounds, my brother-in-law said, "I came all the way from Germany for this guy?" Tyson floored Douglas in the eighth round, but Douglas got back on his feet and the fight continued. At round ten, both fighters came out with a flurry of punches and then Tyson looked hurt. After Douglas delivered a lot of left jabs and one good one to the head, Tyson fell to the mat. The referee counted Tyson out before he could pull himself together, giving Douglas a 10th round technical knockout. We didn't expect that kind of ending to the fight and I'm sure the boxing world was stunned.

Fast forward twenty-three years later, when my wife was taking me to a show at Ruth Eckerd Hall in St. Petersburg, Florida, for my birthday. Guess who was presenting that night? Mike Tyson was live, on-stage with *Undisputed Truth* on April 13, 2013. We had heard about Tyson's struggles throughout his life, but we couldn't wait to hear HIS story.

I'd heard that it was easy to get autographs at Ruth Eckerd Hall, but I understood they had a fence that separated the audience from the performer. If the entertainer didn't come over to you, you'd be out of luck. By then, I was trying to end my autograph collecting (that's what I told everyone), but that night I had a blue and silver Sharpie … just in case.

After we entered the hall, I made my way over to the merchandise booth. I decided to buy a nice program with some phenomenal pictures in it. When the show began, the theatre was completely dark. Then a spotlight shone down on Tyson, who was wearing a white suit and sitting in a high-top chair. I don't know how long his stories went on, but I could have listened all night. He talked about his early life—where he was born, the ugly part of "street life," deaths of family members and friends, marriages, divorces, jail time—he covered it all.

After the show, I told my wife I was going to find that fence where autographers would be waiting. Robin headed to the truck to take a snooze! I looked over the program, and using my fingers, marked some really great pictures I would try to have Tyson sign. I got behind people who waiting by the four-foot-high fence and found a spot that was perfect. I always stayed quiet and acted like I was just checking things out.

From the back door of the building came Iron Mike, tattoos and all. The crowd started begging him to come over. His SUV was parked about fifteen feet away. Right then, a few guys with all their autograph gear started telling me they were going to show me how to get an autograph. I played dumb, like I didn't know what to do. Tyson put some of his things in the SUV and started to walk towards the fence. I had my fingers in place and my Sharpies ready to go.

Then Tyson headed to an area a bit further away from where I thought he would go. I had to move through a couple of people (nicely, of course) to get the program over the fence and in Tyson's eyesight. I dropped one pen against the program, but grabbed the other one right away. Moving up the fence line, I opened the program and Tyson signed the spot right away! I kept moving with the line and he signed another picture!

I had the third picture ready to go, but Tyson was turning away, so I said, "Mr. Tyson, that was a great show you put on for all of us tonight. Thanks for telling it like it is." Tyson turned around, looked at my program, and signed it again. No way did that just happen! I had three autographs!

On the way back to my truck, I happened to see the two autograph guys with their gear. They didn't get any autographs and were going to try to get him to sign at the airport. Those guys should have stuck with me (ha-ha). I jumped into my truck with that "autograph high" I always get. My wife? Well, she knows I'm goofy like that.

Mike Tyson Autograph

Mike Tyson – A fighter of life, love, legend

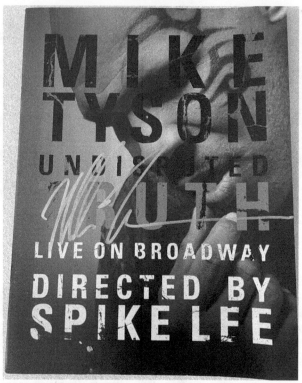

Mike Tyson Signed Program

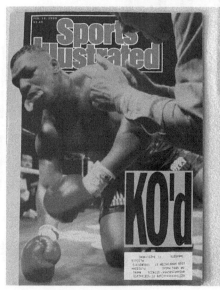

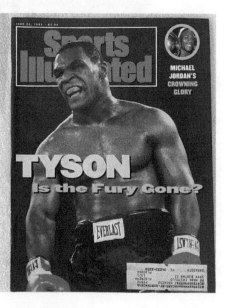

More Than a Friend

Sometime between 2015 and midway through 2016, I reported in for work and had an install scheduled for that day. Wouldn't you know it, as I prepared to leave the shop, my friend, Crazy Tommy, called me. He told me he was working out on Siesta Key, down towards Turtle Beach, at the house of his lady friend, Debbie.

He had stopped at the 7-11 Store, and the clerk had told him that Terry Bradshaw was going to be promoting his new Four Roses Bourbon at Captain Curt's Crab and Oyster Bar. Bottles would be selling for $100, and Bradshaw was autographing them. He would also sign any other items you brought with you. All proceeds would be going to the Wounded Warriors Project, to help veterans and their families.

I told Tommy I couldn't leave work that day and asked him if he could stand in line for an autograph for him and me. We didn't even have anything to be signed, but we could buy the bourbon and have the bottles signed. Tommy said he'd call me back after he got to his job and talked to Debbie. When he called me back, I told him there was definitely no way I could get out of work that day.

Tommy and Debbie were heading out to pick up supplies for their remodel, and on the way back they'd stop in at Captain Curt's to see what was going on. I asked Tommy to go to the Sports Authority and pick up the best-looking NFL football he could find to get signed. I also asked him to bring a silver Sharpie.

He called me back, all fired up. The store didn't have any official NFL footballs, but they had a new replica of one, which was the only one they had. He would get the ball signed for me. He and Debbie were also going to buy a couple of bottles of bourbon for Bradshaw to sign, too!

I told Tommy, "You know this isn't going to be a situation where you're in, and then you're out. There's probably already a line of fifty to a hundred people. You could be waiting a while."

Tommy replied, "That's OK. There's alcohol and food."

"When you get up to Mr. Bradshaw," I said, "slow it down and get a nice big signature with maybe a #12 and HOF 1989. That would be a one-of-a-kind autograph."

"I got it handled," he said. "I'll call you after we get there."

I become over-excited when legends are in town. I couldn't wait for his call, so I called *him* back and asked, "You there yet?"

"No, remember that I said I'd call you when we get there."

"Well, get going! And don't forget to give yourself some space from the person in front of you. Slow it down and also remember to ask for a big signature, #12 and HOF 1989 … Hello?"

Tommy had hung up on me.

Terry Bradshaw, 6'3" inches tall, 209 pounds, was the 1970 first pick, first round out of Louisiana Tech. His career spanned from 1970 to 1983. His awards include three Pro Bowls, one NFL MVP, the 1978 Bert Bell Award, and four Super Bowls rings. Bradshaw, as quarterback, lead the Pittsburg Steelers in back-to-back Super Bowl wins in 1975 and 1975, and again in 1978 and 1979.

Bradshaw was voted into the Pro Football Hall of Fame in 1989. He ran for a total of 30,246 yards, scored 244 touchdowns, was sacked 307 times, and fumbled 84 times, as well as intercepted 210 times. And did I say, four Super Bowls?

Crazy Tommy finally called me back to say he was in line and there was quite a crowd, with about thirty-five people ahead of him. Debbie was supplying him with beers and shots, so I figured Tommy was lighting the place up.

He's a talker, a comedian, and a riot. He told me he was wearing his "gynecologist" shirt. It was navy blue with a white stick figure doctor standing sideways. He had a stethoscope around his neck with lettering that ran down the other side of his shirt that read, "I'm not a gynecologist, but I can take a look."

Tommy said, "Wait 'till Terry gets a look at the shirt. He'll crack up!"

I again reminded him to ask for "HOF 1989." He said, "I got this! Talk to you soon!"

Later on in the afternoon, I got a call from Tommy. He'd had a great time, and Mr. Bradshaw had been really cool with him. They had cracked each other up with some joking around. Bradshaw had gotten a good laugh out of Tommy's shirt. He'd signed the ball just the way Tommy had asked, and Debbie had also bought two bottles of the bourbon and had them signed, too. Tommy told me he would come by the house to drop off the ball.

He came back later that night with the football. I was amazed at the penmanship of the autograph. It was bold and went darn near the length of the ball. It also had the number 12 under it with HOF 1989. I thanked Tommy very much. I told him it was probably one of my top ten autographs now. I told him I owed him big time! But he told me I didn't owe him anything. That's what friends are for, and he is one of the best kinds of friend to have! Thanks Tommy! Thanks Terry!

As a side note, I also have some Steelers blood in my veins as my Uncle Mike Magac did his first five years in the NFL with the '49ers and finished his career with the Steelers, from 1966 to 1967. If he could have stayed three or four more years, he would have been a right guard for Mr. Bradshaw.

I once asked my uncle why he got out of the game so soon. He said back then you sometimes had to play both sides of the ball, and if he hadn't gotten out when he did, he wouldn't have been able to walk later on in life.

I was ring bearer at my uncle's wedding in the mid-60s. One of the only memories I have of that wedding, being only four or five years old, was out at the barbeque grill. They served East Saint Louis-style pig snouts with sauce! That, and I remember all the men at the wedding were huge, especially their big hands. Later in life, I realized they were all his teammates from the University of Missouri and the '49ers. I should have gotten some autographs. Ha, ha!

Terry Bradshaw Signed Football

Steelers Bradshaw Collection

Terry Bradshaw

Tommy making joke's with Terry

Trash Comes to Town

◆ ◆

Dolly Parton—I'd been waiting to cross paths with this amazing lady, as she is one of the top women country music stars—in league with women like Patsy Cline, Loretta Lynn, and the Carter Sisters. They had never come this far south that I know of. In my heart, I really wanted to see Dolly. I read in the newspaper that she had added a stop on her tour to come to the Van Wezel Performing Arts Center in Sarasota.

I looked over to the corner of my bedroom and saw an old guitar in need of some minor repairs. That's all I needed for an autograph—that and a couple of old albums that needed to be dusted off from the collection box. So I set aside the newspaper article and went about my daily life. I reminded myself to mark the calendar and get the guitar ready. I know I've said it before, but there was a high-end desire to get the ink on the guitar, the album, and the photo from the paper.

Lo and behold, I had company coming to town on same day of the show. Shoot! My best friend from Georgia and his wife were coming for a visit. Paul had autographed many a time with me, but he was laid back and there was always the waiting game. When our guests got to Sarasota, the women headed out to go shopping and I looked at Paul. He knew my plan.

We headed to the neighborhood watering hole to have a few cocktails and watch some football. I was ready to go around 4 p.m. The show started at 7, but I had to check to see if buses were on site. We slipped out of the bar and jumped into the truck. Paul told me it was too early. The mile ride across town was quick—let's just say I like to get to where I'm going.

When we pulled into the Van Wezel parking lot, we saw three country music tour buses backed in. I said to Paul, "'Dude, you're never too early!"

As I pulled my truck up, I looked over the situation. One of the buses was surrounded by a chain (you know the loopy things with velvet covering them). I'd never seen barricade rope set up behind this auditorium before.

The two other buses were backed in, catching the sunset. I told Paul, "Come on—let's check it out!"

I grabbed the guitar and one album. Paul clutched the other album. We walked up to the bus backed closest to the stage entrance, the one marked off with the fancy barricade ropes. We weren't that close, but almost immediately a Van Wezel security guard approached us.

"Sorry, guys," he said, "but Ms. Parton doesn't sign autographs. You can wait and see, but you'll have to wait on the sidewalk."

Well, the sidewalk was fifteen feet back from where we wanted to be, so we just moseyed around. I was still checking things out, so we stood there about fifteen minutes or so. When Paul was ready to head back to the truck, we popped some tops and had few beers.

I walked over to Dolly's security guard, and he had the same story—no autographs—she never signs. He told me that Dolly comes off the bus five minutes before show, with a towel held above her head and leaves right when the show is over.

What if she does leave right after the show? Of course, who could blame her for leaving right away? She's what, 70 or 71, still riding buses to sell records? Her Security guys told me the same thing—they showed me the sidewalk and told me I could wait there.

So I was strumming away on the guitar and Paul was in the truck. Of course, the bay waves were splashing the rocks and the sunset was low in the sky.

Suddenly, a gentleman jumped off the steps of one of the buses carrying an armful of dresses and outfits and headed into that very well-guarded bus. I thought, *She's gotta be on that bus.*

I went back to the truck and told Paul that I got Dolly to sign and he missed it—I was joking, of course. Then I told him about the dresses and the exchange I had with the guards. Paul was ready to go back to the Red Barn, but I asked him to give me a little more time.

Paul told me I could have thirty more minutes, so, I went back to the sidewalk and continued strumming the guitar.

All of a sudden, I saw the Security guy, the one who told me Dolly never signs, and he waved me over to the bus. I looked around and then said, "Who, me?" When I walked over, he proceeded to tell me Ms. Parton was going to sign my stuff. He said, "When the bus doors open, do **not** move towards her. She will come to you."

My heart was racing and the high set in. The bus door opened and there she was—really beautiful, wearing a flashy pink V-neck shirt, in her signature tight ankle-high blue jeans and six-inch pink stilettoes.

She asked me if I would like her to sign my guitar. Then she stepped up on the bus a bit higher, leaned on a counter, and signed, "2016 With Love, Dolly Parton."

She asked if I'd like the album signed, and created a very nice signature for me. I told her how my son loved to watch her television show on Saturday evenings back in the 80s, and that my wife was an elementary school principal, and appreciates what she does with the Dolly Parton Imagination Library. I thanked her, she said goodbye, and the door closed. It happened!

Yep, Paul was still in the truck, but this time when I returned, I said, "She signed,"

He was like, "Far Out! Now, let's get back to the bar."

Paul was happy for me—and enjoyed the time we spent together. He didn't mind waiting in the truck, as he understood the waiting game. and the timing. He became part of one of my grand memories.

I called this chapter, "Trash Comes to Town," because I once heard a story Dolly told, of how her family lived by a hollow. Whenever they came to town, there was always a woman standing on the corner. Dolly would tell her mama she wanted to be just like that beautiful woman.

Her mama said, "Darling, that's just trash." So Dolly said that all her life she just wanted to be trash. At 70 plus, she is just as beautiful as ever.

Dolly Parton Collection

Dolly Parton Signed Close-up

Greg Standing by Dolly's Tour Bus after Meeting Her

Hitchin' a Ride

It was April 1976, and I had just turned 16 in February. My family had kind of fallen into the hippie movement of peace and love in the vanishing '60s. Before then I had hooked up with a couple of old friends, to see the Turtles and Jefferson Airplane in concert—it was the only concert I had ever attended.

Someone came up with about ten tickets to see Bob Dylan at the St. Petersburg Bayfront Arts Center. He was starting his 1975—1976 Rolling Thunder Revue Tour, with Joan Baez, Ramblin' Jack Elliot, and other guest musicians.

The evening for the concert came and we loaded up the front and back of a family friend's 1965 International pickup. Mom was coming along and was seated in the middle of the front. My two older sisters, Michaelyn and Kelly, were in the back bed with about five other people and me. I'm not sure if my brother, Steve, was in town and went with us, but I do recall there was not a truer Bob Dylan follower than Steve, being a singer, guitarist, and harmonica player himself.

I remember leaving Sarasota and heading way up over the old Skyway Bridge. Going down the other side of the bridge, those of us in the back were bouncing around. I'm surprised the driver didn't lose control and go over the side!

When we arrived in downtown St. Petersburg, we pulled into a gas station to get directions, use the bathrooms, and buy supplies. We were all getting back into the truck and ready to go, when two of St. Petersburg's finest pulled up in their squad car.

They got out and asked if we were going to the concert. We said yes. They had the driver and two passengers step out of the front of the truck. I don't know if they got consent from the driver to search or if they just started snooping around. They found a baggie with some marijuana seeds in the glove box and then pulled the driver off to the side for a talk. The driver and the officer walked up to the tailgate of the truck. The driver said the officer was going to throw his hat into the middle of all of us sitting in the back bed, so if we had any illegal drugs, we needed to put them into his hat. If we did that, he'd let us be on our way to the concert and not be late.

About three or four finger-sized baggies went into the hat, plus a couple of pre-rolled joints. The officer picked up his hat, and with a smile said, "Now everyone get out of the truck and line up to be searched." Anyone possessing any illegal drugs would go to jail. After searching the first four people or so, they stopped searching and told us to be on our way. They didn't want to make us late.

I tell you one thing—in the mid-1970s Sarasota had a brand of marijuana known as Columbian Gold Bud. I don't know if it was up in the St. Pete area at that time, but those cops got the highest grade that night.

We got to the arena in time for the opening act. I hung with my sister, Michaelyn, because like me, she wanted to get as close to the front as she could, maybe near backstage, 'cause she's beautiful and all that. I had my autograph pad and my ballpoint pen with me. I was hoping for maybe a Bob Dylan autograph or Joan Baez.

We watched most of the concert by the stage area and Michaelyn was talking with some of the roadies during intermissions, but not making any headway toward getting backstage. However, one of the guys gave her two tickets for a private shooting of a video to be used for a TV special. It would be taped April 26, 1976 at the Starlight Ballroom/Belleview Biltmore, in Clearwater, Florida. They had been holding rehearsals in that city with many other musicians getting ready for the spring tour, the *Rolling Thunder Revue*.

The concert ended, but there was no going around back to get autographs. So everyone was ready to hit the road back to Sarasota.

The following day, Michaelyn asked me if I wanted to go Clearwater with her for the show. I said, "Sure, but how we gonna get there?" Kelly, my other older sister, and Michaelyn had blown up the engine in our VW bus, so that was a no-go. Maybe we could borrow a car?

The day came around for the show. No car or truck to borrow. Looks like we were hitchhiking—standing by the side of the road, hoping a passerby would pick us up and not be a serial killer.

Where the hell was Clearwater anyway? We got going early, so I can't remember how many rides it took. I remember it was hot and Clearwater was off the beaten path back then. Would we even make it in time? Holy Moly! I remember arriving at this beautiful country club type of estate. All buildings and fences were painted white and surrounded with luscious green grass. Amidst all this was a white building standing off alone. A line of people had formed at the doors and down the sidewalk. They were just starting to let people in and it looked like we'd made it right on time—this place was not so easy to hitchhike to.

As we entered the building, the floor area in front of the stage was full. However, scaffolding was set up in the back, so you could go up and sit on some wood planking. We were sitting about eight feet above the stage and it was a really cool—a small, personal setting.

The songs played that day were *Hey, Mr. Tambourine Man*, *The Times They Are Changing*, and Joan Baez joined Dylan on stage for *Blowin' in the Wind*. It was pretty awesome. Plus, they were videotaping the show to be aired on a later date—I believe for *The Midnight Special*. MTV wouldn't hit the airwaves until August 1, 1981.

When we made it onto the estate, I had rounded up a couple of white pamphlets with some pictures on the front and some information. I also snatched up a pen. This would be good for a possible signature or two.

The show didn't last too long, but I'd kind of messed up. I should have sat closer to the doors. By the time I got down off the scaffolding and around the back of the building, the musicians were being escorted away on golf carts. Darn! Missed that opportunity.

Oh, well. The sun was getting low in the sky. It was time to get back home. No Dylan autograph! The times, they are a'changin'. Yes, they were.

It was sixteen years later, and I was thirty years old. Mr. Bob Dylan was coming to the Sarasota Van Wezel, on November 9, 1992. Time for me to get a Bob Dylan autograph! I decided I would try out back before and after the show. However, I had heard he didn't like to sign and that he's one of the harder ones to get.

I would get there early the day of the show. The buses had already backed in and a dozen or so other people were waiting to get Dylan's autograph. No one had caught sight of him yet. As it got closer to show time, one of his managers came out and told us Mr. Dylan would not be signing autographs before or after the show.

Nothing like good news, but I'd heard that before, so I stayed—just in case. As Dylan stepped off the bus to enter the stage door, we all yelled to try to get his signature. He waved and went inside. So much for that.

All I needed was a signature on one of the albums I had with me. I hung around the back door of the building and could hear the music—a free concert without seeing the stage.

The show came to an end, and people were leaving. The security wasn't really top of the line back then, but it was enough to keep everyone back, so Dylan could make it to the bus without signing. Mr. Dylan had eluded me again. Zero out of two events. I thought I might as well forget about him.

Fast forward to October 22, 2018—Bob Dylan was coming back to the Van Wezel. I would give it one more try.

The day of the concert I got there early. Two gentlemen dressed in shorts and white security shirts were posted around in the back of the venue. I'd never seen them before. I was the only one there to try for an autograph, so it just goes to show that Dylan's known for not signing.

Security instructed me to stay back on the sidewalk, twenty feet from the bus. I thought to myself, "This is not good."

Right before show time, Dylan exited the bus and headed for the stage door. I decided to go into the lobby and purchase some concert memorabilia. I got a concert poster with the date and city of the show, and Dylan strumming his guitar. I also bought a nice polished steel Hohner harmonica with Bob Dylan's signature engraved on it. This might be the closest I would ever get to an autograph! I was hoping they didn't make too many of the signed harmonicas, so that might be worth some coins in the future. I had dished out $150, which was way over my autographing budget.

When I got back around to the bus, they had repositioned it, backing it into the old stage door. They hadn't used this door since the remodel of the hall. If Dylan used it that night, he'd have eight or so steps to walk down, then the length of the bus to board it. Security had also moved the barricade around so I wouldn't be able to get close unless I hid around a tall row of hedges that surrounded an electrical box.

I went back behind the hedge and the box and tried to keep out of the spotlights. A big, ugly, bald security guard was just on the other side of the bushes by the bus door. The concert was ending, and people were starting to leave out the back entrance.

I'd been hiding out for a while, and more and more people were leaving. It wouldn't be long now, but what would I do about the huge security guard? I wondered what he might do as I came out of the bushes. "Hell," I thought, "I could get shot!"

If I would have had five more minutes, I might have found out. All of a sudden, that big security guard saw me at the edge of the hedge! He was all bent out of shape. "What did I tell you?" he said, and then he pushed me. "You didn't tell me nothing, and don't touch me again," I said to him. He told me, "Get the hell outta there."

I told him I'd have him arrested for pushing me. As I stepped out by the barricades, there came Bob Dylan with his bodyguard walking alongside the bus. They loaded up and were gone.

I got to my truck quickly, and decided to follow. He had a concert in Fort Myers, Florida, the next day, and that was only an hour south. Let's go for a ride!

The bus headed out 3rd Street, to Fruitville Road, and through downtown. It headed east out to I-75, but I was hoping they would stop at a Bob Evans for a late-night breakfast before getting onto the interstate. I wanted to jump out at a red light, beat on the bus door, and yell, "Hook me up!" But the bus kept going up the ramp and onto the interstate.

I'd never followed anyone out of Sarasota to another city before. I could have gotten off at either of the next two exits and called it a night. *Hmmm, what to do?*

I was still following the bus, and we were almost to Venice, Florida. I could still turn back. I didn't, and forty-five minutes later, we were on a main highway going into Fort Myers. The bus made a right-hand turn into a Marriott hotel, right on the corner. I went past the hotel and turned at the light, before pulling into a dark business parking lot.

I had eyes on the two buses. The first bus was unloading band members and roadies at the front entrance. Dylan's bus was back down the side front corner in the darkness of the trees. I decided that when no people were around, I would go sit in the lobby and wait for him to come inside.

I had a guitar, an album, the poster and the harmonica. I would leave the guitar behind and go with the smaller things. Maybe he'd sign the inside of the harmonica box, knowing what I had paid for it. Fat chance!

I waited until no one was around to make my move. In hindsight, I should have waited for the first bus to be moved. When I reached the lobby doors, they didn't open. I guess you had to be coded in or have a room key. As I turned to walk back to my truck, a big guy came off the bus, and looked me over good, so I backed into the darkness of the trees by my truck. As I was standing there, the guy who had come down off the bus yelled over to another fellow by Dylan's bus, informing him that some stranger was standing on the other side of the parking lot.

Then, there he was—the bodyguard. He was about 6'4", 220 pounds, and all muscle. Someone had told me earlier that he was Asian/American and possibly an expert in karate. He had just been on the cover of some magazine. So here he comes, walking towards me, smiling. He asked how I was doing tonight and I said, "Good."

"Did you follow us down from Sarasota? Did you go to the show?" He asked.

"Yes. I just wanted to see if Mr. Dylan would sign this album and my poster."

He said, "As a fan, you should know that Mr. Dylan likes to keep his personal life to himself. He doesn't like to be bothered for autographs."

"I've heard that. But maybe you could take them onto to the bus and have Dylan sign them."

He laughed. "I've only been working for him for ten years, and don't want to get fired."

"What if I don't listen to you, and wait around anyway?"

"You could possibly get hurt or wind up in jail."

Ok, I thought, guess it's back to Sarasota I go. At least I have my pretty harmonica and the poster. Bob Dylan had skunked me three times!

Dylan has since entered the art world and has gallery showings. I could buy a high dollar, signed limited print—maybe or maybe not …

Bob Dylan—singer, songwriter, author, visual artist—he's one of the greatest songwriters of all time, with nearly sixty years of folk, blues, rock, gospel, country, pop, and jazz. He plays guitar, keyboards, and harmonica. He was awarded the Nobel Prize in Literature in 2016.

As the song goes, "The answer, my friend, is blowin' in the wind." Huh!

Bob Dylan Collection

Bob Dylan Harmonica

The Wind Was A'whippin'

❖ ❖

It was winter in Sarasota, and even though it was sunny out, the temperature was in the low '30s. Yes, it gets that cold in Florida! Since moving here in 1974, I've seen snow locally three, maybe four times.

Tony Bennett, a legendary jazz and pop artist would be performing at the Van Wezel Performing Arts Hall. I'd purchased a *Live at Carnegie Hall* album a couple of years back that I'd been trying to get Mr. Bennett to sign, but I had been unsuccessful.

I don't remember the date of this show or the year. I just know it was the winter months because, man, it was cold that night, waiting by the stage door. I stood there in blue jeans, a long-sleeved flannel shirt, and a bomber jacket, while the winds whipped through the back of the building from the northwest.

When exiting through the backstage door at the Van Wezel, attendees followed a sidewalk that led to the parking area, which was surrounded on both sides by two eight-foot block walls. Since it was approximately twenty feet to the parking lot area, folks needing a ride could use this walkway as a secure area in which they reached their bus or limo.

Security personnel almost always sat at that backstage door. However, for whatever reason (the cold?) no one was there that night—just me. I was trying to hide from the wind and the wind chill factor. I had the album zipped inside my jacket to keep it warm, and a silver Sharpie in my pocket, trying to keep that warm, too. I didn't know if the cold would affect the album or the pen, which would mess up the signature.

I started to wonder if Mr. Bennett was already inside, which might be the reason why no one was in the back. I'm nuts. It had been dark for a while and freezing—brrr. I knew I was not supposed to be where I was along this sidewalk, inside these eight-foot walls. However, a person has to try and stay warm somehow!

I unzipped the jacket to check out how the album was doing and again considered just going home. As soon as that thought ran through my head, walking right toward me I saw the legend, Tony Bennett, sporting a black-leather trench coat. We both were startled as we stared at each other. Of course, then I asked if he would sign my album.

When Mr. Bennett said, "Yes," I asked him if he could write something fancy on the album for me.

He wrote something all right, and it looked fancy, but to this day, I still can't read it! His signature on the album is awesome though. I thanked him, climbed into my truck, turned on the heat, and defrosted both me *and* the truck. It was a cold, amazing night ... you never know what the wind will blow in!

Tony Bennett Collection

A Family Affair

I was at a night game for the Tampa Bay Devil Rays, when Sharon Robinson, daughter of the late Jackie Robinson, arrived. He was known for breaking the color barrier in major league baseball and was an amazing player. Sharon was asked to throw out the first pitch before the game.

I was sitting out in left field and I brought a baseball from batting practice for autographing. I watched as she came out from home plate and walked toward the pitcher's mound. I'd thought about Jackie Robinson and the items in my collection, and decided that hers would be a great signature to add to my collection.

I bolted from my seat and headed through the corridor tunnel. I knew she would probably leave from the home plate gate by the Ray's dugout. As I came around the tunnel near that section, there she was, coming off the field and headed toward the gate.

I walked right down to her, past the aisle Security, meeting her halfway up. I asked her if she'd like to sign my baseball, and she said, "Who? Me?"

I told her she was the daughter of a legend! She smiled and signed my ball. I thanked her and noticed that other people were starting to come over to her and ask her to sign their stuff, too. I told her I was sorry for getting her into signing for others, and we laughed.

Jackie Robinson was born in 1919 in Cairo, Georgia, and made his debut in the major leagues with the Brooklyn Dodgers in 1947. The Dodgers were the first MLB team to break the color barrier by integrating black players into the all-white leagues.

Robinson had an amazing career: 1947 Rookie of the Year, 1949 National League Most Valuable Player, six All-Star teams, six pennant titles, 1955 World Series, and was inducted into the Baseball Hall of Fame in 1962.

Mr. Robinson was a man of courage and poise and who once said, "A life is not important except in the impact it has on other's lives."

*Sharon Robinson
autographed baseball
and Jackie Robinson
Collection.*

From One Hand to Another

◆ ◆

We were driving across the Skyway Bridge with my daughter, Mara, and my old friend, Tommy J, and his son, Kyle. We were headed to St. Petersburg to the Florida Suncoast Dome, home of the new expansion team for major league baseball, the Tampa Bay Devil Rays. The organization was recognizing Wade Boggs for reaching his milestone 3,000th hit on August 7, 1999.

At eighteen years of age, Boggs was drafted by the Boston Red Sox. When he didn't win a World Series ring, he became a free agent and signed with the New York Yankees. I'll bet Boston fans burned some of their jerseys over that one!

In 1996, Boggs helped the Yankees win their first World Series in eighteen years. It would be the only one for Boggs. He joined the expansion Devil Rays team in 1998, and headed back to his home town.

The gates to the stadium opened at 11:15, two hours before the game would start. We drove over the Skyway Bridge as the sun was rising, arriving to the stadium early. When we entered, we received a commemorative bat that had the current date and Wade Boggs' autograph burned into the wood. We also received a small "stuffed" Boggs toy and a poster. I was already thinking … maybe we could get Mr. Boggs to sign the bats down on the first-base line.

We headed into the lower section towards the wall along the right-field line. The players were taking batting practice and I could see Boggs by the batting cage. After he swung a few times, he headed out near the dugout to sign a couple of autographs and then disappeared.

By this time my crew was asking to use the bathroom, grab some hotdogs and peanuts, and even have a beer. We headed up the tunnel where I stood alone, waiting for bathroom duty to be over, when a young boy came up to me. He asked me to hold his bat while he went to the bathroom. Of course, I agreed, but when I looked at the bat, I realized it was a game-used Wade Boggs *signed* bat!

When Tommy J, Mara, and Kyle came back after using the facilities, I showed them the bat. Tommy J asked if I was going to take off with it, but of course I wouldn't—he was just a kid!

When the boy returned, I asked him how he had gotten the bat. He replied that Mr. Boggs had given it to him several weeks ago, but he just had it signed today.

I asked him if he wanted to sell the bat for $300, but he told me he already had been offered $300 without the signature on it! I upped my price and offered him $500 for it. The boy smiled and said he'd have to ask his mom and dad. I gave him my phone number and told him to call me, if he decided to sell it. We never did get any autographs that day, but did take home many commemorative items.

A couple of days went by before I finally received a call from that young man. His parents said he could sell the bat! He played ice hockey at the Ellington ice rink and thought he needed some new equipment. We met on a Saturday morning and made the exchange. I had him write down the story of how he acquired the bat. Everyone was happy—I acquired the bat and he used the money to buy his ice hockey equipment.

Wade Boggs retired after eighteen seasons from baseball in 1999 after a knee injury. It's said that his nickname, given to him by Jim Rice, was "Chicken Man," because he ate chicken before every game. Also, it was because he had written a chicken recipe book with his mother and grandmother.

He finished his career with 3,010 hits, a .328 batting average, five American League batting titles, twelve consecutive All Star games, eight Silver Sluggers, two Golden Gloves, and one World Series. Also he was the first player to slam a homerun for his 3,000[th] hit.

*Wade Boggs game used bat, signed,
used during 3000 hit run*

*Letter of Purchase from Young
Rays Fan*

Shh!! "Mums" the Word

◆ ◆

One night between May 9, 1999 and May 13, 1999, I was up late, flipping channels on the TV. I caught something on the news (or maybe ESPN) that Cal Ripken Jr. was heading to a minor league camp for some rehab (I think for his ankle). Well, the Baltimore Orioles minor league camp was only five miles east of my house.

Calvin Edwin Ripken Jr.'s nickname was "Iron Man," which sure went along with the way he played baseball. He was acquired by the Orioles in 1978 in the second round, 48th overall. He would stay with the Orioles for his entire career, starting as their full-time third baseman, and then moving to shortstop in 1982.

Ripken won the World Series with the Orioles in 1983. Then in 1995, he played his 2,131 consecutive game, breaking Lou Gehrig's record of 2,130. With all this history, there was no way they would send Ripken anywhere for rehab, but to the Orioles training camp.

I knew the Orioles organization was trying to get Ripken in some place to rehab where there wouldn't be an invasion of fans, news reporters, and autograph hounds. I gave my old friend, Tommy J, a call and told him I thought Cal Ripken Jr. was coming in town to rehab at the Buck O'Neil Sports Complex in Sarasota. I told him to gather up some autographing items, call in sick to work the next day, and help me chase some ink. It might be all "hush-hush" about Ripken, so I told him not to tell anyone.

I went through some of my collection and found about five items I'd like to get signed. That was a lot, but heck, I'd see what the future held. I was up early the next day, anxious to get moving to the sports complex. I had loaded my car the night before, so all I had left to do was call in sick (cough, cough).

I headed out east with the sun rising in my eyes, toward what then was all country cow pasture. When I reached the complex, not much was going on—just some field workers out doing their jobs.

Tommy J and I knew this one guy who worked on the grounds crew there. We had fished together off the North Siesta Key Bridge at night with him and some minor league players. I just couldn't remember his name. A few other people showed up, including my old friend, Tommy J.

We were hanging out near the back of the building, where all the players come out after eating breakfast. After about an hour, our "fishing buddy" saw us and smiled. He is used to us being there—he knows why we are there, so he'll give us the whole scoop.

We walked over to meet him by the maintenance barn where they kept all the field equipment. Our cars were nearby with all our stuff, so it was good. Our friend told us that Cal Ripken Jr. was coming that day, but he wasn't sure of the time. He told us some supposedly special security would be set up there to keep begging varmints (like us) away from Ripken. We all just laughed.

People came and people went, but there were still a few people hanging around waiting to see if Ripken would show up. Most people were just tourists, checking the place out.

We played the waiting game and saw that the "extra security" showed up, which was a good sign. By then we had gone to our cars, and prepared our items. Security asked some people to leave, but we were hanging out, lying low, so they didn't spot us.

Sometime later, a black SUV pulled in, followed by a white car. We grabbed our stuff and headed to the area between the vehicles, all the while security was telling us to back up.

Sure enough, out stepped "Iron Man," Cal Ripken Jr., heading towards the front entrance of the building. I stepped between Mr. Ripken and security to get an autograph, while Tommy J hung back, watching Mr. Ripken sign a few more. He told all of us that he would take care of everyone when he came back out later in the day. Waiting again, so more people showed up—not good.

Sometime later, Mr. Ripken comes out, and true to his word, he did what he said he would. He told all the people gathered there to relax, because he would sign for everyone. He worked that group of people, so Tommy J got his autograph, and I had about four things signed.

A couple of guys with a game-used Orioles batting helmet were present, so when Mr. Ripken took the helmet to sign, he asked, "Where did you get this from?"

The guys told him they had purchased it from a sports dealer in Baltimore. Mr. Ripken shared that it had been stolen from his locker. He signed the helmet, gave it back, and was done signing for the day. We thanked him and watched as he ran off the field.

That night, I was watching the 6:00 local news and, darn, if we weren't right there on the TV getting signatures! The station showed the same clip over and over every thirty minutes until midnight. Hopefully our bosses at work weren't watching!

Cal Ripken Collection

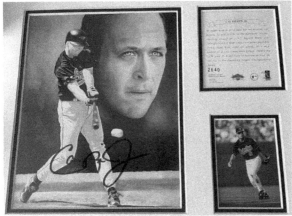

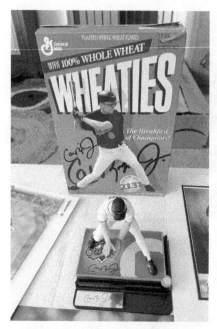

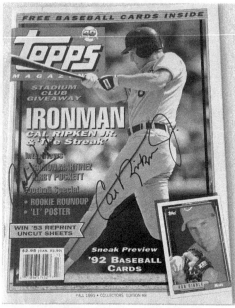

More signed Cal Ripken Stuff

Cal Ripken picture time with Greg, Ed Smith Stadium

Greatest County in the World!

◆◆

It was March 8, 1995, a chilly, rainy Wednesday morning. My cousin, John, was down with his wife, Debbie, from Illinois. We'd spent the last couple of days autographing the St. Louis Cardinals in St. Petersburg, and were doing a little fishing.

In 1994, Emmy-award winning Ken Burns had done a nine-series documentary on baseball. The current Sarasota mayor at that time, Jack Gurney, saw the documentary and learned the story of former Sarasota resident, Buck O'Neil (birth name, John Jordan "Buck" O'Neil, Jr., born in 1911) and the history of the Negro League. The mayor rallied the city to take notice of O'Neil's life and rename the Twin Lakes Sports Complex after O'Neil. At that time, the training complex was where the Baltimore Orioles minor leaguers worked out and it was also the major league Oriole spring training complex.

Buck O'Neil had moved to Sarasota at the age of twelve. His mother was a restaurant manager and his father was a foreman for a farm crew and ran a pool hall in Newtown, an area in Sarasota.

Buck recalled working at the celery fields on Fruitville Road, loading crates onto a truck. Most of the boys working could only carry two crates at a time. However, O'Neil remembered being able to carry four—he was that big and strong. O'Neil was paid $1.25 a day. In the 1920s, the city of Sarasota was segregated, just like most southern cities were back then. Also, at that time, there were only four high schools in the state that blacks could attend.

While in Sarasota, O'Neil's father would take him to Payne Park to watch the New York Giants. At that time, the team had their spring training camp in town. They would also go watch the New York Yankees in St. Pete, where they saw Babe Ruth and Lou Gehrig.

One hot, summer day, O'Neil's father overheard him say, "There's got to be something better than this." His father told him to "grab what he could" out of life and to get an education. The family moved to Jacksonville, where O'Neil completed high school and attended Edward Waters College for two years.

O'Neil left college to play first base for a number of black baseball teams, including the Miami Giants and the Memphis Red Sox. In 1938, O'Neil joined the best team in the Negro League, the Kansas City Monarchs. He played his final game with the team ten years later. O'Neil's baseball record was impressive—he helped the Monarchs win four pennants, while holding a batting average of .353, and had three appearances for the west squad all-star team.

When the Monarchs destiny was disrupted by World War II, O'Neil and several of his teammates were called to duty. O'Neil served in the US Navy for three years and then returned to the Monarchs, where in 1948, he became manager of the team. During his time as manager (1948-1955) he took the Monarchs to two Negro League World Series, won five pennants, and managed five east/west all-star games.

In 1956, O'Neil was signed to be a scout for the Chicago Cubs. The team needed someone to help recruit black players and O'Neil did just that, signing stars like Erie Bank, Lou Brock, Lee Smith, Oscar Gamble, and Joe Carter. In 1962, the Chicago Cubs made O'Neil a manager, so he became the first black manager in the major league history.

On March 8th I rousted up my cousin, John, and informed him that the renaming ceremony, changing Twin Lakes Sports Complex to the Buck O'Neil Sports Complex, was that day. I told John about O'Neil's background and that Frank Robinson (Baseball HOF 1982), and Ken Burns, the director of the Baseball Documentary, would be in attendance.

My cousin was not too happy about going out in the cold rain, so I told my son, Greg Jr., that he could stay home from school if he wanted to go with us. We ate breakfast, grabbed some baseballs, put on our rain gear, and out the door we went. The ceremony was early that afternoon, but the early bird gets the worm, so we headed out early.

When we reached the complex, the parking lot was full of minor league players' cars. There were three buildings on the grounds with no people in sight—most likely because of the rain. John wanted to go back to the house, because he'd driven his 1974 Winnebago down from Illinois, and he wanted to head out the next day.

He told me that for the money he spent on gas, he could've stayed at five-star hotels. Greg Jr. was bellyaching and wanted to go to the Waffle House nearby. I had the heat on in the car and the radio playing music, so I told them to just wait a little bit longer. Patience, calmness, waiting, wondering, timing, the right place and right time—all part of getting the signature.

I had just hit the windshield wipers, when from the building, two men walked out—one tall, one short—it was Frank Robinson and Ken Burns! They were heading toward the minor league locker room and cafeteria. I should have been standing there waiting for them!

They went into the building, so I grabbed my baseballs and told my crew to get moving. As we walked over to the building, the rain was coming down in a steady drizzle. Out of the doors came Frank Robinson, so we asked him to "please" sign our baseballs. He blew us off and kept moving back to the other building. That was kinda mean, but it was okay. He even blew off Greg Jr.—heck, the kid was only eleven.

We checked to see if the doors were unlocked (they were), so we stood outside in the rain for a while, feeling the cold. We noticed a gentleman coming from the parking lot. He was wearing a World Series Ring and looked a lot like Joe Morgan.

When we said, "Hello," he smiled and said, "Hello," back. We still weren't quite sure it was Morgan, so we decided to follow him into the building. That's where we saw several minor league players wearing the Orioles' uniform. We could also see an older gentlemen talking and laughing with the younger players.

I noticed a table by the door that had programs about the event that included date, time, the lineup of speakers, etc. I grabbed a few of those and made my way to the group of men. One of the guys was definitely Ken Burns and his name was on the program.

He moved away from the group, so I realized that was my chance. I asked him if I could get an autograph on the program and told him how I thought his documentary on baseball was great. Burns seemed appreciative and signed my program.

My cousin, John, slid in next to me and asked for an autograph, too. I looked around and sure enough, Buck O'Neil was standing in the group, signing baseballs, and taking pictures with players.

I went over to Greg Jr. and found that he was talking to some newspaper reporters, telling them he was allowed to stay home from school to meet Buck O'Neil. I told the reporter that I was his dad, and yes, I did let him skip school on this rainy day.

Buck O'Neil was heading our way with my cousin, John, right behind him. I gave Greg Jr. a baseball and told him to say, "Mr. O'Neil, would you sign my baseball?"

As O'Neil walked next to us, Greg Jr. asked him just that. O'Neil stopped and smiled and then said, "Aren't you supposed to be in school?"

Greg Jr. replied, "My dad told me I was gonna meet a super star today—a really good man." O'Neil smiled and patted Greg Jr. on his head. Right behind him was my cousin, sliding in to get his baseball signed.

Mr. O'Neil signed the balls and out the door he went. My family wanted to go home, but I wanted one more try for Frank Robinson. It was getting really crowded, as the luncheon was about to start. We'd been there about an hour and a half. This time though, I gave Greg Jr. the baseball and pen to see if Mr. Robinson would sign for him. As he walked closer to us, Greg Jr. asked, "Mr. Robinson, will you sign an autograph for me?"

Mr. Robinson looked at me (not in a happy way), took the ball, signed it, and gave it back. Then John stretched his arm out with a ball and got it signed, too! The waiting game paid off!!

Meeting Buck O'Neil was an honor. The past never wore him down, so he always kept a positive attitude, even in adverse circumstances. When giving his speech that day, he said, "Sarasota, what you've done for me—letting me come home at 83 years of age, proves one thing. This is the greatest country in the world!"

The next day, John's wife, Debbie, began their long drive home in the Winnebago. I went to the store and found the dedication event was on the front page, along with a picture of Greg Jr., sharing his story of meeting Buck O'Neil. Too bad I can't find that newspaper clipping now!

Greg's collection of Buck O'Neil memorabilia

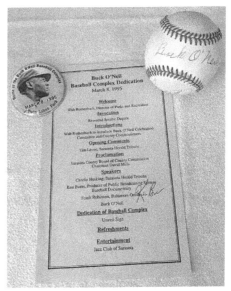

Closeup of Buck O'Neil signature

Buck O'Neil Program autographed by Ken Burns

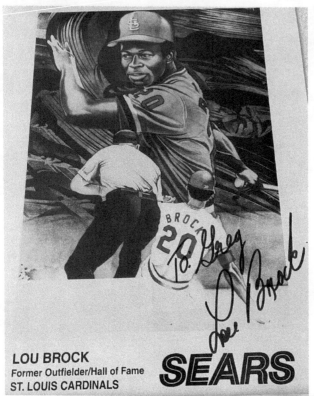

*Lou Brock was scouted
and brought into MLB by
Buck O'Neil.*

LOU BROCK
Former Outfielder/Hall of Fame
ST. LOUIS CARDINALS

Buck O'Neil pin and signed ball.

*Closeup of Frank Robinson and
Buck O'Neil signatures*

The Mountain Man Returns Home

In the late 1990s, my friend, John, who had lived a few streets over from me, uprooted his family and moved to the mountain area of Blairsville, Georgia. Sometime around 2010—2012, John returned with his sons, Josh and Sam, to visit his mother and have some vacation fun. One of the things John wanted to do was take his boys to a Rays' major league baseball game. John wanted me to show them how to get autographs.

We went to a night game at Tropicana Field, when the Detroit Tigers were in town. We arrived at the stadium and I had a couple of baseballs with me. Somehow, we wound up on the third base line by the Tiger's dugout.

As the team came out to warm up, a couple of players came over and signed some autographs. One of the pitchers was wearing those copper beaded "energy" necklaces, so my friend, John, started asking him all kinds of questions about it, while he signed the baseballs. John had the guy cracking up over all the stuff he was asking him. I don't recall who won the game, but I know we didn't get any more signatures at that game.

I told John I knew what hotel the visiting teams stayed, but you weren't allowed to autograph there. If you were lucky, you could sneak in maybe two signatures, but then you would be asked to leave the premises.

John still wanted me to show him, so we climbed into the truck and parked down by the St. Petersburg bayfront, which was near the hotel. I was already thinking … maybe I could get a Justin Verlander, Prince Fielder, or Miguel Cabrera autograph. We grabbed some balls, gloves, and baseballs and started walking down the sidewalk as the team bus rolled into the driveway of the hotel.

Right by the valet stand is a sign that said, "No asking players for autographs." As the players came off the bus, it was a bit hard to tell who was who, as no one wore their team jerseys.

I noticed a fancy car with a woman and kids standing near it. One of the players walked over to them. Wait—it was Prince Fielder, Detroit's first baseman and home run hitter! After I told John who it was, he wanted to go right over, but I told him to wait until Fielder was done talking to his family.

Shortly after, John walked over next to Fielder, talking silly stuff to him. John asked Fielder if he'd sign his son's glove and baseball, which he did. I stepped up and got my glove signed, too. It's always good to have kids with you!

I had already told John what would happen, as soon as we got the autographs. When we were asked to leave the property, none of us cared. John was excited that I had showed him how to stalk the players, and he listened to my stories all the way home.

Prince Fielder was a first round draft pick, and he had a wonderful career: six-times an all-star player, two-time home run derby, three silver sluggers, and 319 home runs.

John (far back) with his sons Josh (left) and Sammy, along with Captain Mattie, fishing in Sarasota Bay

Jon (left) and Greg

Conclusion
5/20/2024

◆ ◆

It's Monday evening, around 7 pm. I met with my publisher, Julie Ann Bakker, today for maybe the 6th time since the start of this process. Julie Ann has been amazing and has worked with me through all my "updates/changes/can we add one more" moments (and there have been a lot of those!). At the meeting I was told this is the "final edit" and reminded that there would be no more pictures and stories added. It's damn near ready for print.

I was lazing around in the 90-degree Florida spring time heat, looking at some pictures on my phone when I realized I'd come full-circle with my oldest granddaughter, Arianna (2008: American League Champs, Tampa Bay Rays). She was a toddler then and now a 17-year-old young woman who had just graduated from Riverview High School in Sarasota.

The graduation was held at the first place my autographing journey started in 1974 with the Harlem Globetrotters…Robarts Arena. Fifty years ago. Wow.

Our family was all seated as the graduating seniors started walking toward the podium, two by two. I thought I could get a better pictures and videos at the back of the arena, so I got up and gathered in with a bunch of other people…just like I did when I was waiting on an autograph. My granddaughter came straight toward me with her big smile, and I got a great picture.

When I went back to my seat, my son-in-law, Ryan asked me if I knew who I was standing next to over there. It was Charles Lester III, who played for Riverview High School and then transferred to

Venice High School, playing cornerback and wide receiver. He is now attending and playing for Florida State University. Right away, my 9-year-old grandson, Owen says, "Gramps, let's go get his autograph on the program."

So here I go, again, passing on the autograph sickness to my grandson. After the ceremony when the caps are being thrown into the air, my grandson and I make our way through the crowd and stand next to Charles Lester. I introduced myself as Arianna's grandpa, and Charles remembered Arianna from Riverview High School. I ask him for his signature on the program and he signs a small one on the top corner. I said, "No, sign a nice, big one," and this time he did just that, adding a #4. I asked Charles if he'd take a picture with Owen. We shook hands and headed back to the family. He was a great guy and I wish him all the best in his life's journey.

After the big weekend, and looking at all the graduation pictures, I was feeling very nostalgic. I felt the need to write one more story. As I reminisced about what has unfolded in the 64 years of my life, I realized I'd gone full circle, *Chasing the Ink*.

I'm finally putting a period in the book (for real this time, Julie Ann).

Gregory Magac Sr.

Sarasota, FL

Granddaughter Arianna's Graduation

Charles Lester Autograph

Owen and Charles Lester

Printed in the USA
CPSIA information can be obtained
at www.ICGtesting.com
LVHW092148160824
788487LV00004B/191/J